Practice*Planners*®

Arthur E. Jongsma, Jr., Series Editor

Helping therapists help their

D1234583

Treatment Planners cover all the necessary elei ....piriy formal treatment plans, including detailed problem definitions, long-term yuais, short-term objectives, therapeutic interventions, and *DSM*™ diagnoses.

❏ The Complete Adult Psychotherapy Treatment Planner, Fifth Edition* ....978-1-118-06786-4 / $55.00
❏ The Child Psychotherapy Treatment Planner, Fifth Edition*..........................978-1-118-06785-7 / $55.00
❏ The Adolescent Psychotherapy Treatment Planner, Fifth Edition* ....978-1-118-06784-0 / $55.00
❏ The Addiction Treatment Planner, Fifth Edition* ....978-1-118-41475-0 / $55.00
❏ The Couples Psychotherapy Treatment Planner, Second Edition..................978-0-470-40695-3 / $55.00
❏ The Group Therapy Treatment Planner, Second Edition................................978-0-471-66791-9 / $55.00
❏ The Family Therapy Treatment Planner, Second Edition...............................978-0-470-44193-0 / $55.00
❏ The Older Adult Psychotherapy Treatment Planner, Second Edition.............978-0-470-55117-2 / $55.00
❏ The Employee Assistance (EAP) Treatment Planner ....978-0-471-24709-8 / $55.00
❏ The Gay and Lesbian Psychotherapy Treatment Planner ....978-0-471-35080-4 / $55.00
❏ The Crisis Counseling and Traumatic Events Treatment Planner,
   Second Edition...978-1-118-05701-8 / $55.00
❏ The Social Work and Human Services Treatment Planner ....978-0-471-37741-2 / $55.00
❏ The Continuum of Care Treatment Planner...978-0-471-19568-9 / $55.00
❏ The Behavioral Medicine Treatment Planner...978-0-471-31923-8 / $55.00
❏ The Mental Retardation and Developmental Disability Treatment Planner ...978-0-471-38253-9 / $55.00
❏ The Special Education Treatment Planner..978-0-471-38872-2 / $55.00
❏ The Severe and Persistent Mental Illness Treatment Planner, Second Edition.....978-0-470-18013-6 / $55.00
❏ The Personality Disorders Treatment Planner ....978-0-471-39403-7 / $55.00
❏ The Rehabilitation Psychology Treatment Planner ....978-0-471-35178-8 / $55.00
❏ The Pastoral Counseling Treatment Planner..978-0-471-25416-4 / $55.00
❏ The Juvenile Justice and Residential Care Treatment Planner ....978-0-471-43320-0 / $55.00
❏ The School Counseling and School Social Work Treatment Planner,
   Second Edition...978-0-470-61817-2 / $55.00
❏ The Psychopharmacology Treatment Planner ....978-0-471-43322-4 / $55.00
❏ The Probation and Parole Treatment Planner..978-0-471-20244-8 / $55.00
❏ The Suicide and Homicide Risk Assessment & Prevention Treatment Planner ..978-0-471-46631-4 / $55.00
❏ The Speech-Language Pathology Treatment Planner.....................................978-0-471-27504-6 / $55.00
❏ The College Student Counseling Treatment Planner ....978-0-471-46708-3 / $55.00
❏ The Parenting Skills Treatment Planner ....978-0-471-48183-6 / $55.00
❏ The Early Childhood Education Intervention Treatment Planner ....978-0-471-65962-4 / $55.00
❏ The Co-Occurring Disorders Treatment Planner ....978-0-471-73081-1 / $55.00
❏ The Sexual Abuse Victim and Sexual Offender Treatment Planner ....978-0-471-21979-8 / $55.00
❏ The Complete Women's Psychotherapy Treatment Planner ....978-0-470-03983-0 / $55.00
❏ The Veterans and Active Duty Military Psychotherapy Treatment Planner ...978-0-470-44098-8 / $55.00

*Updated to *DSM-5*™

The **Complete Treatment and Homework Planners** series of books combines our bestselling *Treatment Planners* and *Homework Planners* into one easy-to-use, all-in-one resource for mental health professionals treating clients suffering from the most commonly diagnosed disorders.

❏ The Complete Depression Treatment and Homework Planner ....978-0-471-64515-3 / $50.00
❏ The Complete Anxiety Treatment and Homework Planner ....978-0-471-64548-1 / $50.00

Practice*Planners*

Homework Planners feature dozens of behaviorally based, ready-to-use assignments that are designed for use between sessions, as well as a CD-ROM (Microsoft Word) containing all of the assignments—allowing you to customize them to suit your unique client needs.

- ❑ Couples Therapy Homework Planner, Second Edition ....978-0-470-52266-0 / $55.00
- ❑ Child Psychotherapy Homework Planner, Fifth Edition* ....978-1-118-07674-3 / $55.00
- ❑ Child Therapy Activity and Homework Planner...978-0-471-25684-7 / $55.00
- ❑ Adolescent Psychotherapy Homework Planner, Fifth Edition*.....................978-1-118-07673-6 / $55.00
- ❑ Addiction Treatment Homework Planner, Fifth Edition*................................978-1-118-56059-4 / $55.00
- ❑ Family Therapy Homework Planner, Second Edition ....978-0-470-50439-0 / $55.00
- ❑ Grief Counseling Homework Planner..978-0-471-43318-7 / $55.00
- ❑ Group Therapy Homework Planner..978-0-471-41822-1 / $55.00
- ❑ School Counseling and School Social Work Homework Planner,
  Second Edition ....978-1-118-41038-7 / $55.00
- ❑ Adolescent Psychotherapy Homework Planner II...978-0-471-27493-3 / $55.00
- ❑ Adult Psychotherapy Homework Planner, Fifth Edition* ....978-1-118-07672-9 / $55.00
- ❑ Parenting Skills Homework Planner ....978-0-471-48182-9 / $55.00
- ❑ Veterans and Active Duty Military Psychotherapy Homework Planner ......978-0-470-89052-3 / $55.00

*Updated to *DSM-5*™

Progress Notes Planners contain complete prewritten progress notes for each presenting problem in the companion Treatment Planners.

- ❑ The Adult Psychotherapy Progress Notes Planner*......................................978-1-118-06675-1 / $55.00
- ❑ The Adolescent Psychotherapy Progress Notes Planner* ....978-1-118-06676-8 / $55.00
- ❑ The Severe and Persistent Mental Illness Progress Notes Planner ....978-0-470-18014-3 / $55.00
- ❑ The Child Psychotherapy Progress Notes Planner*......................................978-1-118-06677-5 / $55.00
- ❑ The Addiction Progress Notes Planner*...978-1-118-54296-5 / $55.00
- ❑ The Couples Psychotherapy Progress Notes Planner...................................978-0-470-93691-7 / $55.00
- ❑ The Family Therapy Progress Notes Planner...978-0-470-44884-7 / $55.00
- ❑ The Veterans and Active Duty Military Psychotherapy Treatment Planner...978-0-470-44097-1 / $55.00

*Updated to *DSM-5*™

Client Education Handout Planners contain elegantly designed handouts that can be printed out from the enclosed CD-ROM and provide information on a wide range of psychological and emotional disorders and life skills issues. Use as patient literature, handouts at presentations, and aids for promoting your mental health practice.

- ❑ Adult Client Education Handout Planner..978-0-471-20232-5 / $55.00
- ❑ Child and Adolescent Client Education Handout Planner ....978-0-471-20233-2 / $55.00
- ❑ Couples and Family Client Education Handout Planner................................978-0-471-20234-9 / $55.00

Adult Psychotherapy Homework Planner
Fifth Edition

Practice*Planners*® Series

Treatment Planners

The Complete Adult Psychotherapy Treatment Planner, Fifth Edition
The Child Psychotherapy Treatment Planner, Fifth Edition
The Adolescent Psychotherapy Treatment Planner, Fifth Edition
The Addiction Treatment Planner, Fifth Edition
The Continuum of Care Treatment Planner
The Couples Psychotherapy Treatment Planner, Second Edition
The Employee Assistance Treatment Planner
The Pastoral Counseling Treatment Planner
The Older Adult Psychotherapy Treatment Planner, Second Edition
The Behavioral Medicine Treatment Planner
The Group Therapy Treatment Planner
The Gay and Lesbian Psychotherapy Treatment Planner
The Family Therapy Treatment Planner, Second Edition
The Severe and Persistent Mental Illness Treatment Planner, Second Edition
The Mental Retardation and Developmental Disability Treatment Planner
The Social Work and Human Services Treatment Planner
The Crisis Counseling and Traumatic Events Treatments Planner, Second Edition
The Personality Disorders Treatment Planner
The Rehabilitation Psychology Treatment Planner
The Special Education Treatment Planner
The Juvenile Justice and Residential Care Treatment Planner
The School Counseling and School Social Work Treatment Planner, Second Edition
The Sexual Abuse Victim and Sexual Offender Treatment Planner
The Probation and Parole Treatment Planner
The Psychopharmacology Treatment Planner
The Speech-Language Pathology Treatment Planner
The Suicide and Homicide Treatment Planner
The College Student Counseling Treatment Planner
The Parenting Skills Treatment Planner
The Early Childhood Intervention Treatment Planner
The Co-Occurring Disorders Treatment Planner
The Complete Women's Psychotherapy Treatment Planner
The Veterans and Active Duty Military Psychotherapy Treatment Planner

Progress Notes Planners

The Child Psychotherapy Progress Notes Planner, Fifth Edition
The Adolescent Psychotherapy Progress Notes Planner, Fifth Edition
The Adult Psychotherapy Progress Notes Planner, Fifth Edition
The Addiction Progress Notes Planner, Fifth Edition
The Severe and Persistent Mental Illness Progress Notes Planner, Second Edition
The Couples Psychotherapy Progress Notes Planner, Second Edition
The Family Therapy Progress Notes Planner, Second Edition
The Veterans and Active Duty Military Psychotherapy Progress Notes Planner

Homework Planners

Couples Therapy Homework Planner, Second Edition
Family Therapy Homework Planner, Second Edition
Grief Counseling Homework Planner
Group Therapy Homework Planner
Divorce Counseling Homework Planner
School Counseling and School Social Work Homework Planner, Second Edition
Child Therapy Activity and Homework Planner
Addiction Treatment Homework Planner, Fifth Edition
Adolescent Psychotherapy Homework Planner, Fifth Edition
Adult Psychotherapy Homework Planner, Fifth Edition
Child Psychotherapy Homework Planner, Fifth Edition
Parenting Skills Homework Planner
Veterans and Active Duty Military Psychotherapy Homework Planner

Client Education Handout Planners

Adult Client Education Handout Planner
Child and Adolescent Client Education Handout Planner
Couples and Family Client Education Handout Planner

Complete Planners

The Complete Depression Treatment and Homework Planner
The Complete Anxiety Treatment and Homework Planner

PracticePlanners®

Adult Psychotherapy
Homework Planner

Fifth Edition

Arthur E. Jongsma, Jr.

WILEY

Published by John Wiley & Sons, Inc., Hoboken, New Jersey
Published simultaneously in Canada

For general information about our other products and services, please contact our Customer Care Department within the United States at (800) 762-2974, outside the United States at (317) 572-3993 or fax (317) 572-4002.

Wiley publishes in a variety of print and electronic formats and by print-on-demand. Some material included with standard print versions of this book may not be included in e-books or in print-on-demand. If this book refers to media such as a CD or DVD that is not included in the version you purchased, you may download this material at http://booksupport.wiley.com. For more information about Wiley products, visit www.wiley.com.

Library of Congress Cataloging-in-Publication Data:

Jongsma, Arthur E., Jr., 1943–
    Adult psychotherapy homework planner / Arthur E. Jongsma, Jr.—Fifth edition.
        pages cm
    Includes index.
    ISBN 978-1-118-07672-9 (pbk.)
    ISBN 978-1-118-83625-5 (ebk.)
    ISBN 978-1-118-83637-8 (ebk.)
    1. Psychotherapy–Planning–Handbooks, manuals, etc. 2. Psychotherapy–Problems, exercises, etc. I. Title.
    RC480.5.J664 2014
    616.89'14—dc23
                                2013027950

Printed in the United States of America

10 9 8 7 6 5 4 3 2 1

To Dave and Lorrie Vander Ark,
whose friendship has enriched our lives and
whose support is more reliable than a fine timepiece

CONTENTS

PRACTICE*PLANNERS*® SERIES PREFACE

Accountability is an important dimension of the practice of psychotherapy. Treatment programs, public agencies, clinics, and practitioners must justify and document their treatment plans to outside review entities in order to be reimbursed for services. The books and software in the Practice*Planners*® series are designed to help practitioners fulfill these documentation requirements efficiently and professionally.

The Practice*Planners*® series includes a wide array of treatment planning books including not only the original *Complete Adult Psychotherapy Treatment Planner*, *Child Psychotherapy Treatment Planner*, and *Adolescent Psychotherapy Treatment Planner*, all now in their fifth editions, but also *Treatment Planners* targeted to specialty areas of practice, including:

- Addictions
- Co-occurring disorders
- Behavioral medicine
- College students
- Couples therapy
- Crisis counseling
- Early childhood education
- Employee assistance
- Family therapy
- Gays and lesbians
- Group therapy
- Juvenile justice and residential care
- Mental retardation and developmental disability
- Neuropsychology
- Older adults
- Parenting skills
- Pastoral counseling
- Personality disorders
- Probation and parole
- Psychopharmacology
- Rehabilitation psychology
- School counseling and school social work
- Severe and persistent mental illness
- Sexual abuse victims and offenders
- Social work and human services
- Special education

- Speech-Language pathology
- Suicide and homicide risk assessment
- Veterans and active duty military
- Women's issues

In addition, there are three branches of companion books that can be used in conjunction with the *Treatment Planners*, or on their own:

- ***Progress Notes Planners*** provide a menu of progress statements that elaborate on the client's symptom presentation and the provider's therapeutic intervention. Each *Progress Notes Planner* statement is directly integrated with the behavioral definitions and therapeutic interventions from its companion *Treatment Planner*.

- ***Homework Planners*** include homework assignments designed around each presenting problem (such as anxiety, depression, substance use, anger control problems, eating disorders, or panic disorder) that is the focus of a chapter in its corresponding *Treatment Planner*.

- ***Client Education Handout Planners*** provide brochures and handouts to help educate and inform clients on presenting problems and mental health issues, as well as life skills techniques. The handouts are included on CD-ROMs for easy printing from your computer and are ideal for use in waiting rooms, in presentations, as newsletters, or as information for clients struggling with mental illness issues. The topics covered by these handouts correspond to the presenting problems in the *Treatment Planners*.

Adjunctive books, such as *The Psychotherapy Documentation Primer* and *The Clinical Documentation Sourcebook*, contain forms and resources to aid the clinician in mental health practice management.

The goal of our series is to provide practitioners with the resources they need in order to provide high quality care in the era of accountability. To put it simply: We seek to help you spend more time on patients, and less time on paperwork.

ARTHUR E. JONGSMA, JR.
Grand Rapids, Michigan

ACKNOWLEDGMENTS

Although only my name appears as the author of this book, the product is the result of the combined efforts of many people. I first would like to acknowledge the contribution of my coauthors on several other books, William McInnis and Mark Peterson. They assisted heavily in the rewrite of this edition of the *Adult Psychotherapy Homework Planner*. They also both previously gave permission for me to borrow and adapt some of the homework exercises we had collaborated on in writing the *Adolescent Psychotherapy Homework Planner*. Several of the assignments in this book have been adapted to the adult focus group from their original creation for the adolescent client. Thank you, Bill and Mark.

I would also like to thank Jim Finley and Brenda Lenz for giving their permission to me to adapt two of their assignments from their *Addiction Treatment Homework Planner* for placement in the Substance Use section of this book.

I am grateful to Sue Rhoda, who was so efficient at transcribing this manuscript in a very timely and professional manner.

My support staff at John Wiley & Sons, Marquita Flemming, Peggy Alexander, Sweta Gupta, and Judi Knott, continues to move the Practice*Planners*® project forward with enthusiasm and professional dedication. Thank you, all.

Finally, my personal support system is grounded in my wife, Judy, who makes me feel important even when I am not, and my children and grandchildren, who consistently show interest in my work. Thank you, family.

A. E. J.

INTRODUCTION

More and more therapists are assigning homework to their clients. Not only have short-term therapy models endorsed this practice, but the benefits are being recognized by many traditional therapists as well.

WHY HOMEWORK?

Assigning homework to psychotherapy clients is beneficial for several reasons. With the advent of managed care, which often requires shorter and fewer treatment sessions, therapists assign between-session homework to help maximize the effectiveness of briefer treatment. Homework is an extension of the treatment process, provides continuity, and allows the client to work between sessions on issues that are the focus of therapy. Homework is also a tool for more fully engaging the client in the treatment process. Assignments place more responsibility on the client to resolve his or her presenting problems, counteracting the expectations that some clients may experience—that it is the therapist alone who can cure him or her. For some, it even may bring a sense of self-empowerment.

Another added benefit of homework is that these assignments give the client the opportunity to implement and evaluate insights or coping behaviors that have been discussed in therapy sessions. Practice often heightens awareness of various issues. Furthermore, homework increases the expectation for the client to follow through with *making* changes rather than just *talking* about change. Exercises require participation, which creates a sense that the client is taking active steps toward change. Homework allows the client to try new behaviors, bringing these experiences back to the next session for processing. Modifications can then be made to the client's thoughts, feelings, or behaviors as the homework is processed in the therapy session.

Occasionally treatment processes can become vague and abstract. By adding focus and structure, homework assignments can reenergize treatment. Moreover, homework can increase the client's motivation to change as it provides something specific to work on. Additionally, homework increases the involvement of family members and significant others in the client's treatment by using assignments that call for their participation. It promotes more efficient treatment by encouraging the client to actively develop insights, positive self-talk, and coping behaviors between therapy sessions. Consequently, many clients express increased satisfaction with the treatment process when homework is given. They are empowered by doing something active that facilitates the change process, and it reinforces their sense of control over the problem. All of these advantages have made the assignment of therapeutic homework increasingly prevalent.

HOW TO USE THIS *HOMEWORK PLANNER*

Creating homework assignments and developing the printed forms for recording responses is a time-consuming process. This *Adult Psychotherapy Homework Planner,* Fifth Edition, follows the lead of psychotherapeutic interventions suggested in *The Complete Adult Psychotherapy Treatment Planner*, Fifth Edition (Jongsma, Peterson, and Bruce, 2014) and provides a menu of homework assignments that can easily be photocopied. In addition to the printed format, the assignments in this *Planner* are provided on a CD-ROM to allow the therapist to access them on a word processor and print them out as is or easily customize them to suit the client's individual needs and/or the therapist's style.

The assignments are grouped under presenting problems that are typical of those found in an adult population. These presenting problems are cross-referenced to every presenting problem found in *The Complete Adult Psychotherapy Treatment Planner*. Although these assignments were created with a specific presenting problem in mind, don't feel locked in by a single problem-oriented chapter when searching for an appropriate assignment. Included with each exercise is a cross-referenced list of suggested presenting problems for which the assignment may be appropriate and useful called *Additional Problems for Which This Exercise May Be Most Useful*. This cross-referenced list can assist you in applying the assignments to other situations that may be relevant to your client's particular presenting problem.

A broader cross-referenced list of assignments is found in Appendix A, *Alternate Assignments for Presenting Problems*. Review this appendix to find relevant assignments beyond the one, two, three, or four exercises found in any specific presenting problem chapter. For example, under the heading of Unipolar Depression in the appendix you will find 27 alternative assignments originally created for other presenting problems but relevant and easily adapted for use with a client struggling with depression issues. In this appendix, with every presenting problem are listed relevant additional assignments from throughout the book. Remember, each assignment is available on the CD-ROM at the back of the book and, therefore, can be quickly edited for use with a specific client. This modified assignment can be saved on your computer's hard disk for repeated later use.

ABOUT THE ASSIGNMENTS

Therapists may introduce the homework assignment with varying degrees of detail and client preparation. Recommendations regarding this preparation and post-exercise discussion are made on the title page of each assignment under the heading "Suggestions for Processing This Exercise with the Client."

Clinical judgment must be used to choose the homework assignments that focus on relevant issues for the client. The title page of each assignment contains a section on "Goals of the Exercise" to guide you in your selection of relevant homework for your client.

CARRYING OUT THE ASSIGNMENT

It is recommended that you review the entire book to familiarize yourself with the broad nature of the type and focus of the various homework exercises. Select a specific assignment from a chapter titled with your client's presenting problem or from the alternative list in the appendix and then review the list of homework goals. Assigning therapy homework is just a beginning step in the therapy treatment process. Carrying out the assignment requires a follow-up exploration of the impact of the assignment on the client's thoughts, feelings, and behavior. What are the results? Was this assignment useful to the client? Can it be redesigned or altered for better results? Examine and search for new and creative ways to actively engage your client in participating in this homework process.

ALTERNATIVES TO DESTRUCTIVE ANGER

GOALS OF THE EXERCISE

1. Increase awareness of how anger is expressed destructively.
2. Decrease the number, intensity, and duration of angry outbursts while increasing the use of new skills for managing anger.
3. Become capable of handling angry feelings in constructive ways that enhance daily functioning.

ADDITIONAL PROBLEMS FOR WHICH THIS EXERCISE MAY BE MOST USEFUL

- Antisocial Behavior
- Attention Deficit Disorder (ADD)—Adult
- Borderline Personality
- Family Conflict
- Posttraumatic Stress Disorder (PTSD)

SUGGESTIONS FOR PROCESSING THIS EXERCISE WITH THE CLIENT

Clients often feel they responded to a frustrating situation in the only way possible. They fail to realize that they have choices and control over their behavior. You may want to review the alternatives to rage listed in the first section of the assignment to help the client understand the alternatives he/she could apply when dealing with frustration or anger. Review the client's journal material and suggest additional constructive ways to respond to frustrating or hurtful situations that prompt his/her mismanaged anger.

ALTERNATIVES TO DESTRUCTIVE ANGER

Destructive anger can take many forms. Anger can be expressed in rage that is out of control, either verbally or physically. We also can express anger by snapping at someone or being unkindly critical. A third form that anger may take is that of cold, icy withdrawal that punishes others by shutting them out, shunning them, or refusing to acknowledge their attempts to relate to us. All of these reactions and many more can be destructive to the relationship and to our own feelings of self-esteem. Destructive expressions of anger often generate later feelings of guilt and shame.

This exercise is designed to briefly identify some *constructive* alternatives to destructive anger by giving a brief description of the positive alternative. The goal is for you to consider these alternatives as you seek to replace destructive anger with more constructive behaviors. You will be asked to keep a journal of situations in your daily life that provoked anger and then note how one or more of these constructive alternatives may have been applied to the situations.

CONSTRUCTIVE ALTERNATIVES

A. *Assertiveness:* Speaking forthrightly in a manner that is very respectful of the other person's needs and rights and does not attack anyone so as to make him/her defensive.

B. *Tune Out/Cool Down:* Recognize that the situation has become volatile and nonproductive and suggest withdrawal from the situation to give each party a chance to cool down and collect his/her thoughts and regain personal control.

C. *Relaxation:* Learn and implement relaxation skills to reduce stress and tension through the use of words that cue relaxation, deep breathing that releases tension, imagining relaxing scenes, or deep muscle relaxation procedures.

D. *Diversion:* When anger is felt to be building, find diversionary activities that stop the buildup and focus the mind on more enjoyable experiences.

E. *Physical Exercise:* When anger and tension levels rise, physical exercise can be a wonderful way to release tension and expel energy as an alternative to losing control or exploding in rage.

F. *Problem-Solving Skills:* Identify or clarify the problem, brainstorm possible solutions, review the pros and cons of each alternative solution, select the best alternative for implementation, evaluate the outcome as to mutual satisfaction, and finally, adjust the solution if necessary to increase mutual satisfaction.

G. *Self-Talk:* Take time to talk to yourself in calming, reasoned, and constructive sentences that move you toward anger control and away from hurtful expressions of anger.

H. *"I" Messages:* Speak to the target of your anger, describing your feelings and needs rather than attacking, labeling, or describing the other person's behavior, motivations, or goals. Begin your sentences with "I feel . . ." or "I need . . . ."

I. *Other:* Describe your own or your counselor's alternative to rage. _____

_____

_____

_____

APPLICATION TO DAILY LIFE

In the columns that follow, describe the date and time, the situation that prompted the angry response, the destructive response, and the alternative constructive response that might have been used. In the final row, instead of writing a full description of the alternative, you may simply enter the alphabetical indicator of the constructive alternative, A through I.

Entry 1 Day/Date and Time: _____ _____	Situation	
	Response	
	Alternative Response	

(**NOTE:** *Please make additional copies of the next page for later entries.*)

Entry ___ (**# of entry**) Day/Date and Time: _____ _____	Situation	
	Response	
	Alternative Response	

Entry ___ (**# of entry**) Day/Date and Time: _____ _____	Situation	
	Response	
	Alternative Response	

ANGER JOURNAL

GOALS OF THE EXERCISE

1. Develop an awareness of current angry behaviors, clarifying origins of and alternatives to aggressive anger.
2. Keep a daily journal of persons, situations, and other triggers of anger; record thoughts, feelings, and actions taken.
3. Decrease the number, intensity, and duration of angry outbursts while increasing the use of new skills for managing anger.

ADDITIONAL PROBLEMS FOR WHICH THIS EXERCISE MAY BE MOST USEFUL

- Antisocial Behavior
- Borderline Personality
- Family Conflict
- Posttraumatic Stress Disorder (PTSD)

SUGGESTIONS FOR PROCESSING THIS EXERCISE WITH THE CLIENT

Some clients deny the degree of anger they feel and express. Other clients may be aware of feelings of anger but need help in understanding the contributing factors and causes for their anger. As you process the journal entries with clients, help them clarify and pinpoint these contributing factors and the causes for their anger. Often the causes for the anger are not those that are initially identified, but lie beneath the surface and can be discovered with some patient processing. Finally, it is helpful to press the client toward describing positive alternative behaviors that could have replaced the maladaptive anger responses that were selected in the heat of the moment. Positive alternatives may include things like assertiveness, time-out, problem solving, "I" messages, or self-talk.

ANGER JOURNAL

To make you more aware of your angry feelings, the circumstances surrounding them, the target of them, the causes for them, and how they were shown, you are being asked to keep an anger journal. This journal will help you record the when, what, who, why, and how of the angry feelings as well as allow you to give some thought to what alternative emotional, behavioral, or cognitive reaction you might have had to the situation. Be as honest as you can be with yourself about your angry feelings, trying not to discount them, excuse them, or deny them. When you conclude that you have experienced anger, that is the time to make an entry into this journal. Your entries do not have to be lengthy; a sentence or two will suffice. You should enter enough information to permit you to discuss each incident with your therapist as you try to process and learn from your anger experiences. Do not forget to include experiences that have generated some anger within you even though you did not express it in words or behavior. The buildup of unexpressed anger can result in an inappropriate outburst at a later time. This journal may help you understand that phenomenon. It is also important for you to give some thought to the last entry; that is, what alternative positive reaction could you have given to the situation instead of burying or blurting out your feelings of anger. Often there is a more constructive response available that you are able to discover when you give the issue some calm consideration and analysis. The heat of the moment leads many of us to make mistakes. Try to make at least one entry per day into your anger journal.

The anger journal that follows asks you to enter the date and time of the experience that generated anger. Second, you are asked to enter a description of the situation, such as where you were and what was happening. Third, you are asked to name the people who were present, and specifically the people with whom you were angry. Next, you are asked to enter a sentence or two indicating your reason(s) for being so angry or the cause of your anger. Then you are asked to describe how your anger was or was not revealed. In the final column, enter your thoughts about how you could have responded to the experience more constructively. (NOTE: *Please make additional copies of the form for later entries.*)

Entry ___ (# of entry) Day/Date and Time: _____ _____	What (Situation)	
	Who (People)	
	Why (Case)	
	How (Reaction)	
	Alternative Positive Reaction	

Entry ___ (# of entry) Day/Date and Time: _____ _____	What (Situation)	
	Who (People)	
	Why (Case)	
	How (Reaction)	
	Alternative Positive Reaction	

ASSERTIVE COMMUNICATION OF ANGER

GOALS OF THE EXERCISE

1. Verbalize feelings of anger in a controlled, assertive way.
2. Decrease overall intensity and frequency of angry feelings, and increase ability to recognize and appropriately express angry feelings as they occur.
3. Demonstrate respect for others and their feelings.

ADDITIONAL PROBLEMS FOR WHICH THIS EXERCISE MAY BE MOST USEFUL

- Antisocial Behavior
- Bipolar—Mania
- Family Conflict
- Impulse Control Disorder

SUGGESTIONS FOR PROCESSING THIS EXERCISE WITH THE CLIENT

The purpose of this exercise is to improve the client's ability to verbally express his/her anger in an assertive manner. Teach the client effective communication skills and/or coping strategies in the therapy sessions to help him/her express feelings of anger in a direct, calm, controlled, yet nonaggressive manner. The client is encouraged to practice the assertive communication techniques on a regular basis at home, at school, and in the workplace. The first page of the assignment identifies several effective communication skills. Feel free to teach the client other effective communication skills that will help him/her to express anger appropriately.

ASSERTIVE COMMUNICATION OF ANGER

In this assignment, you are asked to practice expressing your anger in a calm, controlled, and assertive manner on a regular basis at home, at school, or in the workplace. Assertive communication of anger includes the following characteristics:

1. Use of "I" statements—"I" statements reflect ownership of thoughts and feelings. Effective "I" statements are present-focused and free of manipulative ploys. Use of "I" statements are more likely to reflect statements of personal responsibility.
2. Avoid use of "You" statements that are often blaming, accusatory, or judgmental in nature. "You" statements often focus on the other person's faults and place them on the defensive.
3. Calmly state your reasons for your anger. Refer to specific behaviors and focus more on the present situation and not on past faults of the other person.
4. Use facts instead of judgments.
5. Make requests for positive and specific changes in behavior. For example, "I would appreciate it if you would call and let me know when you are running late."
6. Express your anger as soon after the specific behavior or event as possible so that your expression of anger can be present-oriented.
7. Express anger in a calm and reasonable tone of voice. Clearly, it is best to avoid yelling or talking to the other person in a high-pitched or accusing tone of voice. Avoid nagging and whining as well.
8. Use active listening skills. After you have expressed your thoughts and feelings in a calm and controlled manner, it is important to listen to the other person's point of view. Remember to listen to other people's thoughts without interrupting. Maintain good eye contact while they are speaking to let them know that you are listening intently to their thoughts and feelings. Try to avoid thinking about what you want to say next.
9. If the discussion becomes tense or heated, remember to take a break to regain your composure and organize your thoughts.

Now that you have been taught effective communication techniques, we encourage you to utilize these skills on an everyday basis. Please fill out the Assertive Communication Log to record the incidents where you had the opportunity to practice communicating your feelings of anger.

ASSERTIVE COMMUNICATION LOG

Date: _____ Time: _____

Setting: _____

Person(s) Involved: _____

What were you angry about? _____

_____

_____

How did you express your anger to the other person(s)?_____

_____

_____

_____

How did the other person(s) respond to your expression of anger? _____

_____

_____

_____

How did you, in turn, respond to their statements or feedback? _____

_____

_____

_____

How successful or effective do you feel you were in expressing your anger? Did you resolve the problem? Please explain. _____

_____

_____

_____

_____

What, if anything, would you have said or done differently? _____

_____

_____

_____

_____

HOW I HAVE HURT OTHERS

GOALS OF THE EXERCISE

1. Identify specific behaviors that have been engaged in to hurt others.
2. Identify the consequences of hurtful behavior.
3. Increase awareness of how antisocial behavior has specifically hurt others.
4. Indicate the steps that will be taken to make amends or restitution for hurt caused to others.

ADDITIONAL PROBLEMS FOR WHICH THIS EXERCISE MAY BE MOST USEFUL

- Anger Control Problems
- Legal Conflicts
- Substance Use

SUGGESTIONS FOR PROCESSING THIS EXERCISE WITH THE CLIENT

Minimization and denial are traits that often accompany antisocial behavior patterns. This exercise is designed to increase sensitivity to antisocial behaviors that cause others pain. Confrontation may be necessary to bring the client to acknowledge behaviors that are not included in his/her checklist. Be alert to the antisocial personality trait of projection; that is, the client may try to place blame for his/her behavior on anyone but himself/herself. Role reversal may be necessary to help the client feel the pain of his/her behavior on others.

HOW I HAVE HURT OTHERS

We are capable of hurting others in many different ways. This assignment will help you become more aware of various behaviors that have a hurtful impact on others. Sometimes we are very aware that we are hurting someone with our behavior, while at other times, we do not even seem to notice it. Review the list of hurtful behaviors that follow and put a check mark next to those that you have engaged in and that have resulted in pain for others.

Hurtful Behaviors

_____	Dishonesty	_____	Sex abuse
_____	Disloyalty	_____	Unfaithfulness
_____	Physical assault	_____	Verbal attacks
_____	Stealing	_____	Irresponsibility
_____	Unkindness	_____	Insensitivity
_____	Blaming	_____	Threatening
_____	Illegal acts	_____	Weapon use
_____	Substance abuse	_____	Name calling
_____	Job loss	_____	Unkept promises

1. Describe three situations where you have hurt others through engaging in one of the behaviors listed.

   Situation A: _____

   _____

   Situation B: _____

   _____

   Situation C: _____

   _____

2. Describe how your behavior affected others. How were they hurt?

    Situation A: _____

    _____

    _____

    Situation B: _____

    _____

    _____

    Situation C: _____

    _____

    _____

3. What might you do to make amends for your hurtful behavior toward others in these three situations?

    Situation A: _____

    _____

    _____

    Situation B: _____

    _____

    _____

    Situation C: _____

    _____

    _____

LETTER OF APOLOGY

GOALS OF THE EXERCISE

1. Increase awareness of hurtful behavior toward others.
2. Increase sensitivity toward the impact of hurtful behavior on others.
3. Indicate the steps that will be taken to make amends or restitution for hurt caused to others.
4. Offer sincere apology through written letter for how antisocial or irresponsible behavior has negatively impacted others.

ADDITIONAL PROBLEMS FOR WHICH THIS EXERCISE MAY BE MOST USEFUL

*   Anger Control Problems
*   Family Conflict
*   Intimate Relationship Conflicts
*   Legal Conflicts
*   Substance Use

SUGGESTIONS FOR PROCESSING THIS EXERCISE WITH THE CLIENT

Hurtful behavior toward others is easily minimized or denied in terms of who is responsible for it or the impact it has on others. This assignment increases sensitivity toward the impact that hurtful behavior has had on others. In processing the exercise, it is important that the client include all elements of a constructive apology and avoid projection or minimization. Review each letter of apology to make sure it contains all the necessary elements. Evaluate whether the client demonstrates genuine feelings of regret, shame, or guilt. Clearly confront denial and emphasize the negative impact of insensitive behaviors.

LETTER OF APOLOGY

After we become aware of the pain we have caused someone else due to our own unkind behavior, we must try to find a way to heal the hurt and make amends. Many times just saying "I'm sorry" is not enough. It can be helpful if the apology is accompanied by a written note acknowledging causing the pain and suggesting how you could have done things differently. This assignment asks you to describe three incidents in which you have hurt others. It then asks you to construct a brief letter of apology for each of these incidents.

Three Hurtful Incidents
Describe for each of three incidents who was hurt, what you did to hurt them, how they felt about what you did, how you feel now about what you did, and how you could have acted more kindly.

Incident #1: _____

_____

_____

_____

Incident #2: _____

_____

_____

_____

Incident #3: _____

_____

_____

_____

Apology
Write a letter of apology to each of the people who were hurt in each of the three incidents described (on a separate piece of paper). Include in your letter of apology a description of what you did to hurt them, your perception of how your actions must have affected them, how you feel today about your actions, and what you wished you would have done in the place of your hurtful behavior.

THREE ACTS OF KINDNESS

GOALS OF THE EXERCISE

1. List three actions that will be performed that will be acts of kindness and thoughtfulness toward others.
2. Develop and demonstrate a healthy sense of respect for social norms, the rights of others, and a need for honesty.
3. Demonstrate caring, kindness, and empathy toward other people on a consistent basis.

ADDITIONAL PROBLEMS FOR WHICH THIS EXERCISE MAY BE MOST USEFUL

- Anger Control Problems
- Attention Deficit Disorder (ADD)—Adult
- Impulse Control Disorder
- Legal Conflicts
- Type A Behavior

SUGGESTIONS FOR PROCESSING THIS EXERCISE WITH THE CLIENT

As the name implies, the client is instructed to engage in three acts of kindness, caring, or thoughtfulness over the course of a week. The acts of kindness or caring can be spontaneous or planned. The client can perform the acts of kindness with someone he/she knows very well or with a total stranger. The client may also want to "undo" his/her previous harmful or responsible acts by engaging in thoughtful or responsible behaviors with others. (NOTE: The number of altruistic acts can be modified per week.) It is hoped that the client will develop a routine of helping others or engaging in prosocial behaviors on a regular basis. The client is asked to complete a questionnaire on the following page after performing the altruistic act. Keeping a journal of the altruistic acts will allow the client to process his/her experiences with the therapist. Furthermore, the therapist has the opportunity to reinforce the client's kind or thoughtful behaviors.

THREE ACTS OF KINDNESS

Please record times when you performed an act of kindness for others. Bring the completed questionnaires back to your next therapy session to process with your therapist.

Date _____

Setting (e.g., home, workplace, community) _____

Recipient(s) of kindness _____

What was your specific act of kindness? _____

_____

How did you feel about performing the act of kindness? _____

_____

How did the other person(s) respond to your act of kindness? _____

_____

How did their response make you feel? _____

_____

Would you perform this act of kindness again in the future? _____ yes _____ no

If no, please explain. _____

_____

What are three other acts of kindness you can perform in the future?
(Optional: This question does not have to be answered each time you complete the form.)

_____

_____

_____

ANALYZE THE PROBABILITY OF A FEARED EVENT

GOALS OF THE EXERCISE

1. Develop an awareness of the irrational nature of the fear and anxiety.
2. Examine the probability of the negative expectation occurring and its consequences.
3. Identify distorted self-talk that mediates the anxiety response.
4. Recognize that the feared outcome will not terminate the ability to function.
5. Resolve the core conflict that is the source of the anxiety.

ADDITIONAL PROBLEMS FOR WHICH THIS EXERCISE MAY BE MOST USEFUL

- Dependency
- Low Self-Esteem
- Obsessive-Compulsive Disorder (OCD)
- Phobia
- Social Anxiety
- Suicidal Ideation
- Unipolar Depression

SUGGESTIONS FOR PROCESSING THIS EXERCISE WITH THE CLIENT

Support the client as he/she takes the risk of looking boldly and fairly at the basis for his/her anxiety. Help the client to acknowledge the irrational basis for his/her anxiety and reinforce rational outcomes of feared situations that will not devastate his/her life. Pay special attention to the distorted cognitions that feed the fear and suggest realistic positive self-talk to counteract this strong mediation effect.

ANALYZE THE PROBABILITY OF A FEARED EVENT

Many of our fears grow in their intensity without us ever stopping to analyze their exact nature, their causes, their probabilities of occurrence, the amount of control we might have over the situation, and the very real outcomes that are possible if our fears were realized. This exercise will help you thoroughly review your fears. As you rationally analyze the nature and cause of your fear and its real outcome, the fear will dissipate and your ability to cope will increase. Take this step-by-step approach in looking at two of your greatest fears and then bring this analysis to your counselor for a thorough processing and reinforcement of coping skills.

1. My First Fear is _____

    A. What is the fear or anxiety about? _____

    _____

    _____

    _____

    B. What is the possibility on a scale of 1 (very unlikely) to 10 (inevitable) that the feared outcome will actually happen? Circle one number.

        1   2   3   4   5   6   7   8   9   10

    C. What self-talk messages do you give yourself that make the fear grow?

    _____

    _____

    _____

    D. What are the very real consequences if the feared outcome did occur? _____

    _____

    _____

    _____

    E. What can you do to control the outcome of the situation that you fear? _____

    _____

    _____

    _____

F.   What is the worst possible real outcome if your fear was realized? _____

_____

_____

G.   How would your life be affected if your feared outcome actually happened? How would you cope or continue to function? _____

_____

_____

2.   My Second Fear is _____

A.   What is the fear or anxiety about? _____

_____

_____

B.   What is the possibility on a scale of 1 (very unlikely) to 10 (inevitable) that the feared outcome will actually happen? Circle one number.

1   2   3   4   5   6   7   8   9   10

C.   What self-talk messages do you give yourself that make the fear grow? _____

_____

_____

D.   What are the very real consequences if the feared outcome did occur? _____

_____

_____

E.   What can you do to control the outcome of the situation that you fear? _____

_____

_____

F.   What is the worst possible real outcome if your fear was realized? _____

_____

G.   How would your life be affected if your feared outcome actually happened? How would you cope or continue to function? _____

_____

_____

PAST SUCCESSFUL ANXIETY COPING

GOALS OF THE EXERCISE

1. Identify successful coping strategies used in the past.
2. View yourself as a capable, resourceful person who has been successful at overcoming fear.
3. Apply successful coping strategies from the past to current anxieties.
4. Enhance ability to effectively cope with the full variety of life's anxieties.

ADDITIONAL PROBLEMS FOR WHICH THIS EXERCISE MAY BE MOST USEFUL

- Impulse Control Disorder
- Obsessive-Compulsive Disorder (OCD)
- Panic/Agoraphobia
- Phase of Life Problems
- Phobia
- Social Anxiety
- Suicidal Ideation

SUGGESTIONS FOR PROCESSING THIS EXERCISE WITH THE CLIENT

This solution-focused assignment attempts to get the client to recognize his/her resourcefulness in the past in dealing with anxiety. Helping the client clarify and refine the coping skill that he/she used is the most difficult part of the assignment. Clients are often not aware of what coping mechanism they relied on to deal with their fear. After the successful coping skills have been identified and refined, help the client to apply these successful skills from the past to his/her current anxieties. Monitor and modify the solution as required.

PAST SUCCESSFUL ANXIETY COPING

This assignment leads us to focus on resources and successes that we have demonstrated throughout our past. We tend to forget about our ability to cope when our anxieties and fears seem so real and debilitating. However, all of us have had fears that we have overcome or that we have functioned with in spite of their presence from childhood right into adulthood. We may have feared attending kindergarten, but learned ways to cope with that fear as a child and eventually the fear was eradicated. We may have feared talking to a teenager of the opposite sex, but eventually learned to speak to them in spite of our anxiety. We may have feared going on a job interview, but pressed forward and presented ourselves in the best manner possible. In other words, we learn to cope and to function and to overcome anxiety. We cannot allow our anxieties to cripple us or cause us to avoid circumstances. We must face our anxieties head-on. We may have coped by just "taking a deep breath" or by getting encouragement from our friends or by rehearsing what we were going to do or say so often that it became almost automatic. Whatever coping skill we used, we have been successful in the past and now we must rediscover those coping skills and apply them to the current anxieties.

1. Identify three fears or anxieties that you experienced in the past.
    Fear #1: _____
    _____
    Fear #2: _____
    _____
    Fear #3: _____
    _____
    _____

2. Identify what you did to cope with, or continue to function in spite of, the anxiety.
    Fear #1: _____
    _____
    _____

Fear #2: _____

_____

_____

Fear #3: _____

_____

_____

_____

3. How do you know your coping mechanism identified in question 2 was successful?

Fear #1: _____

_____

_____

_____

Fear #2: _____

_____

_____

_____

Fear #3: _____

_____

_____

_____

4. What other coping skills have you relied on in the past to help you overcome fears?

_____

_____

_____

5. How can you use each of the coping skills identified in question 2 to help you with your current fears? _____

_____

_____

_____

WORRY TIME

GOALS OF THE EXERCISE

1. Reduce overall frequency, intensity, and duration of the anxiety so that daily functioning is not impaired.
2. Learn and implement a strategy to limit the association between various environmental settings and worry, delaying the worry until designated "worry time."
3. Stabilize anxiety level while increasing ability to function on a daily basis.
4. Enhance ability to effectively cope with the full variety of life's anxieties.

ADDITIONAL PROBLEMS FOR WHICH THIS EXERCISE MAY BE MOST USEFUL

- Low Self-Esteem
- Obsessive-Compulsive Disorder
- Panic/Agoraphobia
- Phobia
- Unipolar Depression

SUGGESTIONS FOR PROCESSING THIS EXERCISE WITH THE CLIENT

Clients with a Generalized Anxiety Disorder often spend an excessive amount of time worrying. Furthermore, they have trouble "letting go" of their worries. The goal of this exercise is to decrease the amount of time spent in worrying by restricting worry to a specific time and place. Instruct the client to designate a specific time and place for him/her to worry. Teach the client how to recognize, stop, and delay worry to the agreed-upon "worry time" by using techniques such as deep breathing, deep muscle relaxation, thought-stopping, and refocusing. The client should be trained in the use of these various techniques before implementing the "worry time" intervention. The client is asked to complete a daily "Worry Time" Log to identify how successful he/she was in restricting the amount of time spent in worrying each day.

WORRY TIME
CLIENT'S INSTRUCTIONS

People with generalized anxiety spend a great deal of time worrying about various problems. They have trouble with "letting go" of their worries. Excessive worrying can be draining, both physically and emotionally. It can take away one's energy and interfere with the ability to relax and enjoy life. It is not uncommon for people who experience anxiety to have problems with both falling and staying asleep. High levels of anxiety and excessive worrying can make it difficult to concentrate on one's schoolwork and other tasks in life. Furthermore, people who worry to excess often do not enjoy their time spent with family and friends because they are so focused on their problems.

The purpose of this exercise is to reduce the amount of time you spend each day worrying. The first step in this exercise is to identify the specific stressor or issue that you are worried about in your current life. Next, you will select a specific time and place where you can focus or concentrate on your worries. You are asked to set aside a specific "worry time" for 15–20 minutes each day. Your therapist can help you select a specific time and place. The idea behind this exercise is to limit your worrying to a specific time and place. After your "worry time" has ended, you are instructed to use the strategies or interventions (i.e., deep breathing, relaxation, thought-stopping, or refocusing that you have been taught in the therapy sessions) to manage your anxiety and worries for the remainder of the day. You may find it helpful to engage in some leisure/recreational activity to take your mind off your worries (this is called "refocusing"). Talk with your therapist about which specific strategy you feel is most helpful in limiting the amount of time you spend worrying outside of the "worry time." We realize that this is easier said than done, but with regular practice of these techniques (i.e., deep breathing, relaxation, thought-stopping, or refocusing), the hope is that you will be able to manage your anxiety more effectively. Please fill out the Daily "Worry Time" Log at the end of each day to let your therapist know how successful you have been in limiting the amount of time you spent worrying each day.

DAILY "WORRY TIME" LOG

Date and Time: _____ Place: _____

1. What were you worried about today: _____

    _____

    _____

2. Rate the degree of your anxiety and worry on a scale from 0 to 10 (circle the appropriate number).

0	1	2	3	4	5	6	7	8	9	10

3. What strategy did you use to try and restrict the amount of time you spent worrying? (Please check all that apply.)

    _____ Deep breathing   _____ Relaxation   _____ Positive self-talk

    _____ Thought-stopping   _____ Refocusing   _____ Other (please list)

4. How successful were your strategies in limiting the amount of time you spent worrying?

    _____

    _____

    _____

5. If the strategies were not helpful in limiting the time you spent worrying today, what factors or stressful events interfered with your ability to "let go" of your worries? _____

    _____

    _____

    _____

PROBLEM SOLVING: AN ALTERNATIVE TO IMPULSIVE ACTION

GOALS OF THE EXERCISE

1. Identify the specific ADD behaviors that cause the most difficulty.
2. List the negative consequences of the problematic ADD behavior.
3. Apply problem-solving skills to specific ADD behaviors that are interfering with daily functioning.

ADDITIONAL PROBLEMS FOR WHICH THIS EXERCISE MAY BE MOST USEFUL

- Anger Control Problems
- Bipolar—Mania
- Impulse Control Disorder

SUGGESTIONS FOR PROCESSING THIS EXERCISE WITH THE CLIENT

Clients with Attention Deficit Disorder (ADD) are characterized by their tendency to exercise poor judgment and act without considering the consequences of their actions. The ADD client frequently finds himself/herself in trouble without realizing what caused him/her to get there and fails to recognize the antecedents of his/her negative consequences. In this exercise, the client is taught a basic problem-solving strategy to help inhibit impulses. The client first identifies a problem with impulsivity and then works through the subsequent problem-solving stages. This exercise can be used with clients who do not have ADD, but do have problems with impulse control.

PROBLEM SOLVING: AN ALTERNATIVE TO IMPULSIVE ACTION

People with Attention Deficit Disorder (ADD) often find themselves in trouble without realizing what caused them to get there. It is not uncommon for the person with ADD to try to solve problems by quickly rushing into a situation without stopping and thinking about the possible consequences of his/her actions. The failure to stop and think causes negative consequences for both self and others. If this sounds all too familiar to you and you are tired of finding yourself in trouble because of your failure to stop and think, then this exercise is designed for you. In this exercise, you are taught to use basic problem-solving steps to deal with a stressful situation. By following these steps, you will hopefully find yourself in less trouble with others and feel better about yourself.

1. The first step in solving any problem is to realize that a problem exists. At this beginning stage, you are asked to identify either a major impulsivity problem that you are currently facing or a common reoccurring problem that troubles you and is caused by your impulsive actions.

    Identify the problem. _____

    _____

2. After identifying the problem, consider three different alternative possible courses of action to help you solve or deal with the impulsivity problem. List the pros and cons of each possible course of action. Record at least three different pros and cons for each course of action.

    First possible course of action to be taken: _____

    _____

    Pros _____   **Cons** _____

    _____   _____

    _____   _____

    _____   _____

    Second possible course of action to be taken: _____

    _____

Pros _____   **Cons** _____
_____   _____
_____   _____
_____   _____

Third possible course of action to be taken: _____

Pros _____   **Cons** _____
_____   _____
_____   _____
_____   _____

3. Next, review the pros and cons of each one of your possible courses of action. At this point, talk with your partner, a family member, friend, or peer to help you choose a final plan of action.

4. Identify the course of action that you plan to follow: _____
    _____
    _____

5. What factors influenced you to choose this course of action? _____
    _____
    _____
    _____

6. What advice or input did you receive from others that influenced your decision?
    _____
    _____
    _____

Now you are in the final stage of this exercise. You have identified the problem, considered different possible courses of action, made a decision, and followed through on your plan of action. Your final task is to evaluate the results or success of your plan of action. Please respond to the following questions.

7. What were the results of your plan of action? _____
    _____
    _____

8. How do you feel about the results? _____

_____

_____

9. How did your plan affect both you and others? _____

_____

_____

10. What did you learn from this experience? _____

_____

_____

11. What, if anything, would you do differently if you were faced with the same or a similar problem in the future? _____

_____

_____

SELF-MONITORING/SELF-REWARD PROGRAM

GOALS OF THE EXERCISE

1. Teach the client self-monitoring technique to reduce the effects of his/her inattention, forgetfulness, disorganization, or impulsivity.
2. Assume daily activities or responsibilities at home, school, or work on a regular, consistent basis.
3. Reward self when impulsivity, inattention, or forgetfulness are replaced by positive alternatives.

ADDITIONAL PROBLEMS FOR WHICH THIS EXERCISE MAY BE MOST USEFUL

- Antisocial Behavior
- Bipolar—Depression
- Bipolar—Mania
- Impulse Control Disorder
- Unipolar Depression

SUGGESTIONS FOR PROCESSING THIS EXERCISE WITH THE CLIENT

Adults with ADD have problems completing tasks on a regular basis because of their distractibility, forgetfulness, disorganization, hyperactivity, or impulsivity. This assignment seeks to teach the client a self-monitoring technique to help him/her complete tasks in a timely manner. Talk with the client about whether he/she wants to use the Self-Monitoring/Self-Reward Form to: (1) complete a one-time task that he/she avoided doing for an extended period of time, (2) perform a particular task over a period of time to help build a routine, or (3) complete a long-term project over a period of time by breaking it down into smaller steps. The client is encouraged to reward himself/herself for successfully completing the daily task or responsibility. The client has the option of using tokens that can be accumulated or "cashed in" at a later time to purchase a larger or more meaningful reward. The client is encouraged to utilize the Self-Monitoring/Self-Reward Form to identify the specific reward he/she will receive for successfully performing the activity or responsibility.

SELF-MONITORING/SELF-REWARD PROGRAM

Adults who have been diagnosed with having an Attention Deficit Disorder (ADD) often have difficulty assuming daily responsibilities or completing tasks on a regular basis. Adults with ADD may fail to assume responsibilities or complete a task because they either forgot, became distracted, or actually began the task but switched to another activity. Likewise, they may procrastinate or "put off" doing a mundane, but necessary, task in favor of performing a more enjoyable or less stressful activity. Spouses, family members, and colleagues at work are likely to become irritated and frustrated with the ADD adult's inability to complete tasks in a timely manner. The adult with ADD often becomes frustrated with himself/herself because of his/her failure to complete the activity. This assignment utilizes self-monitoring and self-reward techniques to help the ADD adult complete tasks on a regular basis.

1. Self-Monitoring Technique

One of the primary purposes of this assignment is to teach you a self-monitoring technique to increase your completion of everyday tasks that may not be as interesting or pleasurable as other tasks you perform on a regular basis. In this assignment, you are encouraged to set a realistic goal for yourself and perform at least one designated activity per day. The activity may be performed in the home, school, or work setting. Feel free to consult with your spouse, other family members, college roommates, or colleagues at work about tasks that they would like to see you complete. The task may be a one-time activity. You may also choose to perform one specific task over an extended period of time so that you get into a routine of performing that particular task. On the other hand, you may choose to complete a longer-term project that will need to be broken down into smaller steps and completed over the course of several days or even weeks. Record the specified task on the Self-Monitoring/Self-Reward Form to remind you to complete the identified task. Post the Self-Monitoring/Self-Reward Form in a highly visible place (e.g., refrigerator, desk) to remind you to complete the task.

The following is a suggested list of short-term activities that you may want to perform:

- Balance checkbook or develop filing system for finances
- Study for a specified time period each day
- Sweep the garage
- Clean dishes/mop the kitchen floor
- Plant flowers in the garden
- Call insurance agent(s) about rates for car or home insurance
- Clean and organize desk at work

Below is a suggested list of longer-term projects that may need to be broken down into smaller steps and performed over time:

- Paint bedroom (this may include cleaning walls, sanding, removing wallpaper, applying primer, and applying first and second coats of desired color)
- Organize kitchen or basement (this may include removing and throwing away unnecessary or unused items, sorting and organizing items into groups, and placing groups of items on different shelves in certain sections of the room)
- Build deck (if needed: contact friends or family members for help; purchase construction materials; remove old deck materials; build foundation or set frame; install deck boards, railings, steps; seal or paint deck)

2. Self-Reward

You are strongly encouraged to reward yourself for completing the particular task or steps in a longer-term project. The rewards will hopefully increase your motivation and help you to stay accountable. The rewards need not be expensive, but will hopefully reinforce your efforts for completing the task. Please identify the specific reward you will receive if you complete the task or step in the longer-term project. You may want to reward yourself with tokens that can be accumulated to purchase or receive a larger, more meaningful reward. For example, you may want to reward yourself by going to a favorite local restaurant if you perform a particular task over the course of 5–10 days. Again, feel free to consult with your spouse, family members, or colleagues at work to identify rewards that may motivate you to complete the task. Below is a list of potential rewards:

- Spend 30–60 minutes on the computer without interruption
- Spend one hour of free time without interruption
- Use tokens to purchase tickets for a sporting event
- Use tokens to purchase tickets for a movie or play at a local theater
- Go kayaking on the weekend
- Buy specialty coffee at a local coffee shop
- Go out for lunch one time per week at work
- Receive back rub or massage from spouse
- Purchase bouquet of flowers

Space is provided for you to sign the Self-Monitoring/Self-Reward Form. At the bottom, you have the option of allowing your spouse, another family member, friend, and even therapist to sign the Self-Monitoring/Self-Reward Form. Other signatures may increase your motivation to perform the task. Again, this is optional.

SELF-MONITORING/SELF-REWARD FORM

Date: _____ Time: _____

Setting: _____

1. My goal is to complete the following task on this day: _____

    _____

    _____

2. If I successfully perform or complete this task, then I will receive the following
    reward: _____

    _____

    _____

3. If I am using a token system to: (a) perform a daily task on a regular basis over an
    extended period of time, or (b) complete a longer-term project by breaking it down
    into smaller steps, then I will need to earn the following number of tokens _____
    (number) to receive the following reward: _____

    _____

    _____

_____   _____

Signature of Client   Signature of Spouse/Significant Other

_____   _____

Signature of Family Member or Friend   Signature of Therapist

SYMPTOMS AND FIXES FOR ADD

GOALS OF THE EXERCISE

1. Identify the specific ADD symptoms that have caused the most difficulty.
2. Become familiar with the preliminary elements of some treatment techniques.
3. Understand that treatment involves more than just taking medication.

ADDITIONAL PROBLEMS FOR WHICH THIS EXERCISE MAY BE MOST USEFUL

- None

SUGGESTIONS FOR PROCESSING THIS EXERCISE WITH THE CLIENT

Adult ADD is a syndrome that is revealed in a myriad of different symptoms. Review the client's checklist of symptoms that he/she has experienced and allow him/her to discuss any of them in more detail. It is also important to focus the client's attention on the intervention strategies that are a part of successful treatment. Many clients have the notion that medication alone is the complete answer to their struggles. They may have questions that need to be answered about the coping skills that are briefly described in this homework assignment. Provide the client with as much detail as necessary for their understanding of these techniques. Reinforce those strategies that you believe will be beneficial to them and that will be the focus for future treatment sessions.

SYMPTOMS AND FIXES FOR ADD

Attention Deficit Disorder (ADD) is characterized by a variety of symptoms or signs. Although you may have become aware of having ADD as an adult, the symptoms of distractibility, short attention span, impulsivity, and restlessness most likely began in childhood. This assignment encourages you to review your life and indicate what symptoms are a part of your experience. We then take a brief look at a list of coping skills that commonly help ADD clients.

SYMPTOM CHECKLIST

1. Check all the symptoms that you have experienced within the past 6 months.

_____ Loss of concentration	_____ Disorganized
_____ Easily distracted	_____ Rarely finish projects
_____ Restless and fidgety	_____ Easily irritated (short fuse)
_____ Impulsive actions	_____ Easily frustrated
_____ Rapid mood swings	_____ Low self-esteem
_____ Tendency for addictive behaviors	_____ Interrupt or intrude on others
_____ Inconsistent work and effort	_____ Fail to listen
_____ Poor sense of time	_____ Make careless mistakes
_____ Easily overwhelmed	_____ Poor time management
_____ Difficulty switching activities	_____ Enjoy high-risk behaviors
_____ Feel "driven by a motor"	_____ Chronic lateness
_____ Talk excessively	_____ Easily bored
_____ Frequently lose things	_____ Poor employment history
_____ Blurt out remarks	_____ Feel anxious
_____ Impatient awaiting turn	_____ Often depressed
_____ Forgetful in daily duties	_____ Poor eye contact

2. List the three most problematic symptoms.

   A. _____

   B. _____

   C. _____

3. Why are these symptoms the most problematic? What are the consequences for you of each of these three symptoms?

   A. _____

   B. _____

   C. _____

Fixes

4. Following is a list of coping techniques that are used to assist people who struggle with ADD. Review the list and place a check mark next to those that you think might be most helpful for you to receive further guidance with as your treatment progresses.

   _____ *Medication:* One of the most common treatments for ADD is the prescription of stimulant medication by a physician. There are various types of these medications and they are prescribed in various dosages to fit individual needs.

   _____ *Problem-Solving Skills:* The client is taught how to approach problems in a systematic way and analyze the pros and cons of various solutions before making a decision for action. This approach is a replacement for the impulsivity that characterizes many ADD clients.

   _____ *Stop, Listen, Think, Act:* This technique is also designed to curb impulsivity. The client is taught to listen carefully to the requirements of a situation and then to think about what action should be taken in response to the situation before engaging in a behavior.

   _____ *Positive Self-Talk:* The client is taught to give himself/herself positive messages to counteract feelings of low self-esteem, inadequacy, depression, and anxiety.

   _____ *Time Out:* This procedure is commonly used to help clients reduce their irritability and impulsivity by training them to remove themselves from stimulus situations for a short time before reacting. This allows for consideration of consequences and engaging actions in a more planful manner.

   _____ *Relaxation:* Many clients with ADD are fidgety and restless, anxious, and on edge. Learning to implement relaxation techniques is a major help in reducing stress and reactivity.

_____ *Self-Reward:* Self-reward procedures are implemented to assist ADD clients in completing tasks that are often left incomplete. This procedure is also helpful in motivating clients to be focused in their actions.

_____ *Reminder Aids:* Forgetfulness and lack of organization are common traits of ADD clients. Learning to use checklists, notes written to self, organization calendars, cell phones, and day planners are useful techniques.

_____ *Physical Exercise:* To reduce the restless, fidgety energy that is common to ADD clients, physical exercise on a regular basis is often implemented. The exercise reduces stress and increases relaxation and the ability to focus attention.

_____ *Distraction Reduction:* The client learns to arrange the environment such that sounds, sights, people, or objects that could lead to distraction are minimized or removed.

_____ *Organizational Coach:* Consulting with others is a very helpful technique for those who lack organization in their life. Accepting guidance and advice from others in terms of ways to organize the environment or approach the task can be very beneficial.

_____ *Talk Time:* It is important for many ADD clients to have the opportunity to sit and talk without distractions. This allows for structured time to be set aside where distractions are minimal and thoughts are followed through to completion. Significant others also benefit from this communication opportunity.

5. After you have checked off the techniques that you believe would be helpful for you to learn and implement, explain why you think these would be helpful to you.

_____

_____

_____

_____

_____

_____

_____

_____

_____

_____

_____

_____

_____

EARLY WARNING SIGNS OF DEPRESSION

GOALS OF THE EXERCISE

1. Identify early warning signs of depression.
2. Learn and implement relapse prevention skills.
3. Develop a plan to manage life's stressors and reduce depression.
4. Alleviate depressed mood and return to previous level of effective functioning.

ADDITIONAL PROBLEMS FOR WHICH THIS EXERCISE MAY BE MOST USEFUL

- Bipolar—Mania
- Grief/Loss Unresolved
- Low Self-Esteem
- Medical Issues
- Sleep Disturbance
- Unipolar Depression

SUGGESTIONS FOR PROCESSING THIS EXERCISE WITH THE CLIENT

This exercise is designed for clients who have a history of depression. The primary purpose of the assignment is to help the client recognize the early warning signs of depression. The client is first asked to review a list of depressive symptoms and check the symptoms that he/she has recently been experiencing. In addition, the client is asked to identify previous strategies he/she has learned to alleviate his/her previous bouts of depression. The assignment concludes with the client selecting strategies that he/she feels will be effective in reducing his/her current symptoms of depression.

EARLY WARNING SIGNS OF DEPRESSION

Detecting early warning signs of depression can help prevent a relapse of a prolonged bout of depression. If you are questioning whether you are entering a phase of depression, please review the following list and place a check mark next to the symptoms that you are experiencing.

___ Depressed mood

___ Loss of joy or pleasure in various activities

___ Frequent crying spells

___ Apathy, listlessness, or lethargy

___ Frequent complaints or negative remarks about life

___ Low self-esteem

___ Lack of confidence, give up easily when frustrated

___ Negative or derogatory remarks about self

___ Social withdrawal

___ Loss of motivation

___ Inappropriate guilt or remorse

___ Agitated bodily movements

___ Sluggish or slow bodily movements

___ Loss or increase of appetite

___ Trouble falling asleep

___ Trouble staying asleep

___ Excessive sleeping

___ Nightmares

___ Loss of energy, tiredness, fatigue

___ Poor concentration and indecision

___ Sullen, irritable moods

___ Easily irritated or annoyed

___ Feelings of helplessness/ hopelessness

___ Suicidal thoughts or passive death wishes (e.g., "I wish I had never been born")

___ Self-harmful behavior

___ Other _____

What coping strategies have you learned in the past to manage or alleviate your depression? Please review the list of strategies below and place a check mark next to the strategies you have used in the past to successfully reduce your depression.

___ Trial of antidepressant medication

___ Use of positive self-talk

___ Identify and replace negative self-talk with positive self-talk

___ Thought-stoppage

___ Behavioral activation (e.g., scheduling activities that have a high likelihood of bringing joy or pleasure)

___ Physical exercise

___ Use of role-playing

___ Read self-help book (please list book)

_____

_____

___ Increased social involvement

___ Use of effective communication/assertiveness skills

___ Utilize problem-solving approaches

___ Identify ways to reduce depression

___ Express underlying anger in an assertive manner

Please review the list above and circle the interventions or strategies you would like to learn more about in future therapy sessions.

List three to five strategies that you think will be helpful at the present time in reducing your symptoms of depression.

1. _____
2. _____
3. _____
4. _____
5. _____

Finally, ask three to five people whom you trust for any suggestions that they have about any activities or things you can do to reduce your depression. List some of their ideas below.

1. _____
2. _____
3. _____
4. _____
5. _____

IDENTIFYING AND HANDLING TRIGGERS

GOALS OF THE EXERCISE

1. Develop and demonstrate coping skills to deal with mood swings.
2. Increase awareness of personal triggers and their roots.
3. Develop and implement effective coping skills to carry out normal responsibilities and participate constructively in relationships.
4. Identify specific sources for each trigger.

ADDITIONAL PROBLEMS FOR WHICH THIS EXERCISE MAY BE MOST USEFUL

- Childhood Trauma
- Posttraumatic Stress Disorder (PTSD)
- Sexual Abuse Victim

SUGGESTIONS FOR PROCESSING THIS EXERCISE WITH THE CLIENT

It would be strongly suggested that this exercise be assigned early in a client's treatment, as identifying triggers and their sources are key to cooling down the response, bringing about increased control in the situation, and eventually changing the way the client reacts to the specific triggers. Psychoeducation on triggers needs to be a key part of the processing. It is likely that many of the points will need to be reemphasized along the way. Further, the exercise can be referred back to as the client brings into therapy incidents from his/her week where triggers are clearly involved.

IDENTIFYING AND HANDLING TRIGGERS

Triggers can come in many categories. Two such categories are nontraumatic and traumatic. Nontraumatic triggers would be positive triggers like holiday baking smells, hearing a special friend's laugh, or seeing a special place. On the other hand, traumatic triggers are parts of your past that intrude into your present life. These triggers often activate strong automatic physical and emotional responses that are out of proportion for the presenting situation. This, of course, leads to difficulty related to effectively handling issues and relationships. The exercise below is about beginning to identify as clearly as possible what your triggers are, as identification is the start of bringing them under control.

1. Thoughtfully identify the following:

A. Sounds that trigger me:

    a. _____

        Response: _____

        Thoughts and feelings: _____

        Possible origin: _____

    b. _____

        Response: _____

        Thoughts and feelings: _____

        Possible origin: _____

B. Smells that trigger me:

    a. _____

        Response: _____

        Thoughts and feelings: _____

        Possible origin: _____

    b. _____

        Response: _____

        Thoughts and feelings: _____

        Possible origin: _____

C. Things I see that trigger me:

    a. _____

        Response: _____

        Thoughts and feelings: _____

        Possible origin: _____

    b. _____

        Response: _____

        Thoughts and feelings: _____

        Possible origin: _____

D. Places that trigger me:

    a. _____

        Response: _____

        Thoughts and feelings: _____

        Possible origin: _____

    b. _____

        Response: _____

        Thoughts and feelings: _____

        Possible origin: _____

E. People (faces) that trigger me:

    a. _____

        Response: _____

        Thoughts and feelings: _____

        Possible origin: _____

    b. _____

        Response: _____

        Thoughts and feelings: _____

        Possible origin: _____

F. Time, day of week, or season that triggers me:

    a. _____

        Response: _____

        Thoughts and feelings: _____

        Possible origin: _____

b. _____

    Response: _____

    Thoughts and feelings: _____

    Possible origin: _____

G. Things that are said that trigger me:

a. _____

    Response: _____

    Thoughts and feelings: _____

    Possible origin: _____

b. _____

    Response: _____

    Thoughts and feelings: _____

    Possible origin: _____

2. Now from the triggers that you identified, choose one to address:

    Trigger: _____

3. Choose one approach/technique to implement to address the trigger:

    Relaxation techniques   Grounding

    Deep breathing   Positive self-talk

    Avoiding specific trigger   Thought-stopping

Practice and/or plan with your therapist how you will implement this technique when you experience the trigger.

4. Trigger _____

    Situation(s) I expect to experience _____

    _____

    Strategy I plan to implement _____

    _____

    How I plan to implement the strategy in the situation _____

    _____

Step 1: _____

_____

Step 2: _____

_____

5. After you have implemented the strategy, now evaluate:

How the strategy worked _____

_____

_____

How successful you felt in implementing it _____

_____

_____

Any changes or adjustments you would make _____

_____

_____

KEEPING A DAILY RHYTHM

GOALS OF THE EXERCISE

1. Assist the client in establishing a regular routine of daily activities (e.g., sleeping, eating, exercise, household responsibilities, solitary activities, and social/recreational/ leisure activities).
2. Utilize the Daily Activities Form to schedule, assess, and modify activities so that they occur in a predictable rhythm every day.
3. Achieve stabilization of moods by establishing regular daily rhythm or routine.

ADDITIONAL PROBLEMS FOR WHICH THIS EXERCISE MAY BE MOST USEFUL

- Bipolar—Depression
- Borderline Personality
- Unipolar Depression

SUGGESTIONS FOR CONDUCTING THIS EXERCISE WITH THE CLIENT

Interpersonal and Social Rhythm Therapy uses the Social Rhythm Metric (SRM; see Frank, 2005) to record and construct a daily routine for clients intended to balance and stabilize daily activities so as to not over- or understimulate the client and precipitate manic or depressive symptoms. Therapists can use the SRM or this exercise, which approaches the task somewhat differently than the SRM but toward the same goal. Begin the exercise by educating the client and significant others about Interpersonal and Social Rhythm Therapy and the potential benefits of maintaining a daily routine in stabilizing moods and preventing a relapse of symptoms. After this education, ask the client to use the Daily Activities Form to record when they do various activities such as sleeping, waking, eating, exercising, and working, as well as solitary, social, leisure, and recreational activities. Assessing weekday (or work day) and weekend (or non-working day) activities is preferred. Once daily activities and times have been recorded, review the data with the client toward the goal of constructing a mutually agreed upon schedule that regulates predictable activities. Revisit this task as needed until a satisfactory balance is found. The scale contains the option to record mood type and severity (0–10) associated with activities to assess this relationship and intervene accordingly. Routinely assess the client's success in following the daily routine and problem-solve any obstacles. Options for identifying stressors or disruptions in the schedule and their impact on mood are included.

Frank, E. P. (2005). *Treating bipolar disorder: A clinician's guide to interpersonal and social rhythm therapy*. New York, NY: Guilford Press.

KEEPING A DAILY RHYTHM

Research has shown that Interpersonal and Social Rhythm Therapy, combined with psychotropic medications, has demonstrated benefits in achieving stabilization of moods, reducing the risk for relapse of manic/depressive symptoms, and helping clients manage their everyday demands and stressors. An important part of this therapeutic approach asks you to develop a daily schedule or routine. Having a daily schedule or routine can help stabilize moods. Use the Daily Activities Form to record when you engage in various daily activities such as sleeping, waking, eating, exercising, and working, as well as solitary, social, leisure, and recreational activities. You are encouraged to record your daily activities for both weekdays (or work days) and weekends (or non-working days). The Daily Activities Form that is provided runs from 7:00 a.m. to 11:00 p.m. The times from 11:00 p.m. to 7:00 a.m. have been designated for sleep. However, you may want to adjust the schedule to meet your own specific needs. For example, you may find it best to sleep from 9:30 or 10:00 p.m. until 6:00 or 6:30 a.m. After recording your activities, consult with your therapist about how the information is used to construct your daily routine. You are also encouraged to involve your spouse, significant others, or other family members to help support your new daily schedule on a regular basis. As time goes on, you may find it necessary to modify the schedule to meet your particular needs. You are encouraged to follow the routine regularly. Interruptions inevitably occur in your life; but your goal is to try to be as consistent as possible in following through with the schedule.

You and your therapist should regularly review how successful you have been in following the daily routine or schedule. Your therapist may also ask you to keep close track of your moods and any stressors or disruptions in your life that may cause you to change or adjust your routine. Following a daily routine in this manner has helped others in feeling more stable, productive, and knowledgeable about how activity and mood influence each other.

DAILY ACTIVITIES FORM

(Record when you got out of bed, ate/drank, left your residence, saw another person(s), did work/school/volunteer activities, napped, exercised, watched television, went to bed, and any other activities.)

TIME	ACTIVITY and MOOD (0–10)	TIME	ACTIVITY and MOOD (0–10)
7:00 a.m.		3:30 p.m.	
7:30 a.m.		4:00 p.m.	
8:00 a.m.		4:30 p.m.	
8:30 a.m.		5:00 p.m.	
9:00 a.m.		5:30 p.m.	
9:30 a.m.		6:00 p.m.	
10:00 a.m.		6:30 p.m.	
10:30 a.m.		7:00 p.m.	
11:00 a.m.		7:30 p.m.	
11:30 a.m.		8:00 p.m.	
12:00 p.m.		8:30 p.m.	
12:30 p.m.		9:00 p.m.	

TIME	ACTIVITY and MOOD (0–10)	TIME	ACTIVITY and MOOD (0–10)
1:00 p.m.		9:30 p.m.	
1:30 p.m.		10:00 p.m.	
2:00 p.m.		10:30 p.m.	
2:30 p.m.		11:00 p.m.	
3:00 p.m.		11:00 p.m.–7:00 a.m.	SLEEP

SELF-MONITORING OF MOODS

Date and time: _____

1.   What stressful or life events disrupted or changed your daily routine? _____

_____

_____

_____

_____

2.   a.   What symptoms of mania did you experience as a result of the disruption in your daily routine? (Circle all that apply, or circle *none* if you did not experience any symptoms.)

Expansive/elevated mood	Emotional lability	Increased energy level
Agitated motor movements	Pressured speech	Talking fast/loud
Racing thoughts	Flight of ideas	Grandiose ideas
Little or no appetite	Decreased or loss of sleep	Sexualized behavior or talk
Highly impulsive behavior	Pleasure-seeking behavior	Substance abuse
None	Other: _____	

   b.   Rate each symptom's severity on a scale from 1 to 10.

3. What symptoms of depression did you experience as a result of the disruption in your daily routine? (Circle all that apply, or circle *none* if you did not experience any symptoms.)

Depressed mood	Apathy/listlessness	Hopelessness/helplessness
Negative self-talk	Social withdrawal	Irritability
Suicidal thoughts or gestures	Excessive sleep	Crying spells
Loss of sleep	Lost interest/enjoyment in activities	
Tiredness/fatigue/loss of energy		
None	Other: _____	

   b. Rate each symptom's severity on a scale from 1 to 10.

4. How easily will you be able to return to your normal routine, or will you have to make changes or modifications in your daily schedule? Please elaborate. _____

_____

_____

_____

RECOGNIZING THE NEGATIVE CONSEQUENCES OF IMPULSIVE BEHAVIOR

GOALS OF THE EXERCISE

1. Identify impulsive behavior as distinct from more reasoned, thoughtful behavior.
2. Understand that impulsive behavior has costly negative consequences for yourself and others.
3. Review own behavior and see the impulsive actions and their negative consequences.
4. Think of more reasonable alternative replacement behaviors for those impulsive actions.
5. Terminate self-destructive behaviors, such as promiscuity, substance abuse, and the expression of overt hostility or aggression.

ADDITIONAL PROBLEMS FOR WHICH THIS EXERCISE MAY BE MOST USEFUL

*   Attention-Deficit Disorder (ADD)—Adult
*   Borderline Personality
*   Impulse Control Disorder
*   Substance Use

SUGGESTIONS FOR PROCESSING THIS EXERCISE WITH THE CLIENT

Impulsive behaviors are much more easily recognized by others than by the clients with impulse control problems. They think their behavior is normal and typical. You must try to sensitize them to their pattern of acting before thinking of the consequences. Review this homework with clients slowly, allowing time to process each scene they have described. They will want to quickly dismiss each item and move on to the next. That impulsive action is just the problem you are focusing on.

RECOGNIZING THE NEGATIVE CONSEQUENCES OF IMPULSIVE BEHAVIOR

This exercise is meant to help you think before you act so that you end up with better results. Read the two behavior descriptions for each number and then circle the number of the one that shows a lack of proper control.

Which One Is Impulsive?

1. Purchase two tickets to watch a movie with your favorite actor without reading the reviews in advance.

   _____

2. Waiting your turn patiently at McDonalds.

   _____

3. Grabbing the first piece of clothing to wear in the morning.

   _____

4. Keeping some money for savings.

   _____

5. Waiting for a friend to stop talking before speaking.

   _____

6. Jumping to a new task before another task is finished.

   _____

7. Starting to watch one TV program and then switching to another and another before any are over.

   _____

1. Choose a movie to take your wife/date to after reading the reviews of several movies online.

   _____

2. Complaining loudly about waiting in line and trying to get ahead of others.

   _____

3. Selecting clothes that match and fit the situation.

   _____

4. Spending any and all money as soon as you have it.

   _____

5. Butting into a conversation between two friends, interrupting them.

   _____

6. Completing one task before starting another.

   _____

7. Watching a TV program until it is completed, then choosing another.

   _____

Now return to each of the preceding seven behaviors and write out below what you think the bad consequence or result of the behavior of acting without first thinking about the consequences is for each one. (We did the first one for you.)

Impulsive Behavior Leads to Bad Consequences

1. Your wife/date and you leave the theater very dissatisfied with the movie you sat through and watched.

2. _____

3. _____

4. _____

5. _____

6. _____

7. _____

Pick four out of the seven behaviors described previously and write out a similar scene from your own life when you have been impulsive. Use names and places with which you are familiar.

My Impulsive Behaviors

1. _____

2. _____

3. _____

4. _____

Now describe the bad results of your four impulsive actions.

My Bad Consequences

1. _____

2. _____

3. _____

4. _____

Finally, look at your four impulsive actions and write out a more calm, reasonable, considerate, polite, thoughtful way that you could have acted that would have brought better results.

Good Behavior Choices

1. _____

2. _____

3. _____

4. _____

WHAT ARE MY GOOD QUALITIES?

GOALS OF THE EXERCISE

1. Increase genuine self-esteem through identification of positive character and personality traits.
2. Acknowledge the low self-esteem and fear of rejection that underlie the braggadocio.
3. Decrease the fear of inadequacy that underlies exaggerated claims of ability or social withdrawal and refusal to try new things.

ADDITIONAL PROBLEMS FOR WHICH THIS EXERCISE MAY BE MOST USEFUL

- Bipolar—Depression
- Low Self-Esteem
- Sexual Abuse Victim
- Social Anxiety
- Substance Use
- Unipolar Depression

SUGGESTIONS FOR PROCESSING THIS EXERCISE WITH THE CLIENT

Clients often have a distorted perception of themselves and the world that causes them to see only negative traits and remember only failures. For the manic patient, this underlying core of feeling inadequate is covered with a veneer of exaggerated confidence and willfulness. Genuine self-esteem must be built through realistic self-assessment bolstered by others' support.

WHAT ARE MY GOOD QUALITIES?

Often we are quick to mention our faults and overlook our good qualities. It is now time for you to pay special attention to what is good about you—focus on the aspects of your personality that make you *uniquely a good person*. Look at yourself in an honest and realistic way. You should not try to be polite and deny your strengths, but also you should not have to exaggerate to make up for not feeling good enough to be accepted by others.

1. Find the words that apply to you in the following list of nice things people say about other good people. Circle all those that describe you.

Appreciative	Reliable	Friendly
Humble	Thoughtful	Wise
Creative	Warm	Thorough
Kind	Faithful	Independent
Sensitive	Articulate	Leader
Responsible	Open	Pleasant
Considerate	Communicative	Tolerant
Punctual	Spiritual	Energetic
Attractive	Loving	Includes others
Hardworking	Trustworthy	Physically fit
Intelligent	Reasonable	Conscientious
Sociable	Wide interests	Moral
Decision maker	Easygoing	Humorous
Loyal	Mechanical	Talented
Ethical	Honest	Athletic
Musical	Organized	Artistic
Well-groomed	Well-dressed	Accepting
Insightful	Polite	Complimentary
Practical	Patient	Happy
Approachable	Good listener	Respectful
Obedient	Thrifty	Helpful

Other good things about me that are not on this list are: _____

_____

2. Now give a copy of the form on the following page to two or three people that know you well (parent, friend, teacher, relative) and ask them to circle words that they believe describe you. Fill in their names and your name in the blank spaces.

Dear _____ ,
        (Person's Name)

Because you know me very well, I would like you to tell me what you think are the best things about me. Please circle words that really describe _____ .
                                                                                                      (Your name)

Thank you very much for taking the time to do this for me.

Appreciative	Reliable	Friendly
Humble	Thoughtful	Wise
Creative	Warm	Thorough
Kind	Faithful	Independent
Sensitive	Articulate	Leader
Responsible	Open	Pleasant
Considerate	Communicative	Tolerant
Punctual	Spiritual	Energetic
Attractive	Loving	Includes others
Hardworking	Trustworthy	Physically fit
Intelligent	Reasonable	Conscientious
Sociable	Wide interests	Moral
Decision maker	Easygoing	Humorous
Loyal	Mechanical	Talented
Ethical	Honest	Athletic
Musical	Organized	Artistic
Well-groomed	Well-dressed	Accepting
Insightful	Polite	Complimentary
Practical	Patient	Happy
Approachable	Good listener	Respectful
Obedient	Thrifty	Helpful

Other good things about me that are not on the list of choices are: _____

_____

_____

_____

_____

_____

_____

3.   Now write a list of your 10 best qualities selected from the circled items on your list and the lists completed by others who circled items to describe you.

My Ten Best Qualities

1.   _____

2.   _____

3.   _____

4.   _____

5.   _____

6.   _____

7.   _____

8.   _____

9.   _____

10. _____

4.   Post your list of My Ten Best Qualities on a mirror in your home. Look yourself squarely in the eye as you say each of the words out loud at least one time a day for 7 days in a row. At the end of the week, write a paragraph about how you feel about yourself in the following space.

_____

_____

_____

_____

_____

_____

_____

_____

WHY I DISLIKE TAKING MY MEDICATION

GOALS OF THE EXERCISE

1. Identify reasons for lack of consistency in taking psychotropic medication.
2. Identify reasons to take medication responsibly and reliably.
3. Verbalize acceptance of the need to take psychotropic medication and commit to prescription compliance with blood-level monitoring.

ADDITIONAL PROBLEMS FOR WHICH THIS EXERCISE MAY BE MOST USEFUL

- Attention Deficit Disorder (ADD)—Adult
- Bipolar—Depression
- Paranoid Ideation
- Psychoticism
- Unipolar Depression

SUGGESTIONS FOR PROCESSING THIS EXERCISE WITH THE CLIENT

Medication resistance is a common problem for clients who have been prescribed psychopharmacologic remedies for their symptoms. This exercise is designed to assist the client in identifying his/her reasons for resistance to medication compliance. The client is also asked to examine and explore reasons for taking the prescribed psychotropic medication consistently. Process the completed assignment with the client while addressing his/her reasons for resistance and reinforcing the advantages of prescription compliance.

WHY I DISLIKE TAKING MY MEDICATION

Many people resist taking prescribed medication after they have been diagnosed with an emotional disorder. People offer a variety of reasons for not taking their medication on a consistent basis. This exercise will help you identify the reasons that you may resist taking your medication and help you identify the advantages of taking the medication consistently and responsibly.

Common Reasons for Medication Resistance

_____ Don't feel like myself	_____ Don't need them
_____ Feel lethargic or sluggish	_____ Feel different than other people
_____ Fear getting hooked on pills	_____ Too expensive
_____ Forget to take medication	_____ Too much of a hassle
_____ Side effects (dizzy, sick, etc.)	_____ Fear getting mocked
_____ Lose my creativity	_____ Feel less in control of life

1. Review the list and place a check mark next to those reasons that you resist taking medication for your emotional disorder. What reason(s) might you have other than those listed? _____

   _____

   _____

   _____

   _____

2. What is the main reason that you do not like taking the medication(s)? _____

   _____

   _____

   _____

   _____

3. What specific positive changes would you like to see the medication make in order for you to take it regularly as prescribed? _____

_____

_____

_____

4. Ask a partner, friend, and/or family member to give reasons why they believe it is good for you to take the medication. What differences do they notice in your moods and behavior when you do not take your medication as prescribed? Write down their answers. _____

_____

_____

_____

_____

5. List three reasons you believe you should take the medication. How does the medication help you? _____

_____

_____

_____

6. How can your life be improved with medication helping to control your symptoms?

_____

_____

_____

JOURNAL AND REPLACE SELF-DEFEATING THOUGHTS

GOALS OF THE EXERCISE

1. Identify negative, distorted cognitions that mediate intense negative emotions.
2. Learn new ways to think that are more adaptive.
3. Replace negative thoughts with more positive, realistic interpretations of situations.
4. Replace dichotomous thinking with the ability to tolerate ambiguity and complexity in people and issues.

ADDITIONAL PROBLEMS FOR WHICH THIS EXERCISE MAY BE MOST USEFUL

- Anxiety
- Low Self-Esteem
- Social Anxiety
- Suicidal Ideation
- Unipolar Depression

SUGGESTIONS FOR PROCESSING THIS EXERCISE WITH THE CLIENT

Borderline clients are the epitome of negative, pessimistic thinkers. This exercise helps them acknowledge this pattern and begin to replace these thought patterns with positive, realistic assessments of life. You may want to review the six types of self-defeating thought patterns that are described in the assignment as well as the alternatives to these before the client begins to journal his/her daily life experiences. In reviewing the journal material, you may have to assist the client in finding positive thoughts to replace his/her distorted pessimistic thinking.

JOURNAL AND REPLACE SELF-DEFEATING THOUGHTS

Feeling intense emotions is preceded by the cognitive processing of external situations. When you encounter a troubling situation, you first develop a series of thoughts about that situation as you analyze it. Your emotions evolve based on how you interpret the situation based on your evaluative thoughts. Stimulus situations lead to interpretative thoughts that lead to a variety of different emotions based on those thoughts. This assignment highlights six common self-defeating thoughts that almost always lead to feelings of frustration, sadness, anger, or other negative emotions. Each of these six self-defeating thought patterns can be reversed and you can engage in more realistic positive thinking to produce more calm, confident, and affirming feelings.

1. Definitions of Six Self-Defeating Thought Patterns.

    A. *Black or White Thinking:* Viewing situations, people, or self as entirely bad or entirely good—nothing in between. Such thoughts almost always lead to harsh judgments and alienation from others. Example: "My supervisor is never fair and he has always hated me."

    B. *Hopelessness:* Consistently viewing situations as having no possible positive or even neutral resolution in the future. This leads to despair and refusal to search for solutions to problems. Example: "I'll never make any new friends who accept me and enjoy me."

    C. *Helplessness:* Refusing to acknowledge that he/she has any ability to impact his/her world in a positive fashion, but consistently believes that bad things just happen to him/her. This results in discounting all positive traits, abilities, and successes and refusing to put forth effort to change his/her environment, becoming dependent on others to do it for him/her. Example: "There is nothing I can do to change the situation, so I might as well just give up and let what happens happen."

    D. *Worthlessness:* Viewing self as not worthy of other people's time, interest, or acceptance. This leads to making self-critical remarks in anticipation of rejection from others. Example: "I don't blame them for not liking me because I'm not worth it anyway."

E. *Catastrophizing:* Blowing expected consequences out of proportion in a very negative direction. This results in withdrawal of effort to change things for the better and reacting to a situation as if the negative consequence has already happened. Example: "I'll never be able to get another job. This layoff is the end of the line for me."

F. *Negative Forecasting:* Predicting events will turn out badly without any basis in reality. This type of thinking results in pessimism, depression, and withdrawal of effort. Example: "I'll never get hired, so there's no sense in even going for the interview."

2. Each of the six self-defeating thought patterns listed can be reversed and replaced with a positive alternative.

A. Alternative to *Black or White Thinking:* Recognizing that there are good and bad aspects to almost anything and everyone and refusing to reject someone quickly because of some small flaw or error. This leads to a greater degree of acceptance of other people and acceptance of self. Example: "My supervisor seems to be having a bad day today but I must admit he has been good to me at times."

B. Alternative to *Hopelessness:* Viewing life more realistically and seeing the potential for possible resolution to negative circumstances given increased time and effort. This leads to a sense of empowerment and increased acceptance from others who view you as a "positive thinker." Example: "Everyone needs friends and appreciates kindness, so if I'm patient, friendly, and considerate, I will develop a social network."

C. Alternative to *Helplessness:* Acknowledging personal resources and abilities that can have an impact on negative situations and seeing opportunities to make a difference rather than waiting on others to do it for him/her. This results in taking action and feeling in control of situations. Example: "I will change my approach to this situation and I'm sure that using a different tactic will produce a positive result."

D. Alternative to *Worthlessness:* Seeing self as worthy of acceptance from others and recognizing his/her intrinsic value as a human being with strengths and weaknesses. This results in greater self-acceptance and the expectation of acceptance from others. Example: "I am a good and capable person who deserves respect from others whom I treat with respect."

E. Alternative to *Catastrophizing:* Viewing consequences in a realistic light and keeping negative aspects in a context that includes positive aspects. This type of thinking leads to the ability to build on the positive aspects of any outcome and nurtures a sense of hopefulness. Example: "This layoff is difficult to accept but I have skills and work habits that will allow me to find another job if I am diligent in my search."

F. Alternative to *Negative Forecasting:* Considering that all possible outcomes may occur and recognizing that without effort no positive outcome is possible. This leads to a more optimistic view of the world and generates enthusiasm. Example: "I know there is competition for this job but I'll stay positive in the interview. If I'm not hired for this job, I know there is another job for me in the future."

3. After reviewing the material on self-defeating thoughts and the positive alternatives to these negative patterns, please record up to seven instances of your engaging in self-defeating thoughts and write down a positive alternative thought that could have/should have replaced it.

   Please fill in the information requested: Describe the situation that triggered the self-defeating thought, list the self-defeating thought itself, describe the negative emotion that resulted from this thought, and finally, list an alternative positive thought that could have been used to interpret the situation differently.

Entry 1 Date _____	Situation	
	Self-Defeating Thought	
	Negative Emotional Results	
	Alternative Positive Thought	

Entry 2 Date _____	Situation	
	Self- Defeating Thought	
	Negative Emotional Results	
	Alternative Positive Thought	

Entry 3 Date _____	Situation	
	Self- Defeating Thought	
	Negative Emotional Results	
	Alternative Positive Thought	

Entry 4 Date _____	Situation	
	Self- Defeating Thought	
	Negative Emotional Results	
	Alternative Positive Thought	

Entry 5 Date _____	Situation	
	Self- Defeating Thought	
	Negative Emotional Results	
	Alternative Positive Thought	

Entry 6 Date _____	Situation	
	Self-Defeating Thought	
	Negative Emotional Results	
	Alternative Positive Thought	

Entry 7 Date _____	Situation	
	Self-Defeating Thought	
	Negative Emotional Results	
	Alternative Positive Thought	

PLAN BEFORE ACTING

GOALS OF THE EXERCISE

1. Develop a coping strategy to inhibit the tendency toward impulsive responding.
2. Increase awareness on how impulsive behaviors lead to negative consequences for self and others.
3. Identify problem and explore alternative courses of action before making a final decision to act.
4. Learn to evaluate his/her own behavior and how it affects self and others.
5. Develop the ability to control impulsive behavior.

ADDITIONAL PROBLEMS FOR WHICH THIS EXERCISE MAY BE MOST USEFUL

*   Anger Control Problems
*   Attention Deficit Disorder (ADD)—Adult
*   Bipolar—Mania
*   Type A Behavior

SUGGESTIONS FOR PROCESSING THIS EXERCISE WITH THE CLIENT

Many clients are characterized by their tendency to exercise poor judgment and act without considering the consequences of their actions. The client finds himself/herself in trouble without realizing what caused him/her to get there and fails to recognize the antecedents of his/her negative consequences. In this exercise, the client is taught a basic problem-solving strategy to help inhibit impulses. The client first identifies a problem and then works through the subsequent problem-solving stages. This is a long assignment, so the client will need considerable encouragement and perhaps support in completing the assignment within the therapy session.

PLAN BEFORE ACTING

People often find themselves in trouble without realizing what caused them to get there. This occurs when people try to solve problems by quickly rushing into a situation without stopping and thinking about the possible consequences of their actions. The failure to stop and think causes negative consequences for both self and others. In this exercise, you are taught to use basic problem-solving steps to deal with a stressful situation. By following these steps, you will find yourself in less trouble with others and feel better about yourself.

1. The first step in solving any problem is to realize that a problem exists. At this beginning stage, you are asked to identify either a major problem that you are currently facing or a common recurring problem that troubles you. Talk with your friends, spouse, or family if you have trouble selecting a problem that you would like to focus on solving. Identify the problem below.

    _____

    _____

2. After identifying the problem, consider two different possible courses of action to help you solve or deal with the problem. List the pros and cons of each possible course of action, then record different pros and cons for each course of action.

    First possible course of action to be taken: _____

    _____

    _____

    Pros _____   **Cons** _____

    _____   _____

    _____   _____

    Second possible course of action to be taken: _____

    _____

    _____

    Pros _____   **Cons** _____

    _____   _____

    _____   _____

3. Next, review the pros and cons of each one of your possible courses of action and select the course of action you plan to follow (you are encouraged to talk with your spouse or a friend or family member to help you choose a final plan of action). Now identify the course of action that you plan to follow. _____

_____

_____

4. What factors influenced you to choose this course of action? _____

_____

_____

5. What advice or input did you receive from others that influenced your decision?

_____

_____

6. Now it is time to follow through on your plan of action. Describe the events that occurred when you followed through with your plan of action. What were the results? _____

_____

_____

7. You are in the final stage of this exercise. You have identified the problem, considered different possible courses of action, made a decision, and followed through on your plan of action. Your final task is to evaluate the outcome. How do you feel about the results of your action? _____

_____

_____

8. What did you learn from this experience? _____

_____

_____

9. What, if anything, would you do differently if you were faced with the same or a similar problem in the future? _____

_____

_____

CHANGING FROM VICTIM TO SURVIVOR

GOALS OF THE EXERCISE

1. Identify the traits of a victim versus those of a survivor.
2. Evaluate current status as either a victim or a survivor.
3. Decrease statements of being a victim while increasing statements that reflect personal empowerment.
4. Increase confidence toward facing life with a sense of empowerment.

ADDITIONAL PROBLEMS FOR WHICH THIS EXERCISE MAY BE MOST USEFUL

- Posttraumatic Stress Disorder (PTSD)
- Sexual Abuse Victim

SUGGESTIONS FOR PROCESSING THIS EXERCISE WITH THE CLIENT

The client may be far down the road toward becoming a survivor instead of a victim. On the other hand, the client may be stuck in victim status and this assignment will help him/her sort through traits that keep him/her in that status. Review his/her list of descriptors to make sure that the positive, confident, and healthy descriptors are under the label of "Survivor" while the more negative, self-defeating, depressive descriptors are under the column labeled "Victim." Reinforce motivation to move from victim to survivor and point out the many benefits that accrue as he/she changes this status of perspective.

CHANGING FROM VICTIM TO SURVIVOR

It is natural to view yourself as a victim and to experience all of the feelings and attitudes that accompany that victim status when the abuse has only recently occurred or there has been no opportunity for working through the emotions and thoughts connected to the abuse. It takes time and effort to move from the status of being a victim to becoming a survivor. The feelings and thoughts associated with being a victim are overwhelmingly negative and self-defeating. The feelings and thoughts associated with being a survivor, on the other hand, are more positive, forward looking, and confident. While it is natural and expected that everyone who has been exposed to abuse starts with feeling like a victim, realization of the potential of this person can only be achieved if his/her status changes to that of becoming a survivor. This exercise will help you understand the differences between victims and survivors and help you define your own current status.

1. The following words or phrases describe either a victim or a survivor, but they are presented to you in a mixed-up order. Your task is to look at each word or phrase and rewrite it under the column labeled "Victim" or the column labeled "Survivor" on the next page. You will have to sort through the list to finally end up with a profile of words that describe a victim and words that describe a survivor.

List of Descriptors

Depressed

Has overcome pain

Blames perpetrator

Pessimistic

Hopeless

Empowered

Trauma is in perspective

Defeated

Lives in the present and future

Helpless

Hopeful

Withdrawn socially

Optimistic

Ashamed

Needs sympathy

Preoccupied with trauma

Enjoys living

Lives in the past

Wants understanding

Enjoys people

Letting go of anger

Growing in trust

No energy

Dominated by fear

More smiles than tears

Distrustful

Bitter

Confident

Renewed energy

Focused on the pain

Victim	**Survivor**
_____	_____
_____	_____
_____	_____
_____	_____
_____	_____
_____	_____
_____	_____
_____	_____
_____	_____
_____	_____
_____	_____
_____	_____

2. As you look through your list of words and phrases that describe both the victim and the survivor, do you see yourself more as a victim or as a survivor? Why? _____

_____

_____

3. Which three of the descriptor words or phrases are the most accurate in describing you and your current status? _____

_____

_____

4. What three words or phrases were most accurate in describing you as a child after the trauma occurred? _____

    _____

    _____

    _____

5. What three words or phrases best described you a year ago before you began the journey toward becoming a survivor? _____

    _____

    _____

6. On a scale of 1 to 5, rate your degree of feeling like a victim (1) or a survivor (5).

1	2	3	4	5
Victim				Survivor

7. What has helped you the most in moving from being a victim to becoming a survivor? _____

    _____

    _____

    _____

    _____

8. What person(s) has helped you to move from being a victim to becoming a survivor?

    _____

    _____

    _____

    _____

DEEP BREATHING EXERCISE

GOALS OF THE EXERCISE

1. Learn and practice deep breathing technique.
2. Identify specific situations to use this skill.
3. Demonstrate the ability to use the deep breathing technique in identified situations at home, work, school, and other social situations.
4. Enhance the ability to effectively cope with the full variety of life's anxieties.

ADDITIONAL PROBLEMS FOR WHICH THIS EXERCISE MAY BE MOST USEFUL

- Anxiety
- Phobia
- Posttraumatic Stress Disorder (PTSD)
- Sexual Abuse Victim
- Social Anxiety

SUGGESTIONS FOR PROCESSING THIS EXERCISE WITH THE CLIENT

This is an important technique for many individuals who have heightened levels of anxiety due largely to adverse childhood experiences. As a result of these experiences, they have developed a shallow breathing pattern. Deep breathing helps slow their bodies down when they encounter situations that provoke anxiety, fear, or other threats and make it possible for them to use their skills to assess, process, and problem-solve the situation at hand. Obviously, the therapist is actively involved in this exercise, helping the client to learn, understand, master, and then implement this skill in his/her life situations. The practicing part should be made fun and appropriately competitive with the opportunity to praise the client for effort and the advancement of his/her skill level.

DEEP BREATHING EXERCISE

It is important that when we become nervous, worried, or afraid that we learn to settle our bodies down first. By doing this, we can better handle situations, thus making things better for ourselves and making us feel better about ourselves. Learning deep breathing can help us to do this. Your therapist will help you learn this skill.

STEP 1 (Think 4–4–4)
- Take 4 deep breaths in.
- Hold these breaths for 4 counts.
- Then breathe out 4 counts.
- Repeat two times.

STEP 2
- Using your hand to represent a slice of pizza, identify all of the toppings that are your favorites.
- Now using your hand as the piece of pizza, imagine it coming right out of the oven and how that smells. In order to smell it good, take in 4 deep breaths, holding that great smell for 4 counts.
- Next cool the pizza off so you can eat it by blowing on it for 4 counts.
- Repeat two times.

STEP 3
- To further your skill at deep breathing, practice by using a pinwheel, bubbles, or sunflower seeds.
- Remember the 4–4–4 technique, and in using it, see either how long or fast you can make the pinwheel go or how big a bubble you can blow. You can also practice with the pinwheel, bubbles, or sunflower seeds at home between appointments.

STEP 4
- Now to get this deeper breathing into our brains, teach this to your kids or partner. If they are not available, teach it back to your therapist.

STEP 5

- With the help of your therapist, identify a situation at home and one at work that make you feel anxious/nervous, worried, or afraid.

    At Home: Situation _____

_____

_____

    At Work: Situation _____

_____

_____

Now make a plan for how you will use your deep breathing skills the next time these two situations come up. Plan: _____

_____

_____

_____

_____

STEP 6

- Practice your deep breathing at home during the week by yourself using a pinwheel, bubbles, or sunflower seeds. Report to your therapist how you are doing and how you have used deep breathing in the situations you identified in Step 5.

FEELINGS AND FORGIVENESS LETTER

GOALS OF THE EXERCISE

1. Clarify feelings regarding the childhood traumatic experiences of abuse or neglect.
2. Clarify feelings toward the perpetrator of the childhood abuse or neglect.
3. Increase the level of forgiveness toward the perpetrator and others associated with the childhood trauma.
4. Decrease statements of being a victim while increasing statements that reflect personal empowerment.

ADDITIONAL PROBLEMS FOR WHICH THIS EXERCISE MAY BE MOST USEFUL

*   Low Self-Esteem
*   Posttraumatic Stress Disorder (PTSD)
*   Sexual Abuse Victim

SUGGESTIONS FOR PROCESSING THIS EXERCISE WITH THE CLIENT

This exercise should be assigned in the later stages of therapy after the client has already verbalized and worked through many of his/her feelings surrounding the childhood experiences of abuse or neglect. The client must be ready to offer forgiveness to the perpetrator or significant others and should not be forced into this stage of counseling prematurely. Encourage the client to honestly answer the questions that are meant to help organize his/her thoughts or feelings before writing the actual letter. Some of the questions may not be relevant to a particular client and he/she should exercise his/her judgment about answering them. Be sure to remind the client to return the letter to you for further processing before making any decision about sharing it with the perpetrator or any significant others. The letter may also be used as a basis for a conjoint session with the perpetrator or other family members if that seems clinically appropriate.

FEELINGS AND FORGIVENESS LETTER

In this exercise, you are asked to write a letter of feelings and forgiveness to the perpetrator or other important people connected with your childhood abuse or neglect. You have been given this assignment because you have already done much hard work. You have been able to identify, verbalize, and work through many of your thoughts and feelings surrounding the childhood abuse or neglect. At this point, you are now much stronger emotionally and are ready to offer forgiveness to the perpetrator or significant others associated with your experiences of childhood abuse or neglect.

Before you begin to write the actual letter, please respond to the questions that follow. These questions will help you organize your thoughts and feelings before you write the letter to the perpetrator or significant others. You may find that some of the questions do not apply to you; therefore, leave these items blank. Space is also provided for you at the end of this assignment where you may express any additional thoughts or feelings you may want to include in your letter. Feel free to write down whatever thoughts or feelings come into your mind as you respond to these questions.

1. What impact has the experience of childhood trauma had on your life as an adult?

   _____

   _____

   _____

   _____

2. What feelings did you have as a child toward the perpetrator of the childhood abuse or neglect that you suffered? _____

   _____

   _____

   _____

   _____

3. How did the abuse or neglect make you feel about yourself as a child? _____

   _____

   _____

   _____

   _____

4. How do you feel about yourself as an adult now that you have worked through some of the pain associated with your childhood abuse or neglect? _____

_____

_____

_____

5. What are your present feelings toward the perpetrator of your childhood abuse or neglect? _____

_____

_____

_____

6. What are your feelings about other significant people in the family who witnessed the abuse or neglect but did nothing to stop it? _____

_____

_____

_____

7. What changes have occurred within you that make it possible for you to consider forgiving the perpetrator or other significant persons? _____

_____

_____

_____

8. What, if anything, has the perpetrator or other significant persons said or done that has allowed you to consider forgiveness of them? _____

_____

_____

_____

9. Why are you choosing to begin the process of forgiveness toward the perpetrator or other significant others? _____

_____

_____

_____

10. How would you characterize your present relationship with the perpetrator? _____

_____

_____

_____

11. How would you characterize your relationship with other family members? _____

_____

_____

_____

12. Use the following space to express any other thoughts or feelings that you have about your childhood trauma, yourself, the perpetrator, family members, or the future. _____

_____

_____

_____

_____

_____

_____

_____

_____

_____

_____

_____

13. Review your responses to the questions and then write your letter on a separate piece of paper. Be sure to include your recollection of the facts of the abuse or neglect, how the experience made you feel as a child, how you feel toward yourself as an adult as a result of the trauma, how you have felt toward the perpetrator, your current reason for wanting to begin the process of forgiveness, and what type of relationship (if any) you see in the future with the perpetrator and other family members. Even if the perpetrator is deceased or unavailable for any relationship in the future, writing this letter can still be very beneficial in terms of your own growth and freedom from bitterness. Bring the completed letter to your next therapy session to review it with your therapist. You will have several options to consider about what you want to do with the letter: You may want to destroy it; you may want to save it; you may want to share the letter with the perpetrator or other significant persons through sending it or reading it to them in person. Your therapist can help you reach your decision about these options.

PAIN AND STRESS JOURNAL

GOALS OF THE EXERCISE

1. Discover the relationship between stress, muscle tension, and increased pain levels.
2. Identify any patterns of times, places, or activities that trigger increased pain.
3. Identify and monitor specific pain triggers.
4. Identify patterns of relief activities that are commonly being used to reduce pain or stress.

ADDITIONAL PROBLEMS FOR WHICH THIS EXERCISE MAY BE MOST USEFUL

- Medical Issues
- Phase of Life Problems
- Somatization

SUGGESTIONS FOR PROCESSING THIS EXERCISE WITH THE CLIENT

Review the form for collection of data when this assignment is given to the client. (Please provide the client with sufficient copies of the form in the beginning phases of treatment.) Answer any questions about the type of data that the form requests. Review the completed form with the client to discover any patterns of the place, activity, or time that is associated with increased pain experiences. Note how stress levels may be associated with increased pain. Review the sources of stress that may be triggering pain and prepare the client for training in stress management techniques focused on these sources of stress. Be alert for any adaptive stress reduction techniques the client is currently using so that they can be reinforced.

PAIN AND STRESS JOURNAL

Chronic pain is both a producer of stress and exacerbated by stress. It is important for people suffering from chronic pain to recognize this fact and attempt to minimize the amount of stress in their lives and to develop effective coping skills and techniques to reduce stress that cannot be avoided. The reduction of stress and its accompanying muscle tension will bring about increased pain management and control. This exercise will help you and your therapist discover when chronic pain seems to be most severe and the nature of the stressors that accompany or trigger the increase in pain. Keeping a journal is a difficult task that requires consistent discipline to make entries on a daily basis.

The journal outline form is designed to help you focus your attention on pain and stress management during the treatment process. You are asked to make an entry at least once a day, beginning with writing the date and time in the left-hand column. You may make more than one entry if there are several instances of severe pain during 1 day. After entering the date and time, record where you were when the pain was severe under the Place heading. Next, record the degree of the pain on a scale of 1 to 100, with 100 being the most severe possible, under the Pain Severity heading. Next, record what you were doing while the pain increased in severity under the Activity heading. Record the degree of stress you felt you were under on a scale of 1 to 10, with 10 being the most severe stress in the Stress Severity heading. Next, record the reason you believe you were feeling so much stress under the Stress Source heading. Finally, record any actions you took to relieve the pain or reduce the stress under the Relief Actions heading (include any non-medication or behavioral actions). Repeat these entries on a consistent daily basis and then bring the data to your counselor for review and processing. (Please keep sufficient copies of the form to be used in the future.)

Entry Date and Time: _____	Place	
	Pain Severity (1–100)	

	Activity	
	Stress Severity (1–10)	
	Stress Source	
	Relief Actions	

Entry Date and Time: _____ _____	Place	
	Pain Severity (1–100)	
	Activity	
	Stress Severity (1–10)	
	Stress Source	
	Relief Actions	

MEMORY AID—PERSONAL INFORMATION ORGANIZER

GOALS OF THE EXERCISE

1. Implement memory-enhancing mechanisms.
2. Write down important information that must be remembered to maintain orientation to person, place, and time.
3. Maintain a schedule and keep a history of activities of daily living.

ADDITIONAL PROBLEMS FOR WHICH THIS EXERCISE MAY BE MOST USEFUL

- Attention Deficit Disorder (ADD)—Adult
- Dissociation
- Phase of Life Problems
- Psychoticism
- Unipolar Depression

SUGGESTIONS FOR PROCESSING THIS EXERCISE WITH THE CLIENT

Clients who experience memory deficits related to brain trauma or to psychological issues (e.g., depression, ADD, dissociation) must use coping strategies to help them recall important information and to keep themselves on a productive, structured schedule. These forms can be useful to provide structure to the client and reinforce the habit of writing down important information. It is recommended that the client use either his/her cell phone or a wristwatch with an alarm feature to remind him/her to check the daily scheduler for an important activity to be completed. After a habit is established, the client could consider purchasing a more complete daily organizer.

MEMORY AID—PERSONAL INFORMATION ORGANIZER

It is reassuring when we are accurately oriented to person, place, and time. When memory loss occurs, you must use coping strategies to help you remember information about who you are, where you live, who your supportive friends and family are, what events are scheduled and have already occurred, and what activities are important for you to accomplish. Use the following guide to help you stay organized.

1. **Identifying Personal Information**

   Name: _____

   Address: _____

   Phone: _____

   Birth Date: _____ Age: _____

2. **Names of Supportive People in My Life**

   Parent(s): _____

   Phone: _____

   Spouse/Partner: _____

   Phone: _____

   Brother(s):   1. _____

   Phone: 1A. _____

      2. _____

      2A. _____

   Sister(s):   1. _____

   Phone: 1A. _____

      2. _____

      2A. _____

Neighbor:	1.	_____
Address:	1A.	_____
Phone:	1B.	_____
Friend(s):	1.	_____
Address:	1A.	_____
Phone:	1B.	_____
	2.	_____
	2A.	_____
	2B.	_____
Phone for Police:		_____
Phone for Fire:		_____

3. **Plans for the Month**

Make a copy of this calendar page and write down your appointments for the month. Save your monthly calendars so you can look back to check what you have done in the past.

Sunday	Monday	Tuesday	Wednesday	Thursday	Friday	Saturday

4. **Daily Schedule**

Write down your routine and nonroutine activities that are planned for the day. Make a copy of this page for your reminder or purchase a scheduling book like this.

A.M.	7:00	____		4:00	____
	7:30	____		4:30	____
	8:00	____		5:00	____
	8:30	____		5:30	____
	9:00	____		6:00	____
	9:30	____		6:30	____
	10:00	____		7:00	____
	10:30	____		7:30	____
	11:00	____		8:00	____
	11:30	____		8:30	____
P.M.	12:00	____		9:00	____
	12:30	____		9:30	____
	1:00	____		10:00	____
	1:30	____		10:30	____
	2:00	____		11:00	____
	2:30	____		11:30	____
	3:00	____		12:00	____
	3:30	____		12:30	____

Activities of daily living you may include in your schedule:

- Bathe/shower
- Brush teeth
- Call friend/family member
- Do laundry
- Dust house
- Eat breakfast
- Eat lunch
- Eat supper
- Get dressed
- Get out of bed
- Go grocery shopping
- Go to bed
- Go to doctor appointment
- Grooming
- Make bed
- Pay bills
- Pick up house
- Read e-mail
- Read paper
- Run errand
- Take medication
- Vacuum house
- Wash dishes
- Watch TV

5. **Projects I Need to Do**

Whenever you think of something specific that you must do, write it down and then put it into your schedule later.

TO DO LIST:

_____	_____
_____	_____
_____	_____
_____	_____
_____	_____

6. **Important Things to Remember**

Whenever you read or hear about something important to remember, write it down.

DON'T FORGET:

_____	_____
_____	_____
_____	_____
_____	_____
_____	_____

MEMORY ENHANCEMENT TECHNIQUES

GOALS OF THE EXERCISE

1. Learn the cognitive processes that increase the recall of information.
2. Implement memory-enhancing mechanisms.

ADDITIONAL PROBLEMS FOR WHICH THIS EXERCISE MAY BE MOST USEFUL

- Attention Deficit Disorder (ADD)—Adult
- Educational Deficits

SUGGESTIONS FOR PROCESSING THIS EXERCISE WITH THE CLIENT

You may want to review and process these commonly used memorization techniques in session before asking the client to apply them to his/her daily life. Make suggestions to the client as to when the technique might be implemented. Help the client keep a positive attitude and try to reduce discouragement with his/her memory loss effects. Reinforce instances of the use of techniques to enhance memory.

MEMORY ENHANCEMENT TECHNIQUES

When memory loss occurs, it can be helpful to implement the use of memorization techniques that have proven to be effective over many years. Practice the use of the techniques described to improve your memory.

1. **Chunking:** Grouping information into chunks can be useful when trying to remember a list. The items can be grouped into meaningful pieces. For example, 474965327 is easier to remember if you break the list into smaller groups, such as 474-965-327; or, TWANBCCBSCPRCIA is easier to recall if grouped into familiar chunks, such as TWA NBC CBS CPR CIA.
    List some examples of instances you could use chunking to help you recall information.

    A. _____

    B. _____

    C. _____

2. **Associations:** It is easier to recall something new if you relate it to or pair it with something you already know. For example, if you are trying to remember a person who was just introduced to you as "Holly Weames," you might associate her as "Halloween" and picture her in your mind as having a costume on.
    List some examples of instances you could use association to help you recall information.

    A. _____

    B. _____

    C. _____

3. **Rhyming:** Simple rhymes can help you remember easily forgotten information. For example, if the name of a new acquaintance is Bill Fowler, you could say something silly to yourself like, "Bill Fowler looks like he 'fills his collar.'"
    List some examples of instances you could use rhyming to help you recall information.

    A. _____

    B. _____

    C. _____

4. **Pictures:** It is often easier to remember something if you visualize it. For example, to remember the name of John Runyon, picture in your mind a marathon runner with the sign of "John" on his chest.

   List some examples of instances you could use pictures to help you recall information.

   A. _____

   B. _____

   C. _____

5. **Acronyms:** If you make up a word with the first letter of items that must be remembered, it will make it easier to recall the items. For example, the names of the Great Lakes—Huron, Ontario, Michigan, Erie, and Superior—can be remember as HOMES. We commonly remember information by using the first letters of the words even if the result does not spell a word. For example, WNBA = Women's National Basketball Association.

   List some examples of instances you could use acronyms to help you recall information.

   A. _____

   B. _____

   C. _____

6. **Categorizing:** When faced with a long list of items to recall, it is always helpful to group it into categories. This breaks a long list into smaller parts that are associated with each other and thus easier to recall. For example, consider a long list of sports such as basketball, long jump, tennis, baseball, 100-yard dash, high jump, golf, hurdles, volleyball, and cricket. This list is more easily memorized if it is grouped into two categories—track and field versus sports using a ball.

   List some examples of instances you could use categorizing to help you recall information.

   A. _____

   B. _____

   C. _____

7. **Acrostics:** An acrostic is a sentence that is made by taking the first letter from each word that you want to remember and then inserting another word beginning with that letter. For example, to remember the nine planets, you could create this sentence: *M*an *V*ery *E*arly *M*ade *J*ars *S*tand *U*p *N*early *P*erpendicular (Mercury, Venus, Earth, Mars, Jupiter, Saturn, Uranus, Neptune, Pluto).

List some examples of instances you could use acrostics to help you recall information.

A. _____

B. _____

C. _____

NOTE: The seven techniques described in this homework assignment can be recalled using the acronym CARPACA (*C*hunking, *A*ssociation, *R*hyming, *P*ictures, *A*cronyms, *C*ategorizing, and *A*crostics).

MAKING YOUR OWN DECISIONS

GOALS OF THE EXERCISE

1. Identify decisions that have been avoided.
2. Identify decisions that will be made independently in the future.
3. Implement positive self-talk to build confidence in decision making.
4. Decrease dependence on relationships while beginning to meet own needs, build confidence, and practice assertiveness.

ADDITIONAL PROBLEMS FOR WHICH THIS EXERCISE MAY BE MOST USEFUL

- Grief/Loss Unresolved
- Low Self-Esteem
- Unipolar Depression

SUGGESTIONS FOR PROCESSING THIS EXERCISE WITH THE CLIENT

Decision making is anxiety-producing in people who have developed a pattern of dependency on others or have lost confidence in their own abilities. This exercise is focused on assisting the client to acknowledge the pattern of avoidance of decisions, to commit to making specified decisions, and to build confidence through positive self-talk. Point out the client's distorted cognitive messages that contribute to low self-esteem and assist him/her in listing replacement messages that are more realistic and positive. Reinforce all steps toward independent functioning and decision making.

MAKING YOUR OWN DECISIONS

When you develop a habit of dependence on others, you commonly avoid making your own decisions. You postpone or project responsibility for decisions onto others. Often, this pattern extends to even the small decisions of daily living, such as what time to eat, what meal to prepare, what time to go to bed, or whether to make a small purchase.

1. **Decisions I Have Let Others Make:** List five decisions that you have avoided making in the recent past.

    A. _____

    B. _____

    C. _____

    D. _____

    E. _____

2. **Decisions I Will Make:** List four decisions you will make in the near future without seeking out unnecessary reassurance and direction from others.

    A. _____

    B. _____

    C. _____

    D. _____

3. **Positive Self-Talk:** List four positive messages you can give to yourself that will help you make decisions more confidently (e.g., I am a capable person, I have the intelligence necessary to make reasonable decisions, I have researched this issue enough to make an informed and logical decision).

    A. _____

    B. _____

    C. _____

    D. _____

SATISFYING UNMET EMOTIONAL NEEDS

GOALS OF THE EXERCISE

1. View self as more independent and capable rather than needy and dependent on others.
2. Identify and specify unmet emotional needs.
3. Identify self-help actions to meet emotional needs.
4. Make a commitment to begin self-help action to meet emotional needs.
5. Develop self-confidence so that he/she is capable of meeting own needs and of tolerating being alone.

ADDITIONAL PROBLEMS FOR WHICH THIS EXERCISE MAY BE MOST USEFUL

- Borderline Personality
- Grief/Loss Unresolved
- Intimate Relationship Conflicts
- Low Self-Esteem
- Social Anxiety
- Suicidal Ideation
- Unipolar Depression

SUGGESTIONS FOR PROCESSING THIS EXERCISE WITH THE CLIENT

This exercise helps clients focus on their unmet emotional needs. Clients who struggle with dependency, depression, or feelings of inadequacy often develop a sense of helplessness for doing anything to improve their situation. This assignment challenges the client to think about ways that he/she can commit himself/herself to a self-help action plan. The therapist probably will have to guide the client in listing actions he/she could take to improve the probability of getting his/her needs met. But, it is recommended that the client be allowed to struggle with this issue alone before the therapist provides too much assistance. Actually, this assignment becomes a test of the client's dependency on the therapist to do the assignment for him/her.

SATISFYING UNMET EMOTIONAL NEEDS

All human beings have emotional needs that they want to have fulfilled. When these needs are not satisfied, we feel sad, depressed, lonely, hurt, disappointed, or even worthless. This exercise will help you identify and specify what needs of yours are unmet and will help you design a plan of action by doing something constructive. Too often, people rely on others or life's circumstances to get their needs met and they are disappointed. It is a much healthier approach to do everything you can to assert yourself and arrange your world in such a way that your needs get met through the actions or requests that you make of other people. To be completely dependent on others makes you vulnerable to hurt and disappointment, and it denies your own capabilities and resources to get your needs met.

Unmet Emotional Needs

1. Review the list of common emotional needs and place an X next to the ones that you feel are not met in your life. There are three blank lines for you to write in any unmet needs of yours that were left off the list.

   _____ 1. To feel loved unconditionally by at least a few people.

   _____ 2. To get recognition for accomplishments.

   _____ 3. To be touched, patted, and hugged affectionately.

   _____ 4. To be encouraged to do your best.

   _____ 5. To be listened to, understood, and heard.

   _____ 6. To feel supported when feeling hurt, weak, or vulnerable.

   _____ 7. To be praised and rewarded for your effort to do the right thing.

   _____ 8. To be treated with respect even if you disagree with someone.

   _____ 9. To be forgiven when you do something wrong.

   _____ 10. To feel accepted even with your faults or shortcomings.

   _____ 11. To be asked to join others in social gatherings.

   _____ 12. To be trusted and believed when telling your side of a story.

   _____ 13. To have friends you can trust.

   _____ 14. To have some talent or ability that gets you recognition and builds self-esteem.

_____ 15. To feel accepted and loved by God.

_____ 16. To be treated fairly, equally, and given an opportunity to succeed.

_____ 17. To feel capable of competing adequately against others.

_____ 18. To feel your physical appearance is reasonably attractive.

_____ 19. To have someone believe in your capabilities.

_____ 20. To feel you fit in with a group of friends.

_____ 21. _____

_____ 22. _____

_____ 23. _____

2. You must not rely entirely on others to meet your needs. Next to your top four unmet needs, write one or two things you could do to help yourself move closer to getting your needs met. Perhaps your therapist can help you identify things you can do to help yourself. Write target dates for completing the steps you can take.

Unmet Need	Steps You Can Take	Target Dates
_____	A. _____	A. _____
_____	B. _____	B. _____
_____	A. _____	A. _____
_____	B. _____	B. _____
_____	A. _____	A. _____
_____	B. _____	B. _____
_____	A. _____	A. _____
_____	B. _____	B. _____

3. Write out the consequences of the actions that you have taken to help yourself satisfy your own needs. _____

    _____

    _____

    _____

TAKING STEPS TOWARD INDEPENDENCE

GOALS OF THE EXERCISE

1. Identify and acknowledge fears that inhibit independent actions.
2. Identify events in the past that have taught fear rather than confidence.
3. List steps that can be taken that move in the direction of being more independent.
4. Decrease dependence on relationships while beginning to meet own needs, build confidence, and practice assertiveness.

ADDITIONAL PROBLEMS FOR WHICH THIS EXERCISE MAY BE MOST USEFUL

- Low Self-Esteem

SUGGESTIONS FOR PROCESSING THIS EXERCISE WITH THE CLIENT

The client will be asked to examine his/her history to identify circumstances that contributed to living a life of fear and dependence on others. Give the client support for revealing painful events that have nurtured fear, but also encourage growth in taking steps toward learning to overcome fear and live more independently.

TAKING STEPS TOWARD INDEPENDENCE

Fear and lack of confidence can thwart the normal development of independence. You may look to others to make decisions for you while you seek to please them in any possible way, even if it means taking over activities that clearly belong as the responsibility of others. Explore your fears and ways to overcome those fears by increasing independent actions.

1. **Fear of Disappointing Others:** This is a common fear that inhibits the growth of independence. Describe circumstances in your past that could have taught you to expect that you will disappoint others when you make a decision to act.

    _____
    _____
    _____
    _____
    _____
    _____
    _____

2. **Fear of Failure:** Describe incidents in your past that contribute to your expectation of failure when you take independent action.

    _____
    _____
    _____
    _____
    _____
    _____
    _____

3. **Fear of Abandonment:** What family or social circumstances have caused you to fear that others will leave you alone if you do not constantly try to please them?

_____

_____

_____

_____

_____

_____

_____

4. **Independent Actions:** List actions you can take that will help you overcome your fears and increase your independence. Give a date for implementation.

Action   **Date**

A. _____   _____

   _____

B. _____   _____

   _____

C. _____   _____

   _____

DESCRIBE THE TRAUMA

GOALS OF THE EXERCISE

1. Break down the repression and avoidance of pain.
2. Document details of the traumatic event.
3. Describe the emotions triggered by the event.
4. Regain full memory.

ADDITIONAL PROBLEMS FOR WHICH THIS EXERCISE MAY BE MOST USEFUL

- Antisocial Behavior
- Borderline Personality
- Childhood Trauma
- Posttraumatic Stress Disorder (PTSD)
- Sexual Abuse Victim

SUGGESTIONS FOR PROCESSING THIS EXERCISE WITH THE CLIENT

This assignment must be given to the client only when you are confident that the client has the strength to face his/her demons from the past. You may want to complete this exercise within the session rather than asking the client to fill this out at home between sessions. The data gathered must be processed carefully and often must be processed repeatedly to remove the emotional sting.

DESCRIBE THE TRAUMA

It is often difficult to face the painful events of the past. You may try to avoid pain by avoiding talking about, or even thinking about, such events. Some events may be difficult to recall because you have pushed them away from your conscious memory. But healing comes from facing pain in an atmosphere of acceptance. This exercise leads you to facing the past by detailing the events that have been painful. You may have to consult significant and trusted others to help you recall facts. But make sure that when you record any fact, it is a fact you can vouch for and not just one someone else has told you.

1. **The people involved:**

    A. Who was there when you suffered the pain? _____

    _____

    B. Who have you told about the facts of this incident? _____

    _____

    C. Who was supportive when he/she became aware of the incident or witnessed it? _____

    _____

    D. Who was not supportive? _____

    _____

    E. Who was the person who was responsible for your pain and suffering? _____

    _____

    F. Was there anyone that you believe could have helped you or protected you but did nothing? _____

    _____

2. **Where did the pain occur?**

    A. Describe the location of the incident. _____

    _____

    _____

    B. What time was it when the incident occurred? _____

    _____

    C. How long did the incident last? _____

    D. Did it recur? _____ If so, how often? _____

3. **Your reaction:**

    A.   How did you feel physically and emotionally before the incident occurred? _____

_____

_____

    B.   How did you feel physically and emotionally during the incident? _____

_____

_____

    C.   And how did you feel immediately after the incident? _____

_____

_____

    D.   How do you feel now as you process this incident? _____

_____

_____

    E.   How do you now feel toward the perpetrator of your pain? _____

_____

_____

4. **Others' reactions:**

    A.   How has the perpetrator acted since the incident? _____

_____

    B.   Who has been supportive of you recently? _____

_____

    C.   Who has disappointed you recently because of his/her lack of understanding?

_____

    5.   Write your description of the incident in as much detail as you can. _____

_____

_____

_____

_____

_____

_____

_____

_____

_____

_____

_____

STAYING FOCUSED ON THE PRESENT REALITY

GOALS OF THE EXERCISE

1. Reduce preoccupation with the painful past or confusion with identity.
2. Increase focus on present realities of life.
3. Keep identity focused on reality.
4. Reduce the frequency and duration of dissociative episodes.

ADDITIONAL PROBLEMS FOR WHICH THIS EXERCISE MAY BE MOST USEFUL

- Cognitive Deficits
- Posttraumatic Stress Disorder (PTSD)
- Psychoticism
- Sexual Abuse Victim

SUGGESTIONS FOR PROCESSING THIS EXERCISE WITH THE CLIENT

When a client becomes lost in the issues of the past or loses focus on his/her real identity, this assignment simply reinforces that real identity and present responsibilities. Recognize and reward the client's instances of here-and-now focus to behavior and thoughts.

STAYING FOCUSED ON THE PRESENT REALITY

It is easy to become preoccupied with traumas suffered in the past. But after facing these painful events of the past with openness and sharing the feelings with trusted, supportive people, it is important to not allow the feelings from the past to overwhelm you and cause you to be immobilized. You should have a present-reality focus that should consume most of your energy as you take care of your day-to-day responsibilities. To clarify your focus on daily facets of reality for you, list the facts of your life.

1. **Just the facts:**

   Your name: _____

   Spouse's/Partner's name: _____

   City of residence: _____

   Type of work you do: _____

   Employer: _____

   Hours you work: _____

   Children's names and ages: _____

   _____

   _____

   _____

   Parents' names: _____

   Siblings' names: _____

   _____

   _____

   _____

2. **Projects at home that need attention:**

   _____

   _____

   _____

   _____

3. **Things you should do with or for the kids:**

    _____

    _____

    _____

4. **Things you should do with or for your partner:**

    _____

    _____

    _____

5. **Long-range plans or goals for the future:**

    _____

    _____

    _____

    _____

A REALITY JOURNAL: FOOD, WEIGHT, THOUGHTS, AND FEELINGS

GOALS OF THE EXERCISE

1. Break down denial regarding actual food intake, weight gain, and body size.
2. Identify the distorted thoughts that are associated with eating and the feelings such negative thoughts generate.
3. Reduce the incidence of dysfunctional behaviors used to control weight.
4. Make a concrete pledge to take responsibility for a steady weight gain to be achieved through healthy eating behaviors.

ADDITIONAL PROBLEMS FOR WHICH THIS EXERCISE MAY BE MOST USEFUL

*   None

SUGGESTIONS FOR PROCESSING THIS EXERCISE WITH THE CLIENT

The distorted perception and denial that characterize the client with an eating disorder make it difficult to establish a basis for recovery. This exercise is designed to get the client to face the facts of what and how much has been eaten and how eating sets off a cognitive chain reaction that leads to irrational fear and dysfunctional weight control behaviors (e.g., vomiting, binging, excessive exercise, laxative abuse). You will have to educate the client regarding the relationship between cognitive distortions, negative emotions, and dysfunctional coping behaviors associated with eating. For example, eating three crackers with cheese: "I am going to get fat. My tummy is bloated. I look like a fat pig." After awareness of the destructive pattern is established, the client must be confronted with the personal responsibility to break the cycle and begin to eat normally to gain weight.

A REALITY JOURNAL: FOOD, WEIGHT, THOUGHTS, AND FEELINGS

When you are caught in the web of anorexia or bulimia, it is very easy to distort the reality of what and how much you have eaten, your actual body weight, and reasonable thoughts about food and body image. This journal form is designed to help you stay in touch with reality and not to exaggerate, promote denial, negatively forecast the future, or distort your thinking.

1. Keep a daily record of what foods you eat and the quantity. After each occasion of eating, write your thoughts about the food and yourself. Also, record your feelings connected to the food and yourself. Finally, in the last column, record the common, secret, dysfunctional coping behaviors you engaged in (such as overexercising, forced vomiting, food hoarding, laxative use, lying about eating). On a weekly basis record your weight.

WEEKLY REALITY JOURNAL

Starting Weight: _____

Food Consumed	Thoughts	Feelings	Secret Behavior
DAY 1 Breakfast:			
Lunch:			

Food Consumed	Thoughts	Feelings	Secret Behavior
Dinner:			
Snacks:			
DAY 2 Breakfast:			
Lunch:			
Dinner:			
Snacks:			

Food Consumed	Thoughts	Feelings	Secret Behavior
DAY 3 Breakfast:			
Lunch:			
Dinner:			
Snacks:			
DAY 4 Breakfast:			
Lunch:			

Food Consumed	Thoughts	Feelings	Secret Behavior
Dinner:			
Snacks:			
DAY 5 Breakfast:			
Lunch:			
Dinner:			
Snacks:			

Food Consumed	Thoughts	Feelings	Secret Behavior
DAY 6 Breakfast:			
Lunch:			
Dinner:			
Snacks:			
DAY 7 Breakfast:			
Lunch:			

Food Consumed	Thoughts	Feelings	Secret Behavior
Dinner:			
Snacks:			

2. Hopefully, you are becoming more realistic about the fact that you have not eaten normally, your body is in need of adequate nutrition and calories, and your weight and body size are below average. Denial must be broken and distorted thoughts must be recognized in order for you to get on the road to recovery and break the cycle of treating food as your enemy. The next step is to set goals for increasing weight gradually but steadily through increased food intake (and termination of the secret dysfunctional coping behaviors of excessive exercise, vomiting, lying, and so on). On the following form, record your pledge of a minimum weight gain per week based on healthy eating behavior.

PLEDGE

I, _____ set a goal of gaining _____ per
          (Name of client)   (Weight amount)

week. I will eat meals on a regular schedule and eat normal portions of a balanced diet. I will not engage in secret behaviors to control my weight or calorie intake.

Witness: _____ Signed:_____

Date: _____

HOW FEARS CONTROL MY EATING

GOALS OF THE EXERCISE

1. Identify the fears that exist under the surface of behavior.
2. Identify how these fears control behavior.
3. Accept and implement a plan of facing fears to reduce their influence on the behavior.
4. Develop alternative coping strategies.

ADDITIONAL PROBLEMS FOR WHICH THIS EXERCISE MAY BE MOST USEFUL

*   None

SUGGESTIONS FOR PROCESSING THIS EXERCISE WITH THE CLIENT

A multitude of fears can exert a powerful influence on the client who has an eating disorder. This exercise is designed to help the client identify those fears, note how they impact his/her behavior, and commit to a plan of replacing the negative automatic thoughts associated with each fear. You will have to help the client become aware of how cognitive distortions precipitate fear and then suggest replacement thoughts that are realistic.

HOW FEARS CONTROL MY EATING

Anorexia and bulimia are behavioral problems that are based on fear. The fear may take many forms and can be caused by many distorted thoughts. For this exercise, try to identify the various fears that seem to control your eating behavior. Then focus on the most powerful fears and understand how they are controlling your behavior. Finally, to overcome your fears, you must find ways to face your fears.

1. Review the following list of fears and place a check by those that you struggle with and those that influence your eating behavior. If the list is missing one or more of your fears, add them to the list at the bottom in the blank spaces provided.

   I have a fear of:

   _____ Gaining weight.

   _____ Becoming obese.

   _____ Losing control of my eating and gorging myself.

   _____ Being a failure in many areas of my life.

   _____ Food not being available when I want it.

   _____ Becoming independent and living on my own.

   _____ Developing a sexually attractive body.

   _____ Not being perfect.

   _____ Being rejected by family and/or friends.

   _____ My sexual fantasies leading to impulsive sexual behavior.

   _____ Expressing my thoughts and feelings directly.

   _____ Speaking up for my rights.

   _____ Not having any worth apart from my appearance.

   _____ Becoming close and intimate with someone of the opposite sex.

   _____ Someone else being in control of me.

   _____ _____

   _____ _____

   _____ _____

2. Now list the two most powerful fears in their order of strength.

   A. _____

   B. _____

3. For each of the two fears listed, write about how that fear influences your behavior. What impact does it have on your life? How might it affect your eating?

   Fear #1: _____

   _____

   _____

   Fear #2: _____

   _____

   _____

Most irrational fears are triggered by distorted thoughts. First, people have thoughts about a situation and then these thoughts cause an emotional reaction. Therefore, the fears are reduced or eliminated if the negative thoughts can be changed to thoughts that are more realistic, hopeful, and positive.

4. For each of the fears listed in 2, identify the thoughts that you have that are associated with each fear. For example, if you fear gaining weight, one or more of the following negative thoughts could be triggering this fear:

   • I'm already too fat.
   • I'm going to become fat like my mother.
   • I want to look skinny like a model.
   • If I start to gain, I won't be able to stop.
   • I look pretty when I'm thin.
   • If I eat normally, I'll get fat.
   • I can't eat like most people because I'll get fat.
   • The only way I can stay fit is to constantly diet.
   • It is not healthy to eat regular portions.

When thoughts like these are held onto, the fear of gaining weight grows. Now write your thoughts that help to maintain or trigger each of your fears.

   Fear #1: _____

   _____

   _____

   Fear #2: _____

   _____

   _____

To reduce these fears, you must replace the negative thoughts with positive, realistic thoughts. For example, for fear of gaining weight, the following realistic thoughts could replace the negative thoughts:

- I'm not fat. In fact, I'm underweight.
- I need to gain some weight.
- I can control my weight gain so it is reasonable.
- Being too skinny is not healthy or attractive.
- I will look more attractive when I gain some weight.
- A fit body needs a normal amount of calories.
- Regular portions of food provide the necessary nutrition the body requires.

When thoughts like these are held onto, the fear of normal weight gain disappears.

5. Now write positive replacement thoughts for each fear that will reduce your irrational fear. Remember, thoughts are under *your control* and they cause your feelings.

Fear #1: _____

_____

_____

Fear #2: _____

_____

_____

MY ACADEMIC AND VOCATIONAL STRENGTHS

GOALS OF THE EXERCISE

1. Identify academic and motivational strengths.
2. Brainstorm possibilities that could motivate the pursuit of further education.
3. Develop a plan for future education or training based on strengths.

ADDITIONAL PROBLEMS FOR WHICH THIS EXERCISE MAY BE MOST USEFUL

- Financial Stress
- Phase of Life Problems
- Vocational Stress

SUGGESTIONS FOR PROCESSING THIS EXERCISE WITH THE CLIENT

Encourage the client to think freely or brainstorm when completing this assignment. Process the results with the goal in mind of developing a plan for future education or vocational training. Do not reinforce impulsive shifts into new directions that do not have a solid basis in education, experience, or training.

MY ACADEMIC AND VOCATIONAL STRENGTHS

We all have different talents, abilities, and interests. Some of those strengths can be assets as you look toward increasing your training and education. Many successful people have turned their talents into business ventures after they have received more training that allows them to refine and develop their skills. Use this opportunity to explore your strengths.

1. What subjects did you like in grade, middle, or high school? _____
   _____
   _____

2. What subjects do you like to read about? _____
   _____
   _____
   _____

3. In what areas have you been successful in working with your hands? _____
   _____
   _____
   _____
   _____

4. What abilities do you have that others have recognized in you and for which you have received compliments?
   _____
   _____
   _____
   _____

5. What business idea have you thought about pursuing and what would be the best way to prepare yourself for that business? _____
   _____
   _____
   _____

6. What vocational or professional dreams or fantasies have you had that may be pursued? _____

_____

_____

_____

_____

7. What hobbies or special interests might you develop into a vocation if you had more training or education? _____

_____

_____

_____

_____

8. What types of activities do you really enjoy and feel passionate about? _____

_____

_____

_____

_____

9. What was the most enjoyable thing you have done or the thing you did very well?

_____

_____

_____

_____

10. What are your five greatest talents, gifts, or abilities?

A. _____

B. _____

C. _____

D. _____

E. _____

11. What educational or vocational training plan could take advantage of your identified abilities or interests? _____

_____

_____

_____

THE ADVANTAGES OF EDUCATION

GOALS OF THE EXERCISE

1. Recognize the penalties of a lack of education.
2. Explore the benefits of completing educational goals.
3. State commitment to obtain further academic or vocational training.

ADDITIONAL PROBLEMS FOR WHICH THIS EXERCISE MAY BE MOST USEFUL

*   Financial Stress
*   Substance Use
*   Vocational Stress

SUGGESTIONS FOR PROCESSING THIS EXERCISE WITH THE CLIENT

This assignment is designed to focus the client on the many different ways that life is affected by a lack of or presence of a good education. Process the client's responses to the various aspects of life that are affected by education. Seek a concrete and specific commitment to a realistic plan of action for pursuing educational goals. It is recommended that the client be assigned this exercise after completing the previous homework assignment in this chapter, "My Academic and Vocational Strengths."

THE ADVANTAGES OF EDUCATION

In the following space, explore the negative effects that have accumulated or will accumulate as a result of pursuing and completing your educational goals. Then list the benefits that can result from more education.

1. **Negative effects of a lack of education:**
   A. Financial: _____

   B. Self-esteem (self-pride): _____

   C. Respect from others: _____

   D. Types of work opportunities: _____

   E. Degree of challenge to work opportunities: _____

   F. Amount of time and money available for recreation: _____

2. **Positive effects of completing educational goals:**
   A. Financial: _____

   B. Self-esteem (self-pride): _____

   C. Respect from others: _____

   D. Types of work opportunities: _____

   E. Degree of challenge to work opportunities: _____

F. Amount of time and money available for recreation: _____

_____

3. Identify educational/vocational goals:

A. What are your specific educational/vocational goals? _____

_____

_____

_____

B. What obstacles or life stressors have kept you from pursuing your educational/
vocational goals? _____

_____

_____

_____

C. What steps or courses of action do you need to take to pursue your
educational/vocational goals? _____

_____

_____

_____

_____

D. When do you realistically think you can begin pursuing your goals? _____

_____

_____

E. How much time do you think it will take to complete your goals? _____

_____

_____

APPLYING PROBLEM SOLVING TO INTERPERSONAL CONFLICT

GOALS OF THE EXERCISE

1. Accept responsibility for attempting to find mutually agreeable constructive solutions to conflicts.
2. Brainstorm solutions and analyze their advantages and disadvantages.
3. Implement solutions that are designed to produce "win-win" outcomes.
4. Evaluate the implemented solution as to its degree of mutual acceptance and satisfaction.
5. Decrease the level of present conflict with parents while beginning to let go of or resolve past conflicts with them.

ADDITIONAL PROBLEMS FOR WHICH THIS EXERCISE MAY BE MOST USEFUL

- Anger Control Problems
- Antisocial Behavior
- Intimate Relationship Conflicts
- Phase of Life Problems
- Vocational Stress

SUGGESTIONS FOR PROCESSING THIS EXERCISE WITH THE CLIENT

Many clients need to learn problem-solving skills because they see no solution to problems other than anger, withdrawal, or aggression. This exercise is designed to help the client use classical problem-solving skills to find "win-win" solutions to conflicts with friends, family members, coworkers, spouse, or supervisor. The client may need considerable assistance in completing this assignment since the habit of using dysfunctional problem-solving approaches may be deeply engrained and learned in childhood.

APPLYING PROBLEM SOLVING TO INTERPERSONAL CONFLICT

Getting along with others requires the ability to negotiate solutions to disagreements. All relationships have times of conflict. It is most important that disagreements not trigger immediate anger and withdrawal. A better reaction to conflict is to seek to find a resolution to which both sides agree. This is called a "win-win" situation and results in both parties being satisfied. A conflict that leads to immediate aggression yields a "win-lose" situation and results in hurt, resentment, and anger. This exercise is designed to help you apply problem-solving skills to current conflicts in your life to produce a "win-win" result.

1. Describe a problem of conflict between yourself and the other party in as much detail as possible. _____
   _____
   _____
   _____
   _____

2. Brainstorm all the possible solutions to the problem that you can think of and list them on the following lines. _____
   _____
   _____
   _____
   _____

3. Pick two of the most reasonable and fair solutions from your brainstorm list and list the advantages and disadvantages of each solution.
   Solution #1: _____
   _____

Advantages	Disadvantages

Solution #2: _____

_____

Advantages	Disadvantages
_____	_____
_____	_____
_____	_____
_____	_____
_____	_____

4. Select and write down the best solution option that is apparent from your advantages and disadvantages analysis. _____

_____

_____

_____

5. Indicate when and where you will begin to implement the solution you have selected.

_____

_____

_____

_____

6. After the solution has been implemented, evaluate the outcome of this effort.

_____

_____

_____

_____

7. What changes need to be made in the conflict solution that you selected for it to be even more effective? _____

_____

_____

_____

_____

A STRUCTURED PARENTING PLAN

GOALS OF THE EXERCISE

1. Identify the child's behaviors that are most problematic for parents.
2. Increase parents' focus on interventions for the child's specific targeted problem behaviors.
3. Develop parental consistency in intervening with and giving consequences for undesirable behaviors when they occur.
4. Develop specific positive reinforcements that parents can give for cooperative behaviors or negative consequences they can give for oppositional defiant behaviors.
5. Achieve a reasonable level of family connectiveness and harmony where members support, help, and show concern for each other.

ADDITIONAL PROBLEMS FOR WHICH THIS EXERCISE MAY BE MOST USEFUL

• Parenting

SUGGESTIONS FOR PROCESSING THIS EXERCISE WITH THE CLIENT

Children are masters at manipulation, making parents feel inadequate and constantly on the defensive. To change this, parents must be focused on modifying their child's specific, targeted problematic behaviors in a consistent, nonreactive manner. They will need focus, guidance, and encouragement to stick to this goal. Review parents' interventions and assist them by using modeling and role playing of more effective interventions. Remember to emphasize consistency and positive reinforcement for desired behaviors.

A STRUCTURED PARENTING PLAN

To increase your effectiveness as a parent in guiding and directing your child's behavior, it is most helpful to have an organized plan. A plan provides you with a road map to help you make day-to-day decisions regarding how to respond to your child's behavior patterns. Without a plan, you tend to react rather than act and your parenting lacks consistency and direction. A plan allows you to be specific, focused, and consistent in trying to reach your behavioral goals with your child. This assignment will help you provide structure to your plan as you identify behaviors that you want to see your child increase in frequency, as well as behaviors that you would like to see them stop engaging in. The general principle that will guide you is to reinforce the positive behaviors as strongly and consistently as you can while punishing the unwanted behaviors with consequences that are immediate but short term. To be most effective as a parent, you need to stipulate as precisely as you can the behaviors that you desire to see your children engage in as well as specifying clearly the behaviors you want to see terminated.

Identify Problematic Behaviors

List as specifically as possible several of the problematic behaviors of your child.

_____

_____

_____

_____

_____

_____

_____

_____

Now go over the list and select three of the behaviors that are the most problematic. (It is necessary to limit your focus to maximize your effectiveness.)

1. _____

2. _____

3. _____

Describe Desired Positive Behaviors

For each of the behaviors you selected, describe the desired or expected behavior you would like to see from your child. Make the expectation as specific and as realistic as possible.

Example:

Problem: Always argues then refuses to do any reasonable request or task.

Desired behavior: Comply with request in a reasonable amount of time with minimal resistance.

Problem	Desired Behavior
A. _____	_____
B. _____	_____

Identify Rewards for Positive Behaviors

It is necessary to reward or reinforce the positive behavior when it is done by the child in a reasonable way. This is crucial if you want to see more of that behavior. Remember, the rewards do not have to be big things. (See Reward Examples.) List at least two rewards for the desired behaviors you described in the previous step.

Reward Examples:

1. Thank you for doing that.

2. You sure did a nice job of cleaning up.

Desired behavior: _____

Reward 1: _____

Reward 2: _____

Desired behavior: _____

Reward 1: _____

Reward 2: _____

Identify Consequences for Problem Behaviors

Now develop two or three negative consequences for each of the problem behaviors. Keep in mind that consequences are most effective when they are logical and tied as closely as possible with the behavior/offense. Also, it is best if consequences are brief in nature.

Example of Consequence:

Not allowed to go anywhere or have anyone over until the request/task is done.

Problem behavior: _____

Consequence 1: _____

Consequence 2: _____

Problem behavior: _____

Consequence 1: _____

Consequence 2: _____

Rewards or consequences should be administered in a prompt manner as soon as possible after the achievement or misbehavior. It will take attention and focus to do this consistently.

Plan Ahead to Avoid Problems

To increase your effectiveness, it is helpful to anticipate and plan for possible misbehavior. This will better prepare you to intervene in a timely manner on your terms and make you less likely to overreact. For each of the two problem behaviors, develop a strategy for reinforcing the positive behavior and discouraging the problem behavior.

Example:

Let the child know ahead of time that you have a request or task for him/her to do this afternoon.

1. _____

   _____

   _____

2. _____

   _____

   _____

FACTORS INFLUENCING NEGATIVE SEXUAL ATTITUDES

GOALS OF THE EXERCISE

1. Identify experiences that have influenced sexual attitudes, feelings, and behavior.
2. Acknowledge the influence of childhood experiences on current sexual attitudes.
3. Identify current relational factors that influence sexual attitudes.
4. Verbalize a commitment to change unhealthy attitudes about sexuality to attitudes that are more adaptive.
5. Increase desire for and enjoyment of sexual activity.

ADDITIONAL PROBLEMS FOR WHICH THIS EXERCISE MAY BE MOST USEFUL

- Intimate Relationship Conflicts
- Male Sexual Dysfunction
- Sexual Identity Confusion

SUGGESTIONS FOR PROCESSING THIS EXERCISE WITH THE CLIENT

In reviewing the client's assignment material, provide an atmosphere of acceptance and warmth that will promote openness. Ask questions that will allow the client to elaborate on painful or traumatic sexual experiences from childhood that shape her attitude about current sexual activity. Explore the current relationship with her partner to assess for underlying feelings of anger or hurt that nurture an attitude of rejection toward sexual intimacy.

FACTORS INFLUENCING NEGATIVE SEXUAL ATTITUDES

An adult's attitudes about human sexuality are shaped by many factors, some of which reach back into early childhood. Feelings of fear of and repulsion from sexual activity can be based in subtle or even traumatic experiences of early life. On the other hand, negative attitudes about sexual activity with a partner could be based on more recent dissatisfaction and unhappiness surrounding the relationship itself. This exercise is designed to help you explore your attitudes about sexuality and the possible causes for those attitudes.

1. Explain your current feelings and thoughts regarding sexual activity with your partner. _____

    _____

    _____

    _____

    _____

2. Looking back into your childhood experiences, describe any attitudes of hostility toward sex to which you were exposed. _____

    _____

    _____

    _____

    _____

3. What parental attitudes toward sexuality were displayed in front of you when you were a child growing up in your family? _____

    _____

    _____

    _____

    _____

4. What were your sources of information about sexuality as a young person and what did your parents tell you about sex? _____

    _____

_____

_____

_____

5. Describe any experiences with sexual abuse that contribute to your current feelings about sex. _____

_____

_____

_____

_____

6. Describe the impact on your sexual attitudes of any religious training that you may have received as a child. _____

_____

_____

_____

_____

7. Adolescence is a time of sexual development and exploration. What experiences did you have in adolescence that shaped your current attitudes about sexuality?

_____

_____

_____

_____

8. Describe your reaction and degree of satisfaction with your earliest experiences surrounding intercourse. _____

_____

_____

_____

_____

9. Describe your satisfaction and degree of pleasure surrounding your earliest sexual experiences with your current partner. _____

_____

_____

_____

_____

10. How would you describe your satisfaction with your relationship with your current sexual partner? _____

_____

_____

_____

_____

11. How do your underlying feelings toward your current sexual partner affect your attitudes regarding having sex with that partner? _____

_____

_____

_____

_____

12. What factors do you believe have had the most powerful influence on your current negative attitudes regarding sexual activity? _____

_____

_____

_____

_____

13. Rate your degree of motivation to overcome your lack of desire for sexual activity.

1	2	3	4	5	6	7

No
Motivation

Highly
Motivated

14. Rate your degree of confidence in your ability to overcome your resistance to normal sexual activity with your partner.

1	2	3	4	5	6	7

No
Confidence

Extremely
Confident

STUDY YOUR BODY: CLOTHED AND UNCLOTHED

GOALS OF THE EXERCISE

1. Increase the degree of acceptance of the entire body.
2. Increase the degree of comfort with nudity.
3. Identify positive aspects of your body.
4. Build a positive body image that results in a reduction of sexual inhibitions.
5. Attain and maintain physiological excitement response during sexual intercourse.

ADDITIONAL PROBLEMS FOR WHICH THIS EXERCISE MAY BE MOST USEFUL

- Eating Disorders and Obesity
- Low Self-Esteem
- Sexual Identity Confusion

SUGGESTIONS FOR PROCESSING THIS EXERCISE WITH THE CLIENT

This is a delicate assignment that calls for the client to study her body, beginning with being fully clothed and ending with being fully naked. The assignment asks the client to identify positive aspects of her body and to work toward becoming more comfortable and accepting of her body. Be sure to introduce this exercise with an explanation of what will be expected and answer any questions or provide reassurance about the degree of privacy required. Give permission to the client to focus on her positive physical qualities since our culture discourages boastfulness.

STUDY YOUR BODY: CLOTHED AND UNCLOTHED

A positive body image is critical to overcoming many sexual inhibitions. However, it is very typical for a person to be critical of his/her body and to focus on the flaws. Even though there is no perfect body, many people compare themselves to others and feel inadequate. It is common, however, to discover that a sexual partner focuses on his/her partner's assets or aspects that he/she finds arousing. So while a woman may be critical of her body, her lover is much more pleased with it. The goal of this exercise is to help you develop a greater degree of comfort with your body, both clothed and unclothed. Too often a negative body image leads to a consistent pattern of trying to cover the body under all circumstances. Healthy sexual freedom calls for a high degree of comfort with your own nudity. Being comfortable with yourself and who you are doesn't mean you like everything about yourself or think you are special, but instead means that you feel accepting of yourself for who you are and what you look like.

1. Locate a mirror in your home where you can be alone and undisturbed for about 3 minutes each day for 5 days. Have a watch/timepiece with you to track the time. Note the time, center yourself directly in front of the mirror, and look straight into it at yourself for the time designated.

   Day 1 Time: 3 minutes Focus: Study your head and face, beginning with your hair and forehead, and work down to your shoulders.

   Record what you saw that you liked, what you thought, and any feelings you experienced. _____

   _____

   _____

   _____

   Comfort Scale: Place an **X** on the comfort scale that reflects your level of comfort looking at your head and face in the mirror.

Very	Quite	So-So	Little	Not

Day 2   Time: 3 minutes   Focus: Study entire body while clothed in a bathing suit.
Record what you saw that you liked, what you thought, and any feelings you experienced. _____

_____

_____

Comfort Scale: Place an **X** on the comfort scale that reflects your level of comfort looking at your body in the mirror.

Very	Quite	So-So	Little	Not

Day 3   Time: 3 minutes   Focus: Study body from waist up while unclothed.
Record what you saw that you liked, what you thought, and any feelings you experienced. _____

_____

_____

Comfort Scale: Place an **X** on the comfort scale that reflects your level of comfort looking at your body in the mirror.

Very	Quite	So-So	Little	Not

Day 4   Time: 3 minutes   Focus: Study body from waist down while clothed.
Record what you saw that you liked, what you thought, and any feelings you experienced. _____

_____

_____

Comfort Scale: Place an **X** on the comfort scale that reflects your level of comfort looking at your body in the mirror.

Very	Quite	So-So	Little	Not

Day 5   Time: 3 minutes   Focus: Study entire body while unclothed.
Record what you saw that you liked, what you thought, and any feelings you experienced. _____

_____

_____

Comfort Scale: Place an **X** on the comfort scale that reflects your level of comfort looking at your body in the mirror.

Very	Quite	So-So	Little	Not

2. Describe how the overall experience of the exercise affected you. _____

    _____

    _____

    _____

    What do you think you have gained from this experience? _____

    _____

    _____

    _____

    When you look at yourself in the mirror now, how comfortable do you feel with your body?

    Comfort Scale: Place an **X** on the comfort scale that reflects your level of comfort looking at your body in the mirror.

Very	Quite	So-So	Little	Not

3. How important is it for you to feel comfortable with your body in order to enjoy sexual interaction?

1	2	3	4	5	6	7
Not Important						Very Important

4. List the assets of your body without being discounting or critical. Be bold and brag about yourself! _____

    _____

    _____

    _____

PLAN A BUDGET

GOALS OF THE EXERCISE

1. Itemize and identify monthly income and expense, monthly totals by category.
2. Calculate any difference between projected (budgeted) expenses and income amounts and actual amounts for each category.
3. Make a plan to reduce differences between projected and actual amounts in order to balance the budget and reduce financial stress.
4. Make a plan to reduce expenses or increase income in order to balance the budget.
5. Establish a clear income and expense budget that will meet bill payment demands.

ADDITIONAL PROBLEMS FOR WHICH THIS EXERCISE MAY BE MOST USEFUL

- Family Conflict
- Phase of Life Problems

SUGGESTIONS FOR PROCESSING THIS EXERCISE WITH THE CLIENT

Preparing a budget and tracking actual financial data takes considerable discipline that may require significant encouragement from the therapist. Review the client's figures on a regular basis to reinforce the recording of data. Make decisions about a new financial plan based on how the budget amounts are different from actual amounts. Review the client's budget as to reasonableness and completeness before he/she moves toward implementation and comparison with actual figures.

PLAN A BUDGET

Preparing a structured budget allows for the tracking of cash flow into and out of your household. It is essential to resolving financial stress that a clear understanding is developed as to where money is being spent and what changes are possible to balance income with expense. The following basic budget allows you to enter projected monthly income and expense amounts and then enter the actual amounts that develop and evolve through the month. The final column allows you to calculate any difference between what was projected and what actually evolved for income and expense. Perhaps you would like to make several copies of the worksheet before you begin to fill in amounts so that expenses can be tracked for several months.

1. First enter monthly budget amounts for each category and then, after these have been reviewed thoroughly, begin to enter actual amounts spent or received in a month.

Category	Monthly Budget Amount	Monthly Actual Amount	Difference
Income:			
Wages			
Bonuses			
Interest income			
Capital gains income			
Dividend income			
Miscellaneous income			
INCOME SUBTOTAL			
Expenses:			
Mortgage or rent			
Heating			

Electricity			
Water/sewer			
Trash			
Cable TV			
Telephone			
Home repair/maintenance			
Car payments			
Car gasoline/oil			
Car repairs			
Other transportation			
Child care			
Auto insurance			
Home owner/renter's insurance			
Health insurance			
Computer expense			
Internet service provider expense			
Entertainment/recreation			
Groceries			
Household products			
Clothing			
Eating out			
Gifts/donations			
Medical/dental/vision/medications			
Hobbies			
Vacation fund			
Emergency fund			

College fund			
Retirement			
Credit card payment			
Magazines/newspapers			
Taxes			
Pets			
Miscellaneous			
EXPENSES SUBTOTAL			
NET INCOME (Income less Expenses)			

2. After reviewing the budget, what areas of expense do you feel have been out of control? Where does spending need to be cut back? _____

_____

_____

_____

3. Can you think of ways to increase the amount of income that would help balance the budget? _____

_____

_____

_____

_____

4. If more than one person is living off of this budget, what agreements have been reached with the other parties as to sticking with the budget? _____

_____

_____

_____

_____

5. Now use your new input and track a second month. Note improvement or new areas of overspending.

CREATING A MEMORIAL COLLAGE

GOALS OF THE EXERCISE

1. Begin verbalizing feelings associated with the loss.
2. Express thoughts and feelings about the deceased.
3. Resolve issues of conflict related to the lost loved one.
4. Create positive memories of the lost loved one that can balance the pain of the loss.

ADDITIONAL PROBLEMS FOR WHICH THIS EXERCISE MAY BE MOST USEFUL

- Intimate Relationship Conflicts
- Unipolar Depression

SUGGESTIONS FOR PROCESSING THIS EXERCISE WITH THE CLIENT

The processing of the collage and accompanying questions are best done in a slow-paced, reflective manner. Ask numerous questions about the collage to elicit more information and feelings from the client. You may point out themes and patterns that reflect a positive, warm connection to the lost loved one so that these good memories can be supported as a balance against the painful feelings of the client's grief. This assignment could be used for loss associated with death or loss associated with the breakup of a significant relationship.

CREATING A MEMORIAL COLLAGE

To begin to balance the pain of your loss with pleasurable memories, you need to start uncovering and remembering the warm and special things about that person so you can hold on to those key memories. By completing the collage, you can begin to find that balance. To help yourself work through the stages of grief, complete the following exercises.

1. Use an **X** to indicate where you are now in working through the grief cycle (you can use more than one **X**).

    |_____|_____|_____|_____|

    Shock/   Guilt/   Anger   Depression   Acceptance
    Denial   Loneliness

2. Create a collage.

    A. Obtain a poster board 24 inches by 36 inches.

    B. Carefully search through family photos and select those of your lost loved one that are meaningful to you.

    C. Next look in magazines/newspapers and cut out words, phrases, and other pictures that reflect your feelings about the lost loved one.

    D. Arrange the pictures and words/phrases and secure them on the poster board in any way you feel best expresses your feelings.

3. When you have completed your collage, respond to the following:

    A. Explain briefly the pictures you chose and which two have greatest significance for you. _____

    _____

    _____

    _____

    _____

    B. Explain the reasons for the words/phrases you chose. _____

    _____

    _____

    _____

    _____

C. Looking over the collage you've created, what does it say to you about the person and your feelings? _____

_____

_____

_____

D. Do the pictures bring back any of the following feelings? (Circle any that apply.)

Anger	Disappointment	Other: _____
Hurt	Abandonment	Other: _____
Guilt	Regret	
Worry	Rejection	

Explain: _____

_____

_____

_____

E. Does looking at the pictures bring to the surface any thoughts of regret about things you wish you had said or done or things you wish you had *not* said or done? List them.

_____

_____

_____

_____

F. Do the pictures bring back any of the following feelings? (Circle any that apply.)

Joy	Love	Other: _____
Gratitude	Empowerment	Other: _____
Satisfaction	Amazement	
Peace	Forgiveness	

Explain: _____

_____

_____

_____

DEAR _____: A LETTER TO A LOST LOVED ONE

GOALS OF THE EXERCISE

1. Express feelings connected with the loss of a loved one.
2. Clarify thoughts, feelings, and experiences surrounding the lost loved one.
3. Express thoughts and feelings about the deceased that went unexpressed while the deceased was alive.
4. Begin a healthy grieving process for the loss of a significant other.

ADDITIONAL PROBLEMS FOR WHICH THIS EXERCISE MAY BE MOST USEFUL

- Intimate Relationship Conflicts
- Phase of Life Problems
- Unipolar Depression
- Vocational Stress

SUGGESTIONS FOR PROCESSING THIS EXERCISE WITH THE CLIENT

Traumatic loss can take many forms: death of a loved one, loss of a job, divorce from a loved one, breakup of a significant relationship, loss of a friend, loss of a significant other to a debilitating medical condition, and so on. This letter can be appropriately written and adapted to any of these types of loss as the feelings of grief attached to these losses are similar in many respects. The client is first asked to respond to a series of questions before actually writing the letter to the lost loved one. These questions are designed to help organize his/her thoughts and clarify his/her feelings. After the client responds to the questions, he/she can then begin writing the actual letter. Instruct the client to bring the letter to the next therapy session for processing. It may be helpful to ask the client to read the letter to you to allow for more expression of affect. Allow the client to elaborate on any of the aspects of the letter that you feel are important and tied to unresolved grief issues.

DEAR _____: A LETTER TO A LOST LOVED ONE

Writing letters can be a way to help you identify and express your thoughts and feelings. This is especially true when you need to work through your feelings surrounding the loss of an important person in your life. In this homework assignment, you are asked to write a letter to the lost loved one to help you identify and express your own feelings about the significant loss in your life.

1. First, find a quiet or relaxing place where you can write the letter. This will help you concentrate on writing down your thoughts and feelings without distractions. Perhaps you can write the letter in a quiet room in your house, at the library, or in a favorite outdoor place such as a park or beach.

2. Respond to the following questions designed to help you organize your thoughts and feelings before you begin to actually write the letter. You may find that some of these questions do not apply to you; therefore, leave those items blank. Space is also provided for you to express any additional thoughts or feelings that you may want to include in your letter. Feel free to write down whatever thoughts come into your mind at this stage in the assignment. You can decide later as to whether you want to include these thoughts in your final letter.

   A. What thoughts and feelings did you experience when you learned of the loss of your loved one? _____

   _____

   _____

   _____

   B. What are some of the positive things you miss about your loved one? _____

   _____

   _____

   _____

   C. What are some of the hurts, problems, or disappointments that you had in your relationship with your loved one? _____

   _____

   _____

   _____

D. It is not uncommon to experience guilt or remorse about not having said or done something with a person before the relationship ended. What, if anything, do you wish you could have said or done? _____

_____

_____

_____

E. Do you feel that the loss of your loved one was in any way your fault? If so, please describe why you feel responsible. _____

_____

_____

_____

F. Are you sorry about some of the things that happened between you and your loved one? Describe. _____

_____

_____

_____

G. How has the death of your loved one affected your present life? _____

_____

_____

_____

H. What are some of the important events that have occurred since the loss of your loved one that you would have liked to have shared with him/her? _____

_____

_____

_____

I. What fond memories of your loved one do you cherish? _____

_____

_____

_____

J. How do you feel about your loved one today? _____

_____

_____

_____

K. How would your loved one want you to live your life now? _____

_____

_____

L. How do you feel about your life now? What is good and bad about your life now? _____

_____

_____

_____

M. Use the following space to express any other thoughts or feelings that you would like to include in the letter. _____

_____

_____

_____

3. Next, review your responses and begin to write the letter. Use the following space or write on separate paper. Bring the completed letter to your next therapy session to discuss with your therapist. After discussing the letter, consider what you would like to do with the letter—do you want to keep it or throw the letter away? Your therapist can help you answer these questions.

_____

_____

_____

_____

_____

_____

_____

_____

_____

_____

_____

_____

_____

_____

_____

_____

_____

_____

IMPULSIVE BEHAVIOR JOURNAL

GOALS OF THE EXERCISE

1. Increase awareness of impulsive behaviors.
2. Identify impulsive behavior's antecedents, mediators, and consequences.
3. List the negative consequences that accrue to self and others as a result of impulsive behavior.
4. Acknowledge that impulsive behavior leads to negative consequences for self and others.

ADDITIONAL PROBLEMS FOR WHICH THIS EXERCISE MAY BE MOST USEFUL

- Attention Deficit Disorder (ADD)—Adult
- Bipolar—Mania
- Borderline Personality
- Financial Stress
- Legal Conflicts
- Substance Use
- Type A Behavior

SUGGESTIONS FOR PROCESSING THIS EXERCISE WITH THE CLIENT

You may need to review the details of this assignment to help the client better understand what the homework calls for. The client may tend toward minimization and/or may be out of touch with his/her feelings. Examine the completed journal material for unrealistic, distorted thoughts that trigger feelings and actions of an impulsive nature. Use cognitive change techniques to counteract these distorted thoughts and replace them with more realistic cognitions. Reinforce all verbalizations of acceptance of responsibility for negative consequences related to impulsive actions.

IMPULSIVE BEHAVIOR JOURNAL

It is sometimes difficult to become aware of our own patterns of behavior, the triggers for those behaviors, and the results of those behaviors. We tend to be blind to our own behavior patterns and their results. Often other people have to confront us with our behavior and the painful consequences caused by our actions. We tend to minimize the negative consequences and to highlight the positive results that we see. This exercise is designed to increase your awareness of your own behavior patterns related to impulsive actions and their results. You will need to tune in to your own thoughts and feelings as well as be vigilant about the consequences of your actions.

1. Please enter information regarding incidents in which you acted impulsively in the Impulsive Behavior Journal form on the next page. (Please make additional copies of this form for further impulsive actions.) To begin, you may want to select one incident per day over the next week. For each incident enter the Day/Date and Time that the incident occurred. Describe where you were when the incident occurred (Place). Describe what was going on around you prior to your impulsive action (Situation). Next, describe what you were thinking (Thoughts) and what your emotions were (Feelings). Then describe the behavior that you engaged in that was done without thoroughly thinking it through (Impulsive Act). Finally, describe what you saw as the consequences of your behavior (Result). Repeat the entry of this data for the future impulsive behavior incidents.

IMPULSIVE BEHAVIOR JOURNAL

Entry ___ Day/Date and Time: _____ _____	Place	
	Situation	
	Thoughts	
	Feelings	
	Impulsive Act	
	Result	

Entry ___ Day/Date and Time: _____ _____	Place	
	Situation	
	Thoughts	
	Feelings	
	Impulsive Act	
	Result	

2. List the results of your impulsive actions (e.g., made me feel better, reduced my anger, got back at somebody, felt more relaxed afterwards). _____
    _____
    _____
    _____
    _____

3. List all of the negative consequences that have occurred because of your impulsive behavior (e.g., loss of money, embarrassment to self or others, injury to self or others, broken promises, lost friendships). _____
    _____
    _____
    _____
    _____

4. As you review your impulsive behavior, what triggers for these actions can you identify (e.g., thoughts or feelings, a particular situation, a person or place)? _____
    _____
    _____
    _____
    _____

5. What connection do you see between your impulsive behavior and the painful consequences for yourself or others? _____
    _____
    _____
    _____
    _____

6. What strategies can you use to avoid experiencing some of the same painful consequences?
    _____
    _____
    _____
    _____

HOW CAN WE MEET EACH OTHER'S NEEDS AND DESIRES?

GOALS OF THE EXERCISE

1. Identify needs of both partner and self that are expected to be met within the relationship.
2. Identify means to meet each other's needs and desires.
3. Focus energy on meeting the partner's needs and desires rather than exclusively focusing on your own needs.
4. Increase the frequency of participating in mutually enjoyable activities.
5. Develop the necessary skills for effective, open communication, mutually satisfying sexual intimacy, and enjoyable companionship time within the relationship.

ADDITIONAL PROBLEMS FOR WHICH THIS EXERCISE MAY BE MOST USEFUL

- Dependency
- Female Sexual Dysfunction
- Male Sexual Dysfunction

SUGGESTIONS FOR PROCESSING THIS EXERCISE WITH THE CLIENT

This assignment is designed to be completed by each of the partners within the relationship. It is recommended that each partner complete the homework independently and bring the results back for sharing and processing within a conjoint session. Take the opportunity to teach both partners the key concept that mutually satisfying relationships necessitate each partner being willing at times to sacrifice his/her own needs and desires and choose to meet the needs and desires of the partner. Also teach the partners that each of them should take personal responsibility for finding satisfaction for some needs outside of the relationship.

HOW CAN WE MEET EACH OTHER'S NEEDS AND DESIRES?

GENERAL INTRODUCTION FOR BOTH PARTNERS

A successful and healthy intimate relationship requires that each partner invest some of his/her time and energy into satisfying the needs and desires of his/her partner. When relational needs are not being met satisfactorily, the relationship is in serious trouble and eventually may break. However, all needs cannot be met by one partner. Each must take some responsibility for satisfying needs apart from the relationship. This exercise helps you identify and clarify your needs as well as the needs of your partner.

Partner 1 Perspective

1. List the needs and desires that you expect the relationship to meet.

   A. _____

   B. _____

   C. _____

   D. _____

   E. _____

2. List your partner's needs and desires (as you understand them) that he/she expects the relationship to meet.

   A. _____

   B. _____

   C. _____

   D. _____

   E. _____

3. List what you are willing to do to meet your partner's needs and desires.

   A. _____

   B. _____

   C. _____

D. _____

E. _____

4. List what you expect your partner to do to meet your needs and desires.

   A. _____

   B. _____

   C. _____

   D. _____

   E. _____

5. How have you let your partner down in meeting his/her needs and desires?

   A. _____

   B. _____

   C. _____

   D. _____

   E. _____

6. How has your partner let you down in meeting your needs and desires?

   A. _____

   B. _____

   C. _____

   D. _____

   E. _____

7. What could you do to get some of your needs met outside of the relationship, by yourself or with the help of others?

   A. _____

   B. _____

   C. _____

   D. _____

   E. _____

8. Describe three instances in which you feel that you sacrificed your own needs and desires to meet the needs and desires of your partner instead.

   A. _____

   B. _____

   C. _____

9. List at least three enjoyable and rewarding activities that you feel would help you and your partner satisfy each other's need for social contact.

A. _____

B. _____

C. _____

Partner 2 Perspective

1. List the needs and desires that you expect the relationship to meet.

A. _____

B. _____

C. _____

D. _____

E. _____

2. List your partner's needs and desires (as you understand them) that he/she expects the relationship to meet.

A. _____

B. _____

C. _____

D. _____

E. _____

3. List what you are willing to do to meet your partner's needs and desires.

A. _____

B. _____

C. _____

D. _____

E. _____

4. List what you expect your partner to do to meet your needs and desires.

A. _____

B. _____

C. _____

D. _____

E. _____

5. How have you let your partner down in meeting his/her needs and desires?

A. _____

B. _____

C. _____

D. _____

E. _____

6. How has your partner let you down by not meeting your needs and desires?

A. _____

B. _____

C. _____

D. _____

E. _____

7. What could you do to get some of your needs met outside of the relationship, by yourself or with the help of others?

A. _____

B. _____

C. _____

D. _____

E. _____

8. Describe three instances in which you feel that you sacrificed your own needs and desires to meet the needs and desires of your partner instead.

A. _____

B. _____

C. _____

9. List at least three enjoyable and rewarding activities that you feel would help you and your partner satisfy each other's need for social contact.

A. _____

B. _____

C. _____

POSITIVE AND NEGATIVE CONTRIBUTIONS TO THE RELATIONSHIP: MINE AND YOURS

GOALS OF THE EXERCISE

1. Each partner identifies the positive things he/she and the partner contribute to the relationship.
2. Each partner identifies changes he/she and the partner should make to improve the relationship.
3. Establish a balanced perspective on the relationship rather than focusing on partner's negatives.
4. Develop the necessary skills for effective open communication, mutually satisfying sexual intimacy, and enjoyable time for companionship within the relationship.

ADDITIONAL PROBLEMS FOR WHICH THIS EXERCISE MAY BE MOST USEFUL

- Female Sexual Dysfunction
- Male Sexual Dysfunction

SUGGESTIONS FOR PROCESSING THIS EXERCISE WITH THE CLIENT

This exercise has a separate page to be filled out by each of the partners in the relationship. Ask each partner to complete the exercise independently and to bring it to a subsequent conjoint session. Review each partner's list and attempt to clarify the language and to put the changes requested in positive terms. Clients generally indicate what they would like not to happen rather than what they would like to happen. Ask each client for a commitment to work on making the changes that are called for in his/her own behavior.

POSITIVE AND NEGATIVE CONTRIBUTIONS TO THE RELATIONSHIP: MINE AND YOURS

GENERAL INTRODUCTION FOR BOTH PARTNERS

When conflicts predominate in a relationship, an exaggerated focus gets placed on the negative aspects of the partner. Defenses keep us from evaluating our own contributions to the conflict and from noticing the positive things that the partner does to enhance the relationship. We become so focused on the negative aspects and primarily see the partner as the cause of the failure of the relationship. This assignment attempts to put things in perspective by asking each partner to take an honest look at himself/herself as well as evaluating the partner's contribution to conflict. Additional balance is sought by attempting to have each partner list the positive things that are brought to the relationship by each partner.

Partner Lists

Each partner is to complete the following four lists on the form on the next page. In the first list, itemize those things that you do that contribute positively to the relationship. In the second list, itemize those things that your partner does that enhance the relationship. Third, list the things that you need to do to improve the relationship and make it stronger. Finally (and this is always the easiest part), list the things that you believe your partner needs to do to make the relationship better.

PARTNER'S LIST FORM

1. What I do to enhance the relationship:

    A. _____

    B. _____

    C. _____

    D. _____

    E. _____

2. What does my partner do to enhance the relationship?

    A. _____

    B. _____

    C. _____

    D. _____

    E. _____

3. Things I need to do to improve the relationship:

    A. _____

    B. _____

    C. _____

    D. _____

    E. _____

4. What does my partner need to do to make the relationship better?

    A. _____

    B. _____

    C. _____

    D. _____

    E. _____

ACCEPT RESPONSIBILITY FOR ILLEGAL BEHAVIOR

GOALS OF THE EXERCISE

1. Describe the behavior that led to current involvement with the court system.
2. Accept responsibility for decisions and actions that have led to arrests and develop higher moral and ethical standards to govern behavior.
3. Verbalize and accept responsibility for the series of decisions and actions that eventually led to illegal activity.

ADDITIONAL PROBLEMS FOR WHICH THIS EXERCISE MAY BE MOST USEFUL

- Anger Control Problems
- Antisocial Behavior
- Impulse Control Disorder

SUGGESTIONS FOR PROCESSING THIS EXERCISE WITH THE CLIENT

Be alert to the client's attempts to project blame onto others for his/her illegal behavior. Try to highlight the series of decisions that were made that eventually led to the illegal activity. Reinforce acceptance of full responsibility for decisions and actions.

ACCEPT RESPONSIBILITY FOR ILLEGAL BEHAVIOR

When a change in behavior pattern is necessary, the first step to be taken is to accept responsibility for the actions taken previously. Therefore, this assignment is directed toward having you honestly and completely acknowledge that what you did was illegal, who was hurt by your behavior, and what decisions led to this choice of activity on your part.

1. Describe in detail the illegal behavior that you engaged in. _____

   _____

   _____

   _____

   _____

   _____

   _____

   _____

2. List who was harmed by your behavior and how they were affected.

   Who   **Harmful Effect**

   _____   _____

   _____   _____

   _____   _____

   _____   _____

   _____   _____

   _____   _____

   _____   _____

3. Describe the series of steps that led to your illegal action (when you thought of doing it, who you discussed it with, what preparations you made before initiating the action, etc.). _____

_____

_____

_____

_____

_____

_____

_____

_____

_____

4. Describe how you feel about having acted illegally. _____

_____

_____

_____

_____

_____

_____

_____

5. Why is it important for you to take full responsibility for your illegal behavior without blaming others or excusing yourself? _____

_____

_____

_____

_____

_____

_____

_____

_____

CROOKED THINKING LEADS TO CROOKED BEHAVIOR

GOALS OF THE EXERCISE

1. Identify and replace cognitive distortions that foster antisocial behavior.
2. Create and implement positive thoughts that promote prosocial behavior.

ADDITIONAL PROBLEMS FOR WHICH THIS EXERCISE MAY BE MOST USEFUL

- Anger Control Problems
- Antisocial Behavior

SUGGESTIONS FOR PROCESSING THIS EXERCISE WITH THE CLIENT

The client may need assistance in working through this assignment. Explore his/her distorted thoughts that foster antisocial behavior by reviewing past behavior and the thought process or basic beliefs that preceded the behavior. Help the client develop prosocial thoughts that foster adaptive, legal behavior choices.

CROOKED THINKING LEADS TO CROOKED BEHAVIOR

People take action based on thoughts that precede that action. These thoughts often serve to justify illegal behavior even when the thinking pattern is distorted and based in unreasonable beliefs. Use this assignment to identify the thinking pattern or beliefs that foster your engagement in illegal behavior.

1. Check off your distorted or unrealistic thoughts that foster breaking the law. Add your own thoughts if they are not listed.

    _____ I have to take things into my own hands to get what I want, regardless if it is illegal to do so.

    _____ I take the things I want because I deserve to have them.

    _____ Other people get away with breaking the law; I should be able to do it, too.

    _____ The police are just out to get me.

    _____ If I get away without getting arrested, then the action was okay.

    _____ I don't have any choice; this action is my only alternative.

    _____ I *had* to do this to get out of a jam.

    _____ When I am drunk or high, I do crazy things that I'm not responsible for.

    _____ Life is not fair to me, so I have to break the law just to get by.

    _____ If I don't break the law, I will not fit in or get accepted.

    _____ The world is a cruel place, so you need to grab everything you can.

    _____ They (i.e., victim of crime) ticked me off, so they got what they deserved.

    _____ If they're dumb enough to let you get away with it, then it is their own fault.

    _____ I love taking chances and seeing whether I can get away with it.

    _____ _____

    _____ _____

2. What are some of the distorted or unrealistic thoughts that have contributed to your past illegal actions? Please give examples.

A. _____

_____

_____

_____

B. _____

_____

_____

_____

C. _____

_____

_____

_____

3. Replacing thoughts that trigger illegal behavior is hard work. You must catch yourself thinking the trigger thoughts and then talk to yourself in a more positive, prosocial, realistic manner. Focus on two of your trigger thoughts from the previous section and write several positive thoughts to replace the distorted ones.

Trigger Thought: _____

_____

Positive Replacement Thoughts: _____

_____

_____

Trigger Thought: _____

_____

Positive Replacement Thoughts: _____

_____

_____

ACKNOWLEDGING MY STRENGTHS

GOALS OF THE EXERCISE

1. Identify individual accomplishments, traits, and skills.
2. Use positive self-talk messages to build self-esteem.
3. Decrease the frequency of negative self-descriptive statements and increase frequency of positive self-descriptive statements.
4. Elevate self-esteem.

ADDITIONAL PROBLEMS FOR WHICH THIS EXERCISE MAY BE MOST USEFUL

- Bipolar—Mania
- Social Anxiety
- Suicidal Ideation
- Unipolar Depression

SUGGESTIONS FOR PROCESSING THIS EXERCISE WITH THE CLIENT

Clients with low self-esteem often discount or minimize their accomplishments, positive traits, and skills. Encourage them to include all of these in their completion of this assignment. The concept of accomplishments should be processed to expand the client's scope to include *all* the things he/she does well every day and not to just consider major accomplishments. Encourage the client to overcome his/her resistance to saying good things about himself/herself in the mirror exercise part of the assignment. While processing the results of the homework with the client, reinforce all signs that the client is showing integration of his/her positive accomplishments, traits, and skills into his/her concept of self.

ACKNOWLEDGING MY STRENGTHS

When we view ourselves as lovable, valuable, and capable, we are recognizing key things about ourselves that add to our self-esteem. Completing the exercise that follows will help you recognize your accomplishments, positive personal traits, and skills.

1. Over the next week, identify three positive things you accomplish each day (e.g., cooked a good meal, found a job, cheered up a friend).

<table>
<tr><td>Day 1</td><td>Day 2</td></tr>
<tr><td>A. _____</td><td>A. _____</td></tr>
<tr><td>B. _____</td><td>B. _____</td></tr>
<tr><td>C. _____</td><td>C. _____</td></tr>
<tr><td>Day 3</td><td>Day 4</td></tr>
<tr><td>A. _____</td><td>A. _____</td></tr>
<tr><td>B. _____</td><td>B. _____</td></tr>
<tr><td>C. _____</td><td>C. _____</td></tr>
<tr><td>Day 5</td><td>Day 6</td></tr>
<tr><td>A. _____</td><td>A. _____</td></tr>
<tr><td>B. _____</td><td>B. _____</td></tr>
<tr><td>C. _____</td><td>C. _____</td></tr>
<tr><td>Day 7</td><td></td></tr>
<tr><td>A. _____</td><td></td></tr>
<tr><td>B. _____</td><td></td></tr>
<tr><td>C. _____</td><td></td></tr>
</table>

2. List five personal traits that you value about yourself (e.g., friendly, trustworthy, accepting). Then ask friends, family, and others for five more.

<table>
<tr><td>My List</td><td>Others' List</td></tr>
<tr><td>A. _____</td><td>A. _____</td></tr>
<tr><td>B. _____</td><td>B. _____</td></tr>
<tr><td>C. _____</td><td>C. _____</td></tr>
</table>

D. _____   D. _____

E. _____   E. _____

3. Now list five skills that you believe you have (e.g., play piano, can fix things, good housekeeper).

    A. _____

    B. _____

    C. _____

    D. _____

    E. _____

4. Reviewing the three areas of accomplishments, traits, and skills, what do you believe are your most valuable assets? _____

_____

_____

_____

5. Write each of your 15 positive skills and traits on a 3 × 5 card and post them around your home so that you are reminded of them regularly.

6. Take three cards with positive skills or traits written on them and stand in front of a mirror. Look yourself in the eye while repeating the statements "I am _____" (filling in one of your positive qualities). Repeat this mirror exercise for 2 minutes each day for a week. Rate how comfortable you were with saying good things about yourself.

```
└────────┴────────┴────────┴────────┴────────┴────────┘
1        2        3        4        5        6        7
```

Very   Very
Uncomfortable   Comfortable

7. Rate how your self-esteem has grown after completing this exercise for 1 week.

```
└────────┴────────┴────────┴────────┴────────┴────────┘
1        2        3        4        5        6        7
```

No   Maximum
Growth   Growth

REPLACING FEARS WITH POSITIVE MESSAGES

GOALS OF THE EXERCISE

1. Identify fearful thoughts that foster low self-esteem.
2. Identify coping techniques to resist the impact of fear on behavior.
3. Use positive self-talk messages.
4. Develop a consistent positive self-image.

ADDITIONAL PROBLEMS FOR WHICH THIS EXERCISE MAY BE MOST USEFUL

- Anxiety
- Dependency
- Panic/Agoraphobia
- Sexual Abuse Victim
- Social Anxiety
- Suicidal Ideation
- Unipolar Depression

SUGGESTIONS FOR PROCESSING THIS EXERCISE WITH THE CLIENT

It may be helpful to review the list of coping techniques that is presented in the exercise prior to asking the client to complete the homework. You may elaborate on some of these techniques and answer any questions that might arise. Upon completion of the exercise, you may focus on teaching the details of some of the anxiety-reduction coping techniques that are mentioned and/or selected by the client. You may also have to help the client in the development of ways that he/she can keep positive affirmation statements in mind. Continue to reinforce the client's use of these positive statements to cope with his/her slide back into low self-esteem thought patterns.

REPLACING FEARS WITH POSITIVE MESSAGES

It is very important after you start feeling good about yourself that you work to maintain that attitude. To do this, you need to be prepared to terminate the negative/fearful thoughts that can set you back and, at the same time, you need to keep supportive thoughts at the forefront of your mind. The exercise that follows will help you develop ways to address these factors and maintain your self-esteem.

1. Negative and fearful thoughts can undermine self-esteem by holding people back from doing things.

    A. Circle the fearful thoughts that you have.

Making a mistake	Being left out or behind
Failing at something	Others getting mad at me
Being criticized	Not being liked
Going crazy	Others seeing me in a panic
Saying/doing something stupid	Others seeing me as unattractive
Others thinking I'm bad	Others hurting my feelings
Having a heart attack	Getting fired at work

    Add your own fearful thoughts to the list.

    _____

    _____

    B. Now from the fearful thoughts you circled, select the two thoughts that you have most frequently. List them here and then answer the questions that follow.

    1. First fearful thought: _____

    _____

    _____

    What is the worst that could happen if the feared event actually occurred?

    _____

    _____

    _____

    _____

Review the following list of coping techniques and put an **X** next to two that you believe could help you overcome your fear.

____ Do a reality check with self or others.

____ Replace fearful thought with a positive, realistic thought.

____ Share the fear with others to get reassurance.

____ Affirm your own ability to cope using positive self-talk.

____ Distract yourself with a pleasurable activity.

____ Use relaxation exercises to reduce tension.

____ Accept the fear and forge ahead with action.

____ Engage in aerobic exercise.

____ Visualize yourself as being successful at the feared task.

____ Withdraw from the feared situation temporarily, and then return to it.

____ Gradually face the feared situation until the fear is overcome.

____ Use problem-solving skills to address the feared situation.

____ Implement assertiveness skills to address the feared situation.

____ Reward yourself for facing the feared situation.

Describe why you think the two techniques you selected will help you and how you will apply those techniques to your life.

Technique 1: _____

_____

Technique 2: _____

_____

2. Second fearful thought: _____

_____

What is the worst that could happen if the feared event actually occurred?

_____

_____

_____

Review the list of coping techniques again and put an **X** next to two that you believe could help you overcome this second fear.

Describe why you think the two techniques you selected will help you and how you will apply those techniques to your life.

Technique 1: _____

_____

Technique 2: _____

_____

2. As a way of maintaining your self-esteem, it is important to keep in mind certain important thoughts.

    A. Circle the affirmations that you most need to remember.

God doesn't make junk.	I expect good things.
I like myself.	I am a good person.
Mistakes are learning opportunities.	I have things to offer.
I know I can do it.	I can trust myself.
I am lovable.	I feel good about me.
I can make good decisions.	I value myself.
No one is perfect.	I can say no.
I can be a friend to someone.	I don't have to be perfect.
I can deal with my fears.	I am a child of God.
I can grow and change.	My family loves me.
With God all things are possible.	With God I can let go of fear.
With God I can face anything.	I can find strength in God's spirit.
I can forgive others.	With God I'm never alone.
Others do like me.	

    B. Now develop three ways you can keep these thoughts at the front of your mind (e.g., write two or three thoughts on a note card, carry the card with you, and read it four times during your day).

    1. _____
    2. _____
    3. _____

3. Evaluate your progress over the next 2 weeks in each of these three areas.

    A. Stopping fearful thoughts

Week 1 (circle):	Great	Good	Okay	Poor
Comment: _____				
Week 2 (circle):	Great	Good	Okay	Poor
Comment: _____				

    B. Daily affirmations

Week 1 (circle):	Great	Good	Okay	Poor
Comment: _____				
Week 2 (circle):	Great	Good	Okay	Poor
Comment: _____				

JOURNALING THE RESPONSE TO NONDEMAND SEXUAL PLEASURING (SENSATE FOCUS)

GOALS OF THE EXERCISE

1. Participate in nondemand sexual pleasuring exercises.
2. Record thoughts and feelings generated by the sexual pleasuring exercise.
3. Share and process thoughts and feelings associated with each step in the sexual pleasuring activities.
4. Experience decreased inhibition and performance anxiety and increased sexual arousal and sexual pleasure.
5. Increase the desire for and enjoyment of sexual activity.

ADDITIONAL PROBLEMS FOR WHICH THIS EXERCISE MAY BE MOST USEFUL

• Female Sexual Dysfunction

SUGGESTIONS FOR PROCESSING THIS EXERCISE WITH THE CLIENT

This assignment requires that you provide the client with some direction in locating material on sexual pleasuring exercises that are fairly standard for treating such things as hypoactive sexual desire or high anxiety associated with sexual performance. You may give directions for sexual pleasuring within the session or direct the client to read material that contains a description of nondemand sexual pleasuring. Two books are referred to within the directions for the client, but you may suggest others. The power of the sexual pleasuring exercise increases dramatically as the partners learn to share their thoughts and feelings regarding their sexual interplay. This exercise provides some structure to allow partners to describe their thoughts and feelings and then to return to a conjoint session to process this information. You may also encourage them to share thoughts and feelings freely during the sensate focus experience itself. The form for journaling must be copied so that each partner can have his/her own form to complete.

JOURNALING THE RESPONSE TO NONDEMAND SEXUAL PLEASURING (SENSATE FOCUS)

This exercise is designed to help you describe your thoughts and feelings that are associated with participation in a nondemand sexual pleasuring activity often called "sensate focus." Rather than describe all of the aspects of nondemand sexual pleasuring exercising, you are referred to books on human sexuality that describe this standard approach to sexual interaction that is designed to reduce inhibition, desensitize sexual aversion, increase arousal, and enhance sexual pleasure. Many books on human sexuality contain a description of this type of sexual exercise (e.g., *Rekindling Desire: A Step-by-Step Program to Help Low-Sex and No-Sex Marriages* by McCarthy and McCarthy [Brunner-Routledge, 2003] or *Resurrecting Sex: Resolving Sexual Problems and Rejuvenating Your Relationship* by Schnarch [HarperCollins, 2002]). Your therapist may want to suggest a specific resource book for you to consult to obtain the specifics of a nondemand sexual pleasuring exercise.

One of the most important aspects of engaging in the nondemand sexual pleasuring exercise is processing the feelings that are generated by the exercise and sharing them openly with your partner. After you have agreed on how to implement the sexual pleasuring exercise and established a schedule for doing so, record the steps that you will be taking together under Question 1 on this form. As you implement each step of the exercise, each partner should complete the questions independently and bring the form back to a conjoint counseling session for review and processing.

1. Outline the four steps that you will implement in a nondemand sexual pleasuring exercise often referred to as "sensate focus." **(Partners complete this section together.)**

   A. _____

   _____

   B. _____

   _____

   C. _____

   _____

   D. _____

   _____

Journal of Thoughts and Feelings

Step 1: Date(s) implemented: _____

1. Describe your thoughts and feelings before the exercise began.

    Toward the exercise: _____

    Toward your partner: _____

2. Describe your thoughts and feelings during the exercise.

    Toward the exercise: _____

    Toward your partner: _____

3. What was the best aspect of the exercise? _____

    _____

    _____

    _____

4. What would have made the exercise experience better? _____

    _____

    _____

    _____

5. What benefit did you get from this step of the pleasuring exercise? _____

    _____

    _____

    _____

6. Rate your degree of sexual arousal during this exercise.

1	2	3	4	5	6	7

    None   Very
                                                                            High

7. How ready are you to move to the next step in the pleasuring sequence?

1	2	3	4	5	6	7

    Not   Very
    Ready   Ready

Step 2: Date(s) implemented: _____

1. Describe your thoughts and feelings before the exercise began.

   Toward the exercise: _____

   Toward your partner: _____

2. Describe your thoughts and feelings during the exercise.

   Toward the exercise: _____

   Toward your partner: _____

3. What was the best aspect of the exercise? _____

   _____

   _____

   _____

4. What would have made the exercise experience better? _____

   _____

   _____

   _____

5. What benefit did you get from this step of the pleasuring exercise? _____

   _____

   _____

   _____

6. Rate your degree of sexual arousal during this exercise.

1	2	3	4	5	6	7

   None   Very
                                                                        High

7. How ready are you to move to the next step in the pleasuring sequence?

1	2	3	4	5	6	7

   Not   Very
   Ready   Ready

Step 3: Date(s) implemented: _____

1.   Describe your thoughts and feelings before the exercise began.

Toward the exercise: _____

Toward your partner: _____

2.   Describe your thoughts and feelings during the exercise.

Toward the exercise: _____

Toward your partner: _____

3.   What was the best aspect of the exercise? _____

_____

_____

_____

4.   What would have made the exercise experience better? _____

_____

_____

_____

5.   What benefit did you get from this step of the pleasuring exercise? _____

_____

_____

_____

6.   Rate your degree of sexual arousal during this exercise.

1	2	3	4	5	6	7

None   Very
                                                                                  High

7.   How ready are you to move to the next step in the pleasuring sequence?

1	2	3	4	5	6	7

Not   Very
Ready   Ready

Step 4: Date(s) implemented: _____

1. Describe your thoughts and feelings before the exercise began.
   Toward the exercise: _____
   Toward your partner: _____

2. Describe your thoughts and feelings during the exercise.
   Toward the exercise: _____
   Toward your partner: _____

3. What was the best aspect of the exercise? _____
   _____
   _____
   _____

4. What would have made the exercise experience better? _____
   _____
   _____
   _____

5. What benefit did you get from this step of the pleasuring exercise? _____
   _____
   _____
   _____

6. Rate your degree of sexual arousal during this exercise.

1	2	3	4	5	6	7

   None   Very
                                                           High

7. How ready are you to move to the next step in the pleasuring sequence?

1	2	3	4	5	6	7

   Not   Very
   Ready   Ready

HOW I FEEL ABOUT MY MEDICAL TREATMENT

GOALS OF THE EXERCISE

1. Verbalize thoughts and feelings about having to receive treatment for a serious or chronic illness.
2. Explore and identify reasons for resistance to receiving treatment.
3. Cooperate with medical treatment regimen without passive-aggressive or active resistance.
4. Verbalize acceptance of the reality of the medical condition and the need for treatment.

ADDITIONAL PROBLEMS FOR WHICH THIS EXERCISE MAY BE MOST USEFUL

• Psychoticism

SUGGESTIONS FOR PROCESSING THIS EXERCISE WITH THE CLIENT

This exercise not only provides the client with the opportunity to openly express his/her thoughts and feelings, but can also be used to uncover the reasons for his/her resistance to cooperating with the medical treatment regimen. Process the expression of feelings and the reasons for resistance in complying with the medical interventions. You may also want to share the client's responses with his/her physician (after obtaining the necessary releases) to help the physician become aware of the client's thoughts and feelings. The physician could also address the client's resistance and explain the reasons why the client is receiving the current medical treatment regimen.

HOW I FEEL ABOUT MY MEDICAL TREATMENT

Please take a few minutes to answer the questions that follow. Your answers will help your therapist better understand your thoughts and feelings about having to receive regular medical treatment.

1. What medication(s) do you currently take for your illness? Please give dosage and frequency.

Medication Name	Dosage	Frequency

2. What other types of treatment (besides taking medication) do you receive for your illness? Hospitalizations? How frequent? _____

_____

_____

_____

_____

3. What do you dislike about receiving the treatment? _____

_____

_____

_____

_____

4. What are the consequences of not cooperating with your treatment regimen as recommended? _____

_____

_____

_____

_____

5. How does your family react if you do not cooperate with your treatment regimen?

_____

_____

_____

_____

6. What would you like to tell your doctor about your treatment? _____

_____

_____

_____

_____

7. How much say or control do you feel you have in your current treatment? Place an **X** above the space that best describes how you feel.

| None | Very Little | Some | Fair Amount | A Lot |

8. What would you like to tell your friends or family members about how you feel about receiving the medical treatment? _____

_____

_____

_____

_____

9. What advice would you give yourself about cooperating with the treatment? _____

_____

_____

_____

_____

THE IMPACT OF MY ILLNESS

GOALS OF THE EXERCISE

1. Identify the emotional, physical, and relational impact of the medical condition.
2. Identify feelings associated with the medical condition.
3. Identify people who can be turned to or relied on in time of illness for emotional help and support.
4. Reduce fear, anxiety, and worry associated with the medical condition.

ADDITIONAL PROBLEMS FOR WHICH THIS EXERCISE MAY BE MOST USEFUL

- Bipolar—Mania
- Psychoticism

SUGGESTIONS FOR PROCESSING THIS EXERCISE WITH THE CLIENT

The purpose of this exercise is to help the client identify the impact of the illness on his/her life and then to encourage expression of his/her feelings about his/her serious or chronic illness. The client should be encouraged to express these feelings in the therapy sessions and to other family members or trusted individuals. The exercise identifies key people the client can turn to for emotional support and help. Finally, the client is asked to identify what coping strategies or activities help him/her to cope with or manage the symptoms or effects of the illness.

THE IMPACT OF MY ILLNESS

In dealing with a serious or long-term illness, it is very important that the person suffering from the illness express his/her feelings. This exercise helps your therapist, family members, and other important people in your life better understand your feelings about your illness. Please respond to the following questions or items.

1. What is your illness? _____

   _____

   _____

2. How long have you had this illness? _____

   _____

   _____

3. List three adjectives to describe your illness.

   _____ _____ _____

4. What feelings do you have about your illness? Place a check mark in front of the words that describe how you feel. Add any other feelings in the blank spaces.

   ____ Afraid   _____ Sad   _____ Angry

   ____ Nervous   _____ Helpless   _____ Rage

   ____ Worried   _____ Hopeless   _____ Frustrated

   ____ Confused   _____ Trapped   _____ Guilty

   ____ Uncertain   _____ Different   _____ Lonely

   ____ Inferior   _____ Embarrassed _____ Apathetic ("I don't care")

   ____ Calm   _____ Content   _____ Rage

   ____ ____   _____ ____   _____ ____

5. What is your biggest concern or worry about your illness? _____

   _____

   _____

   _____

6. What impact do your feelings and stress have on your illness? _____

    _____

    _____

7. Who understands how you feel about your illness (e.g., parents, partner, siblings, doctor, friends)? _____

    _____

    _____

8. How do you think your partner or family members feel about your illness? How does your illness affect your relationships with them? _____

    _____

    _____

9. How do you think your friends view you and your illness? How does your illness affect your relationships with them? _____

    _____

    _____

10. Who can you turn to for emotional help and support in dealing with your illness?

    _____

    _____

11. What are the limitations caused by your illness? _____

    _____

    _____

12. How do you feel about these limitations? _____

    _____

    _____

13. Describe your strengths, interests, and abilities that continue in spite of your illness. _____

    _____

    _____

14. What coping strategies or activities have you found helpful in learning to deal with or manage your feelings about your illness (e.g., writing, talking, distracting activities, prayer, meditation)? _____

    _____

    _____

INTERRUPTING YOUR OBSESSIONS/COMPULSIONS

GOALS OF THE EXERCISE

1. Develop and implement a daily ritual that interrupts the current pattern of compulsions.
2. Reduce interference from or time involved with obsessions and compulsions.
3. Function daily at a consistent level with minimal interference from obsessions and compulsions.

ADDITIONAL PROBLEMS FOR WHICH THIS EXERCISE MAY BE MOST USEFUL

- Anxiety
- Unipolar Depression

SUGGESTIONS FOR PROCESSING THIS EXERCISE WITH THE CLIENT

This intervention seeks to interrupt the client's obsessive thoughts or compulsive behaviors by having him/her perform an unpleasant job or task. The assignment has three parts. The client is first asked to identify a list of three to five unpleasant jobs or tasks that he/she can perform when the obsessive thoughts or compulsive behaviors emerge. Brainstorm with the client a list of various unpleasant tasks that he/she can perform in a variety of settings (e.g., home, school, or workplace). Explain the purpose of the intervention if the client expresses any resistance about following through with this unconventional intervention. The second part of the assignment asks the client to evaluate the effectiveness of the intervention after at least 1–2 weeks have passed. Finally, the client is requested to identify any modifications that can be made to the intervention. The client is encouraged to consult with the therapist about any possible modification(s).

INTERRUPTING YOUR OBSESSIONS/COMPULSIONS

The purpose of this intervention is to reduce the frequency and intensity of your obsessive thoughts or compulsive behaviors by having you perform an unpleasant job or task. We realize that this approach seems unusual, as most people are not eager or highly motivated to perform an unpleasant task. Yet, it is hoped that by committing to perform various unpleasant tasks on a regular basis, you will be rewarded by experiencing a decrease in the frequency of your obsessive thoughts or compulsive behaviors (which over time can be more unpleasant or anxiety-producing).

This assignment actually contains three different parts. The first part asks you to create a list of unpleasant tasks that you can perform at home, work, or in the school setting (if you are a college student). The second part involves evaluating the success of the intervention, while the third part seeks to identify any modifications that need to be made to the intervention.

I.   Identification of Unpleasant Jobs or Tasks

Please take some time to think about some possible unpleasant jobs or tasks that you can perform when the obsessions/compulsions emerge. Feel free to talk with your therapist, spouse, family members, friends, or colleagues at work about various tasks that you can perform. The task need not be time consuming, but hopefully will be unpleasant in nature so that it interrupts your obsessions/compulsions. Examples of unpleasant tasks include, but certainly are not restricted to: sweeping the garage, weeding, scrubbing the toilet or cleaning different parts of the bathroom, stripping wallpaper in a room (this can be performed over time), performing an act of kindness to an annoying colleague at work or student in one of your college courses, and engaging in small talk for a brief period of time with an annoying person.

You are asked to create a list of three to five unpleasant tasks because you will not always be able to perform the same task in different settings. For example, it would be difficult to clean the bathroom at work. Not all jobs or tasks will work in every setting or situation. Keep in mind that some days will be better than others. Try not to be discouraged if you regress and experience an increase in the frequency of your obsessions/compulsions on a particular day.

1. What are three to five unpleasant tasks that you can perform to interrupt your obsessions/compulsions? (Please feel free to add more jobs or tasks on the back of this page if you choose.)

    A. _____

    B. _____

    C. _____

    D. _____

    E. _____

2. After reviewing the list, what job(s) or task(s) do you feel would be most effective at home? _____

    _____

    _____

    At school or work? _____

    _____

    In a public setting? _____

    _____

II. Evaluation of the Effectiveness of the Intervention

Please answer the following questions approximately 1 to 2 weeks after you have performed the unpleasant job(s) or task(s).

1. What percentage of the time did you perform the unpleasant jobs or tasks when you began to experience the obsessions/compulsions?

    ___ 0–20%   ___ 20–40%   ___ 40–60%   ___ 60–80%   ___ 80–100%

2. If you were not able to perform the unpleasant job(s) or task(s) on a consistent basis (less than 60%), what stressors or factors interfered with your ability to perform the unpleasant jobs or tasks? _____

    _____

3. Overall, how successful were the unpleasant jobs or tasks in interrupting or managing your obsessions/compulsions?

1	2	3	4	5	6	7

    | Totally | | | No Change | | | Highly |
    | Unsuccessful | | | | | | Successful |

4. Which of the unpleasant jobs or tasks were helpful in interrupting your obsessions/ compulsions?

    _____

    _____

5. What unpleasant jobs or tasks were not effective in interrupting your obsessions/ compulsions? _____

    _____

6. What stressful events interfered with the effectiveness of this intervention and caused you to experience an increase in the frequency of your symptoms (optional)?

    _____

    _____

    _____

    _____

    _____

III. Modifications of the Intervention

1. After evaluating your progress, what changes or modifications would you make to this intervention?

    A. _____
    B. _____
    C. _____
    D. _____
    E. _____

2. What other unpleasant jobs or tasks can you perform to reduce the frequency of your obsessions/compulsions? List three to five other tasks (again, feel free to consult with your therapist, family members, or friends).

    A. _____
    B. _____
    C. _____
    D. _____
    E. _____

MAKING USE OF THE THOUGHT-STOPPING TECHNIQUE

GOALS OF THE EXERCISE

1. Identify obsessive thoughts that produce anxiety and interfere with normal functioning.
2. Implement the use of the thought-stopping technique to reduce the frequency of obsessive thoughts.
3. Rate the degree of success at reducing obsessive thoughts and the concomitant anxiety.
4. Reduce the frequency, intensity, and duration of obsessions.

ADDITIONAL PROBLEMS FOR WHICH THIS EXERCISE MAY BE MOST USEFUL

- Anxiety
- Eating Disorders and Obesity

SUGGESTIONS FOR PROCESSING THIS EXERCISE WITH THE CLIENT

Thought-stopping is a simple but effective technique to reduce the impact of obsessive rumination. You may want to review the essential elements of the thought-stopping technique with the client and practice its implementation in the office prior to giving this homework assignment. Review the client's implementation after 1 week and adjust the technique as necessary to increase its effectiveness. You may want to add the element of having the client snap a rubber band around his/her wrist at the time of shouting "STOP."

MAKING USE OF THE THOUGHT-STOPPING TECHNIQUE

Obsessive thoughts that recur on a frequent and regular basis can be very frustrating and interfere with normal functioning. You can become preoccupied with these thoughts and therefore unable to focus on other issues. These recurring thoughts can also produce considerable anxiety and they often are connected to worries that a harmful or embarrassing event will occur. A simple but effective technique for coping with obsessive thoughts and reducing their ability to raise anxiety is the "thought-stopping" technique. This exercise guides you through the implementation of this technique and assesses its effectiveness.

1. List any obsessive thoughts that recur regularly and interfere with your normal functioning.

    _____

    _____

    _____

2. Rate the degree of interference of the obsessive thought on your normal routine.

    | 1 | 2 | 3 | 4 | 5 |

    Very Strong   No
    and Frequent   Interference

3. List three positive, calming scenes that you could place in your mind to replace the obsessive thought (e.g., sunning yourself all alone on a warm beach, fishing on a quiet lake as the sun sets).

    Scene 1:

    _____

    _____

    Scene 2:

    _____

    _____

Scene 3:

_____

_____

4. Over the next week, each time that the obsessive thought occurs, shout "STOP!" to yourself in your head without making a sound. Picture a large red traffic sign, and then begin to think about one of the calming scenes from the previous question while breathing deeply and relaxing your muscle tension. Rate on a daily basis the degree of your success at implementing this technique to stop and replace the obsessive thought.

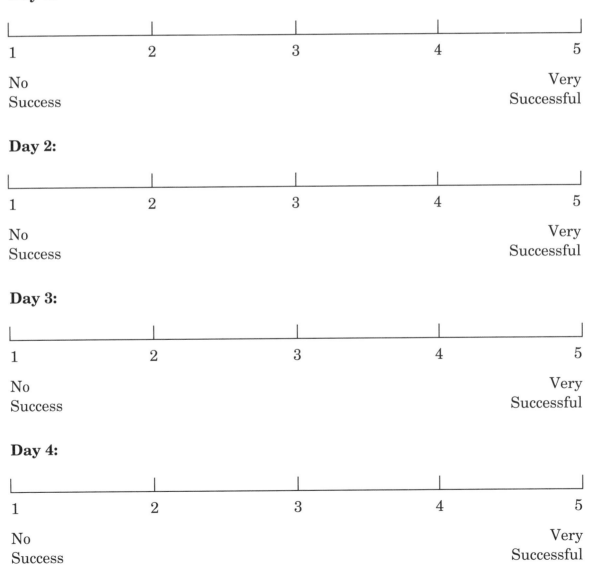

Day 1:

1	2	3	4	5

No   Very
Success   Successful

Day 2:

1	2	3	4	5

No   Very
Success   Successful

Day 3:

1	2	3	4	5

No   Very
Success   Successful

Day 4:

1	2	3	4	5

No   Very
Success   Successful

Day 5:

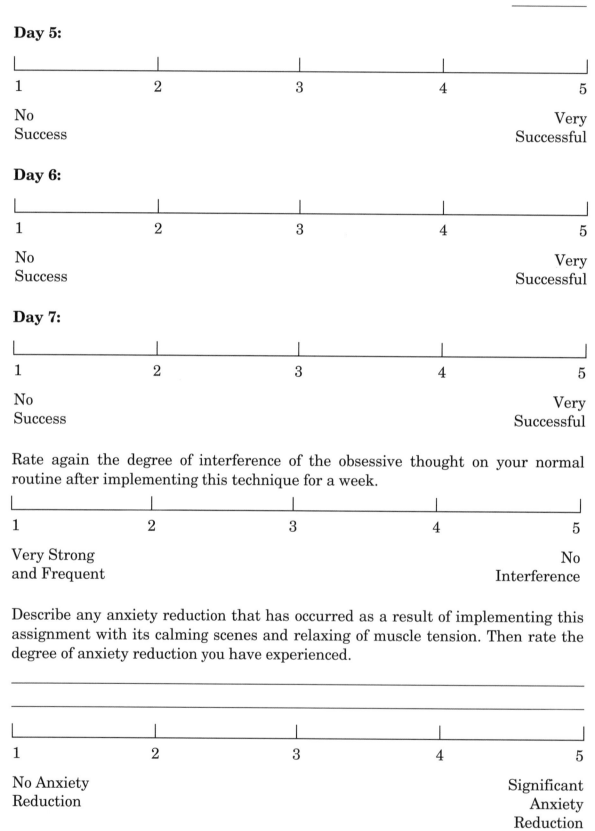

| 1 | 2 | 3 | 4 | 5 |

No
Success

Very
Successful

Day 6:

| 1 | 2 | 3 | 4 | 5 |

No
Success

Very
Successful

Day 7:

| 1 | 2 | 3 | 4 | 5 |

No
Success

Very
Successful

5. Rate again the degree of interference of the obsessive thought on your normal routine after implementing this technique for a week.

| 1 | 2 | 3 | 4 | 5 |

Very Strong
and Frequent

No
Interference

6. Describe any anxiety reduction that has occurred as a result of implementing this assignment with its calming scenes and relaxing of muscle tension. Then rate the degree of anxiety reduction you have experienced.

_____

_____

| 1 | 2 | 3 | 4 | 5 |

No Anxiety
Reduction

Significant
Anxiety
Reduction

REDUCING THE STRENGTH OF COMPULSIVE BEHAVIORS

GOALS OF THE EXERCISE

1. Identify compulsive behaviors and their irrational basis.
2. Develop and implement realistic self-talk techniques to reduce the frequency of compulsive behaviors.
3. Develop and implement a daily ritual that interrupts the current pattern of compulsions.
4. Develop a greater sense of control over compulsive behavior rituals and reduce their frequency.

ADDITIONAL PROBLEMS FOR WHICH THIS EXERCISE MAY BE MOST USEFUL

- Eating Disorders and Obesity
- Substance Use

SUGGESTIONS FOR PROCESSING THIS EXERCISE WITH THE CLIENT

Most often clients suffering from Obsessive-Compulsive Disorder (OCD) enter treatment believing that they have no control over their behavior patterns or thought patterns. This exercise is designed to increase their sense of control and reduce the frequency of compulsive behaviors. You may want to review the main elements of this homework assignment with the client before it is given, helping him/her to understand positive self-talk and behavioral interruption principles. Review the client's success at implementation and make any necessary adjustments in the therapeutic techniques as needed.

REDUCING THE STRENGTH OF COMPULSIVE BEHAVIORS

Compulsive behaviors are repetitive and intentional behaviors that are done in response to obsessive thoughts or according to eccentric rules. They are often done to neutralize or prevent discomfort or some dreaded situation in the future. None of these compulsive behavior rituals are connected in any realistic way with what they are designed to neutralize or prevent. This assignment helps you to examine your compulsive behavior rituals and provides you with two powerful techniques to increase your control over these compulsive behaviors and reduce their frequency of occurrence.

1. List the compulsive behaviors you engage in on a frequent and repeated basis.

    _____

    _____

    _____

    _____

2. Rate the degree of control you believe that you have over these compulsive behaviors.

1	2	3	4	5

    No   Total
    Control   Control

3. Describe why you believe engaging in these repetitive behaviors is of benefit to you (e.g., it's relaxing, feel less anxious or worried, stops my thinking about it).

    _____

    _____

    _____

    _____

4. Rate how rational you believe your compulsive behavior is (e.g., Is it reasonable? Is it really effective at reassuring you? Does it make sense?).

```
|_____|_____|_____|_____|
1               2               3               4               5
```

Irrational and   Very
Unreasonable   Rational

5. Positive realistic self-talk can be effective at counteracting the urge to engage in compulsive behavior. Review the following self-talk messages and write any additional messages you believe could be effective for your use.

   A. This behavior is not reasonable and I will not do it.

   B. I can resist this urge and it will go away eventually.

   C. I can think and act rationally about this urge.

   D. Anxious feelings will return after I perform this action, so I'm not going to do it.

   E. If I implement relaxation techniques, I will settle down.

   F. I'm going to think of a pleasant, calm scene until this urge passes.

   G. I'm going to focus my attention on another task so that the urge passes.

   H. _____

   I. _____

6. From the list, select the two or three self-talk messages that you think would be most effective for you. Write their letters below.

   _____   _____   _____

7. It is often effective to develop and implement a ritual that interrupts the current pattern of compulsive behavior. This behavior becomes a substitute for the compulsive behavior, but it is one that is under your control more directly. Describe two or three behaviors that you could engage in when the urge to perform the compulsive behavior becomes strong (e.g., vacuum the house, take a walk or perform some other exercise, call a friend, write in a journal).

   A. _____

   B. _____

   C. _____

8. For the next week, implement positive self-talk and ritual behavioral interruption to reduce the frequency of engaging in the compulsive behavior. Rate your degree of success at implementing these techniques.

Day 1:

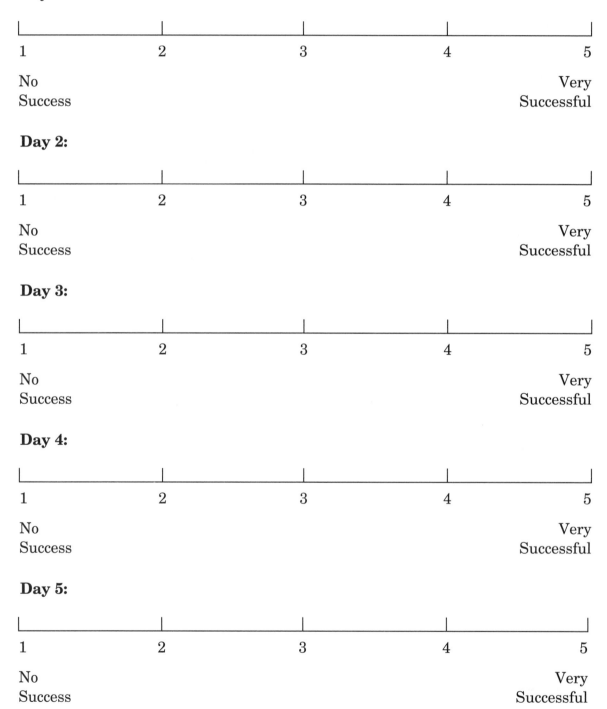

| 1 | 2 | 3 | 4 | 5 |

No
Success

Very
Successful

Day 2:

| 1 | 2 | 3 | 4 | 5 |

No
Success

Very
Successful

Day 3:

| 1 | 2 | 3 | 4 | 5 |

No
Success

Very
Successful

Day 4:

| 1 | 2 | 3 | 4 | 5 |

No
Success

Very
Successful

Day 5:

| 1 | 2 | 3 | 4 | 5 |

No
Success

Very
Successful

Day 6:

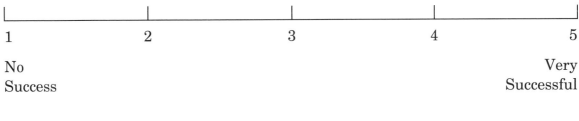

1   2   3   4   5

No   Very
Success   Successful

Day 7:

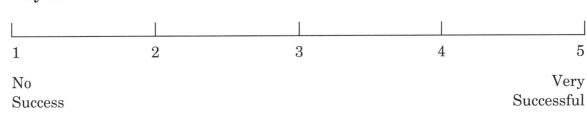

1   2   3   4   5

No   Very
Success   Successful

9. Now that you have implemented cognitive and behavioral control techniques, rate the degree of control you believe you have over your compulsive behaviors.

1   2   3   4   5

No   Total
Control   Control

COPING CARD

GOALS OF THE EXERCISE

1. Reduce the frequency, intensity, and duration of panic attacks.
2. Reduce the fear that panic symptoms will recur without the ability to manage them.
3. Implement relapse prevention strategies for managing possible future anxiety symptoms.

ADDITIONAL PROBLEMS FOR WHICH THIS EXERCISE MAY BE MOST USEFUL

*   Anxiety
*   Obsessive-Compulsive Disorder (OCD)
*   Phobia
*   Social Anxiety

SUGGESTIONS FOR PROCESSING THIS EXERCISE WITH THE CLIENT

In this assignment, the client is encouraged to utilize a "coping card" that identifies different strategies he/she can use to reduce the frequency, intensity, and duration of his/her panic attacks. Instruct the client to develop a list of coping strategies and write them down on the coping card. The client should place the coping card in a readily accessible place so that he/she can easily review the list when the symptoms of panic begin to emerge. The client should be encouraged to use positive self-talk or engage in calming or relaxing activities to help manage the panic attack. The therapist should train the client in the use of various anxiety-reduction techniques (e.g., deep breathing, progressive muscle relaxation, refocusing, replacing negative, distorted self-talk with reality-based, positive self-talk, etc.).

COPING CARD

Panic attacks can be very frightening, especially when they are intense and "come out of the blue." Millions of people like you have experienced panic attacks, but the good news is that they can be effectively managed or treated through various anxiety reduction techniques such as deep breathing, progressive muscle relaxation, refocusing, system desensitization, and replacing distorted, negative self-talk with positive, reality-based self-talk. Hopefully you have already received training in the use of some of these strategies or techniques.

In this assignment you are asked to use a "coping card" to manage your panic attacks. Write down various coping strategies on your coping card to remind you of different strategies that you can use when your symptoms of panic begin to appear. Keep the coping card in a readily accessible place (e.g., in your purse or wallet, posted on the refrigerator or a bulletin board) so that you can review the list when you begin to feel highly anxious or stressed. You are encouraged to record at least five different coping strategies that you can use at different times. We encourage you to write down several strategies because no one single coping strategy, by itself, will be successful all the time or in every situation. The more strategies you have listed on your coping card, the greater the chance you will be able to use a strategy that works for a certain stressful event or situation. Remember, different strategies work for different people at different times.

Below is a list of different strategies you can use to record on your coping card. Talk with your therapist about what strategies best fit your situation or personality style.

1. Go with the anxiety, don't fight it
Tell yourself to go with the anxiety and don't fight it. You can tell that you are fighting the panic attack when you tense your muscles, become more frantic in your movements, and express such statements as "Why is this happening to me?" Remember, fighting the anxiety often only increases the intensity of the panic attack.

2. Utilize reality-based, positive self-talk to help replace distorted, negative self-talk
When the symptoms of panic begin to come on, it is helpful to use positive self-talk. Below are some examples of positive self-talk that you can use or tell yourself when the panic attacks emerge:
- "Pace your breathing and slow your body down."
- "You can manage this panic attack."
- "This panic attack won't last forever" or "It will go away."
- "You've survived other panic attacks before."
- "Just stop what you're doing and take a few minutes to relax."

We encourage you to talk with your therapist about what specific self-statements you can use to manage your panic attacks.

3.   Refocusing

Oftentimes, it helps to refocus your attention on calming activities to help reduce your anxiety. You are encouraged to relax while you are performing these calming activities. Examples of calming or relaxing activities include:

- Going for a walk
- Playing a guitar, piano, or another instrument
- Gardening
- Knitting or crocheting
- Playing a video game
- Singing your favorite song
- Dancing

4.   Deep breathing and progressive relaxation

You are strongly encouraged to use deep breathing or progressive muscle relaxation to help slow your body down and reduce your stress. Ask your therapist to train you in the use of these techniques if you are not familiar with them.

5.   Record strategies on a "coping card"

After reviewing the list of various strategies and talking with your therapist, please record at least five different strategies on your coping card (you may record them on a 4 × 6 index card or the form below).

COPING CARD

The following is a list of strategies I can use to manage my panic attacks:

1. _____
   _____
1. _____
   _____
3. _____
   _____
4. _____
   _____
5. _____
   _____
6. _____
   _____
7. _____
   _____

MONITORING MY PANIC ATTACK EXPERIENCES

GOALS OF THE EXERCISE

1. Identify changes in panic attack severity.
2. Identify thoughts or experiences that trigger panic attacks.
3. Note reinforcing reactions of others to the panic attack experience.
4. Track the effectiveness of panic attack coping strategies.
5. Reduce the frequency, intensity, and duration of panic attacks.

ADDITIONAL PROBLEMS FOR WHICH THIS EXERCISE MAY BE MOST USEFUL

- Anxiety
- Phobia
- Social Anxiety

SUGGESTIONS FOR PROCESSING THIS EXERCISE WITH THE CLIENT

This rating form may be used with the client after coping strategies have been thoroughly reviewed and taught. After the client is familiar with such coping strategies as relaxation, deep breathing, positive self-talk, attention diversion, behavioral substitution, and cognitive restructuring, he/she can use the form to track his/her implementation of and success with these techniques in reducing the severity of panic symptoms. Provide the client with seven copies of the form so he/she can complete one on a daily basis to rate his/her experience of panic and the progress toward rehabilitation. The client should also be alerted to the need to monitor internal and external triggering stimuli for his/her panic experience.

MONITORING MY PANIC ATTACK EXPERIENCES

Make copies of this form and answer the questions for each panic attack experience.

Anxiety Scale

0	10	20	30	40	50	60	70	80	90	100

None   Mild   Moderate   High   Severe

1. Using the 0 to 100 scale, what number would you use to rate the overall level of your anxiety during the panic attack? _____

2. What symptoms of panic did you experience? _____
    _____
    _____

3. Approximately how long did your panic attack last? _____

4. What problems or stressful events were you experiencing shortly *before* your panic attack? _____
    _____
    _____
    _____
    _____

5. What anxious or negative thoughts were you experiencing shortly *before* the panic attack? _____
    _____
    _____
    _____
    _____

6. How did your family members, friends, or others react *during* and *after* your panic attack? _____

_____

_____

_____

_____

7. What strategies did you use to deal with your anxiety? _____

_____

_____

_____

_____

8. How did the strategies help in managing your anxiety? _____

_____

_____

_____

_____

9. What will you do differently, in the future, if you have another panic attack? _____

_____

_____

_____

_____

CHECK SUSPICIONS AGAINST REALITY

GOALS OF THE EXERCISE

1. Verbalize an understanding that fears or suspicions can grow to become irrational.
2. Examine suspicions against history, others' perception, and logic.
3. Acknowledge that some personal fears/suspicions are unreasonable.
4. Report reduced vigilance and suspicion around others as well as more relaxed, trusting, and open interactions.

ADDITIONAL PROBLEMS FOR WHICH THIS EXERCISE MAY BE MOST USEFUL

*   Intimate Relationship Conflicts
*   Psychoticism
*   Sleep Disturbance
*   Social Anxiety

SUGGESTIONS FOR PROCESSING THIS EXERCISE WITH THE CLIENT

If the client's paranoia is severe and the client is not open to challenging his/her beliefs, then you will have to be very actively involved in assisting the client in completing this exercise. Review each step of the assignment to help the client yield the irrational belief in the face of contradictory evidence from history, others' perceptions, and logic.

CHECK SUSPICIONS AGAINST REALITY

Fear and suspicion have a way of growing in strength and breadth or scope when the fear is not checked against reality. If we ponder our fears alone, the risk is that they can become irrational, unreasonable, and illogical. It is common to feel more anxious in the middle of the night when worries are on your mind and it is dark, quiet, and lonely. Burdens seem reduced when the light of day arrives and the concerns can be shared with others. We regain a realistic perspective.

Use this exercise to examine the fears and suspicions that plague you and interfere with your feeling of trust, peace, and happiness. Check out your suspicious beliefs against reality viewed from a different perspective.

1. Check out your fears/suspicions by thinking about the history of the suspected person or agency in terms of dealings with you. Have you, for the most part, been dealt with fairly, reasonably, respectfully, and kindly? _____

   _____

   _____

   _____

   _____

   _____

2. Check out your fears/suspicions by writing about the history of the suspected person or agency in terms of dealings with others. Have others, for the most part, been dealt with fairly, reasonably, respectfully, and kindly? _____

   _____

   _____

   _____

   _____

3. Check out your fears/suspicions by writing about how others perceive the suspected person or agency. Ask others about whether they share your beliefs and record their responses. _____

_____

_____

_____

_____

_____

_____

4. Check out your fears/suspicions by considering whether your fear is logical, rational, or reasonable. Can you acknowledge that your suspicions are irrational and should be discounted and revised? _____

_____

_____

_____

_____

_____

_____

_____

LEARNING TO PARENT AS A TEAM

GOALS OF THE EXERCISE

1. Each parent identifies his/her own parenting strengths and weaknesses.
2. Each parent identifies the parenting strengths and weaknesses of his/her partner.
3. Acknowledge areas where parenting weaknesses exist and request help in these areas.
4. Each parent identifies ways that he/she can be supportive of his/her partner in the parenting process.
5. Implement a scheduled list of family activities to promote connectedness and harmony.
6. Achieve a level of competent effective parenting.

ADDITIONAL PROBLEMS FOR WHICH THIS EXERCISE MAY BE MOST USEFUL

*   Family Conflict

SUGGESTIONS FOR PROCESSING THIS EXERCISE WITH THE CLIENT

Encourage the parents to work on the first step of this exercise independently before sharing the results with each other in a discussion format. Encourage them to come to you with requests for specific kinds of help they need as they try to improve their parenting. Reinforce their attempts to support one another as members of the parenting team. Encourage them to involve the children in finding family activities that will promote family connectedness.

LEARNING TO PARENT AS A TEAM

Parenting is a difficult task that requires good communication between partners as well as good cooperation and consistency. Each of us is a unique human being who brings his/her own strengths and weaknesses to bear on the task of parenting. To be an effective parenting team, you must help your partner in his/her area of weakness while your partner helps you in your area of weakness. Each of you must also support each other in your area of strengths. This exercise is meant to help you identify your strengths and weaknesses and describe ways that you can support each other to become a stronger parenting team. The exercise also calls for you to implement increased family activities to promote a feeling of connectedness between family members and promote harmony between parents as leaders of this family.

1. Each parent lists three to five of his/her own parenting strengths (e.g., playing with the children, making the children do their homework) and weaknesses (e.g., not enforcing the rules, talking to the children, supporting my spouse in parenting). Then list three to five strengths and weaknesses of your partner. Write your lists without consulting your partner. After all lists have been created, transfer the data to this page.

MOTHER'S LIST

Her Own

Strengths	Weaknesses
_____	_____
_____	_____
_____	_____
_____	_____

Her Partner's

Strengths	Weaknesses
_____	_____
_____	_____
_____	_____
_____	_____

FATHER'S LIST

His Own

Strengths	Weaknesses
_____	_____
_____	_____
_____	_____
_____	_____

His Partner's

Strengths	Weaknesses
_____	_____
_____	_____
_____	_____
_____	_____

2. After sharing your lists with each other, discuss and describe what kind of help you need from your counselor to improve your parenting as a team. _____

    _____

    _____

3. List three ways that each of you wishes the other partner would show support for you as a parent (e.g., join me when I discipline, calm me when I'm upset, listen to me when I'm frustrated).

MOTHER'S WISHES

A. _____
B. _____
C. _____

FATHER'S WISHES

A. _____
B. _____
C. _____

4. In a family meeting, construct a list of activities that members would enjoy doing together. Use a brainstorming technique where no idea is rejected to create a list of at least eight possible activities.

    _____   _____

    _____   _____

    _____   _____

    _____   _____

5. Select two activities to be implemented per week for the next 2 weeks. Schedule them for a date and time when all will be available to participate.

    Week 1   Activity 1: _____

              Date/Time: _____

              Activity 2: _____

              Date/Time: _____

    Week 2   Activity 1: _____

              Date/Time: _____

              Activity 2: _____

              Date/Time: _____

6. Describe the reaction of yourself and other family members to the family activity schedule.

    _____

    _____

    _____

    _____

THE TWO SIDES OF PARENTING
(BEING PARENTED AND BEING A PARENT)

GOALS OF THE EXERCISE

1. Achieve a level of competent, effective parenting.
2. Develop the client's awareness of the thoughts and feelings connected to how they were parented.
3. Identify and resolve any issues from childhood related to how the client was parented.

ADDITIONAL PROBLEMS FOR WHICH THIS EXERCISE MAY BE MOST USEFUL

- Anger Control Problems
- Childhood Trauma
- Posttraumatic Stress Disorder (PTSD)
- Substance Use

SUGGESTIONS FOR PROCESSING THIS EXERCISE WITH THE CLIENT

The two main things to keep in front of you during the processing of this exercise are psychoeducational. The first thing is to keep the client aware that the love of parents for a child and vice versa is a given and that we are looking at how the client was parented and the feelings and perspective he/she holds related to that experience. Most of us do not examine this experience unless it has been clearly a bad one and thus miss and overlook key information and insights. Secondly, as with all exercises adults complete, this exercise should be reviewed the following week because opening the door in these areas often leads to the client recalling more and this is missed in many cases unless we follow up.

THE TWO SIDES OF PARENTING
(BEING PARENTED AND BEING A PARENT)

Becoming a parent is a significant event and a cause for us in most circumstances to start thinking about how we will be as a parent and to look back at how we were parented. This exercise is meant to expand our insight into parenting and being parented, not to look specifically for issues. This exercise seeks to look beyond and further than a parent's love for his/her child. Each parent is to complete this exercise individually.

Being Parented

1. I generally think of my childhood as: (circle one)

   Happy/carefree   Okay   Better than others   Decent
   Unhappy   Troubled   Unpleasant   Terrible

   Briefly explain: _____

   _____

2. My parents were: (check two for mom and circle two for dad)

   Strict   Easygoing   Passive   Controlling
   Uninterested   Mean   Negative   Concerned
   Fair   Uninvolved   Adoring (could do no wrong)   Stern

   Briefly explain: _____

   _____

3. The lead parent in my home when I was growing up was:

   Dad   Mom   Stepparent

   Briefly explain: _____

   _____

4. What do you know about how each of them was parented?

   Dad: _____

   _____

   Mom: _____

   _____

5. How did they discipline and/or correct you?

As a child: _____

_____

As a teen: _____

_____

6. What were the basic house/family rules? _____

_____

_____

7. What were "hot buttons" for each of your parents?

Mom: _____

Dad: _____

8. What did you like about how they parented? _____

_____

_____

9. What is one thing that you would have liked them to do differently? _____

_____

10. How frequently did your mom and dad praise or recognize you for what you did?

Often   Regularly   Occasionally   Rarely   Never

Being a Parent

1. What were your thoughts and feelings about becoming a parent? _____

_____

_____

2. What were your concerns, worries, and/or fears? _____

_____

_____

3. How do you feel about being a parent now? _____

_____

_____

4. What do you feel that you do well as a parent? _____

_____

_____

5. What would you like to do better in terms of your parenting? _____

_____

_____

6. Describe one way in which you parent like your parents. _____

_____

_____

7. Describe one thing they did as parents that you consciously do not do. _____

_____

_____

8. What method do you use to discipline and/or correct your children? How often do you do this? _____

_____

_____

_____

_____

9. How frequently do you praise or recognize your children for what they have done?

    Often   Regularly   Occasionally   Rarely   Never

10. Complete the following sentence: When I become a parent, I will never _____

_____

_____

_____

USING REINFORCEMENT PRINCIPLES IN PARENTING

GOALS OF THE EXERCISE

1. Parents learn some basic tools of behavior modification.
2. Parents learn to write clear, behaviorally specific, positively directed rules.
3. Parents focus more on rule-keeping behavior and develop a repertoire of positive reinforcements for the child.
4. Parents learn to confront rule-breaking in a calm, controlled, reasonable, behaviorally focused, respectful manner and develop a list of potential logical consequences.
5. Effectively manage challenging problem behavior of the child.

ADDITIONAL PROBLEMS FOR WHICH THIS EXERCISE MAY BE MOST USEFUL

- Anger Control Problems
- Family Conflict
- Intimate Relationship Conflicts

SUGGESTIONS FOR PROCESSING THIS EXERCISE WITH THE CLIENT

Parents find it difficult to express expectations in behaviorally specific language—so do therapists. We must patiently try to shape parents' behavior as we process the rules that they develop. Also, be careful to bring to light unspoken rules that are left unlisted, but actually are very important for harmony in the household. Use counseling sessions to review lists and to model or role-play positive reinforcement of rule-keeping behavior. Watch out for negative consequences for rule-breaking that are not "tied to the crime" and are too protracted.

USING REINFORCEMENT PRINCIPLES IN PARENTING

Rules are best kept when there are as few as possible; they are stated clearly and in a positive direction; obedience is recognized by reward; and disobedience is either ignored (if a minor violation) or met with a consequence that is swiftly administered, brief, not harsh, focuses on the offensive behavior and not on the child, and is somehow related to the broken rule. This exercise helps you think about what your rules are for your child and what the consequences are for his/her obedience and disobedience.

Think about, discuss, and then write out the four most important rules of the household for your child. Write them concisely and clearly so there is no misunderstanding as to what is expected from the child. Also, be sure to write them in observable terms and in a positive direction. For example:

EXAMPLE A

Bad Rule: Johnny must stop causing so much trouble with his sister.

Better Rule: Johnny must keep his hands off his sister, talk to her softly and politely, and allow her to finish her TV program before asking to change the channel to his preference.

EXAMPLE B

Bad Rule: Johnny must take his schoolwork more seriously and be more responsible about homework assignments.

Better Rule: Johnny must attend all his classes promptly and regularly, complete and hand in each assignment on time, keep the rules of the classroom, reserve at least 1 hour per night for quiet study, and obtain no grade below C–.

EXAMPLE C

Bad Rule: Johnny must not explode in anger whenever he is told he may not do some activity or must stop some activity he is doing.

Better Rule: When Johnny is told what he may or may not do, he must accept the parental or teacher limits calmly and respectfully, carrying out the request within 30 seconds or less.

Four Most Important Rules

1. _____
_____
2. _____
_____
3. _____
_____
4. _____
_____

When rules are kept or reasonably obeyed, it is easy to take this behavior for granted and not acknowledge it. But when the goal is to build self-esteem, increase compliance, and reduce conflict with authority, then it is advisable to focus positive attention on obedience or compliance. Find ways to reward obedient behavior whenever and wherever it occurs. Rewards do not have to be elaborate, expensive, or even concrete. The reward can be as simple as "Thanks, I appreciate that" or an affectionate pat on the back. At times, it may be appropriate to stop and talk about how pleasant it is for everyone when rules are kept, respect is shown, and conflict is at a minimum. Finally, some rewards may be more concrete such as a small gift, a favorite meal, a special outing, a privilege granted, or an appreciative note left on his/her pillow.

Now list five ways that you could show positive recognition to your child for keeping the rules.

1. _____
_____
2. _____
_____
3. _____
_____
4. _____
_____
5. _____
_____

Obviously, rules are not going to be kept 100 percent of the time by any child. The difficult task for a parent is to decide how to respond to disobedience most effectively and reasonably. Two cardinal rules for punishment: First, do not react when and if your anger is not well controlled; postpone action but make it known that you are doing so. Second, keep your focus on the child's behavior that is out of bounds and do not disparage, name-call, swear at, or belittle the child; give consequences with an attitude of respect.

Consequences should be given as soon as reasonably possible after the disobedience—long delays before consequences reduce effectiveness significantly. Consequences should be brief and tied to the offensive behavior, if possible. Long and extended consequences breed resentment, cause hardship for the enforcers of the consequences, and are not any more effective than something more pointed and brief. Finally, be sure to be consistent in giving consequences; both parents have to work together. Misbehavior should not be overlooked one time and addressed the next nor should it be overlooked by one parent and punished by the other.

Now list two possible consequences for disobeying each of the Four Most Important Rules that you listed previously.

1a. _____

_____

1b. _____

_____

2a. _____

_____

2b. _____

_____

3a. _____

_____

3b. _____

_____

4a. _____

_____

4b. _____

_____

WHAT NEEDS TO BE CHANGED IN MY LIFE?

GOALS OF THE EXERCISE

1. Identify sources of stress, dissatisfaction, or frustration.
2. Identify responsibilities that are perceived as overwhelming.
3. Identify potential resources that have been overlooked and can reduce stress and increase shared responsibilities.
4. Resolve conflicted feelings and adapt to the new life circumstances.

ADDITIONAL PROBLEMS FOR WHICH THIS EXERCISE MAY BE MOST USEFUL

*   Suicidal Ideation
*   Unipolar Depression

SUGGESTIONS FOR PROCESSING THIS EXERCISE WITH THE CLIENT

A central role for the therapist in helping the client with a phase of life problem is that of assisting him/her in clarifying the problem and identifying resources to help reduce dissatisfaction in life. This assignment is best used in early stages of counseling. You may want to consider the option of completing the assignment with the client during the session, but if the client has significant strengths, it would be helpful to challenge him/her to work on this assignment between sessions and then process the results together. If his/her list of potential resources is not complete, you may focus on this issue in item number 7 and help him/her expand his/her thinking about this issue.

WHAT NEEDS TO BE CHANGED IN MY LIFE?

Your life may be disrupted by circumstances that you wish were different. Or, there may be a set of circumstances that you wish were present in your life that are absent. You may also be searching for resources that can provide you with some assistance to resolve the problems facing you. This assignment is designed to help you clarify those issues and bring you closer to making changes to improve your life.

1. List those circumstances that are present in your life that are contributing to your dissatisfaction, stress, or frustration. _____

    _____

    _____

    _____

2. Describe why each of the circumstances listed leads to dissatisfaction. _____

    _____

    _____

    _____

3. List those circumstances that you wish were present in your life and that you believe would increase your sense of fulfillment. _____

    _____

    _____

    _____

4. List those activities that you wish you were involved in and that you believe would increase your quality of life. _____

    _____

    _____

    _____

5. What changes would you like to occur for you to be less stressed and more happy?

_____

_____

6. What, if any, responsibilities would you like to share with others in order to reduce your burden? _____

_____

_____

7. Now it is time for you to brainstorm possibilities that exist in your life that may have been overlooked. These possibilities include resources that could be helpful to you to resolve crises that you face. In the following spaces, fill in the names of people, organizations, or activities in the various categories listed that could be sources of support.

Family members: _____

Friends: _____

Neighbors: _____

Self-help group members: _____

Counselor: _____

Coworkers: _____

Clergy: _____

Service organizations: _____

Church members or groups: _____

Educational classes: _____

Other resources: _____

8. Select three resources from your list and describe how these could be helpful to you and how you might begin to include them in your daily life.

Resource 1: _____

_____

_____

Resource 2: _____

_____

_____

Resource 3: _____

_____

_____

WHAT'S GOOD ABOUT ME AND MY LIFE?

GOALS OF THE EXERCISE

1. Identify advantages of current life situation.
2. Identify personal strengths and positive traits or talents.
3. Develop an action plan to increase activities that give meaning and satisfaction to life.
4. Balance life activities between consideration of others and the development of own interests.

ADDITIONAL PROBLEMS FOR WHICH THIS EXERCISE MAY BE MOST USEFUL

*   Chronic Pain
*   Dependency
*   Suicidal Ideation
*   Unipolar Depression

SUGGESTIONS FOR PROCESSING THIS EXERCISE WITH THE CLIENT

This assignment is best given at middle stages of counseling after the problems have been clarified and the client has the potential for establishing some balanced perspective to his/her life. If the client returns the assignment without having fulfilled all of the requests for information, review the items and brainstorm additional data that could have been included. Some clients find it very difficult to see anything positive about their life situation or their own personal strengths. Clients may also need help in developing the action plan called for in the final item of the assignment.

WHAT'S GOOD ABOUT ME AND MY LIFE?

Many people get stuck in a negative perception of themselves or their life circumstances and lose a balanced perspective that includes positive aspects of their lives. This assignment is designed to help you focus on your strengths and how you might use them to empower yourself toward greater satisfaction with your life. You need to make a concerted effort to overcome your belief that your life circumstances are overwhelmingly negative.

1. Describe at least four advantages to your current life circumstance (e.g., opportunity to make own decisions, opportunity for intimacy and sharing with a partner, a time for developing personal interests, meeting the needs of a significant other).

    A. _____

    B. _____

    C. _____

    D. _____

2. List at least four of your strengths, positive traits, or talents that you can use to enrich your life and the lives of others.

    A. _____

    B. _____

    C. _____

    D. _____

3. What changes do you believe you could make to help restore balance to your life?

    _____

    _____

    _____

4. What steps will you commit to for using your strengths, interests, and talents to begin to make the changes you feel are necessary for increased satisfaction? Describe actions and set target dates for implementation.

    Action   **Date**

    _____   _____

    _____   _____

    _____   _____

    _____   _____

    _____   _____

    _____   _____

FOUR WAYS TO REDUCE FEAR

GOALS OF THE EXERCISE

1. Identify and develop specific strategies to resolve the fear.
2. Implement a specific strategy on a consistent basis to minimize the impact of the fear.
3. Increase confidence and effectiveness in coping with the fear.
4. Reduce fear of the specific stimulus object or situation that previously provoked phobic anxiety.

ADDITIONAL PROBLEMS FOR WHICH THIS EXERCISE MAY BE MOST USEFUL

- Anxiety
- Panic/Agoraphobia
- Social Anxiety

SUGGESTIONS FOR PROCESSING THIS EXERCISE WITH THE CLIENT

The focus in processing this exercise should be placed on assisting the client in completely developing each of the resolution strategies and in helping him/her to fully implement a strategy to reduce his/her fear. Offer encouragement, feedback, and direction as needed as you follow up on the strategy. If the first strategy chosen does not seem to be effective despite the client's best efforts, another option should be chosen and implemented.

FOUR WAYS TO REDUCE FEAR

This exercise helps you develop four different ways to minimize your fear. After developing the four ways, you will then choose the one that you feel would be best for you and try it for the following week when encountering your fear.

1. Develop fully each of the following methods for resolving your fear.

    A. **Exaggeration:** Start with identifying your fear; then imagine it as big, scary, ugly, and so on. Use as many negative descriptive words as possible in describing the fear in the worst possible way and with the most dire consequences.

        _____

        _____

        _____

        Application: By imagining the worst that can happen in the worst possible way, the things I face don't seem so big or terrible.

    B. **Thought Restructuring:** Record the three most common thoughts you have that lead to increased feelings of fear (e.g., "I'm going to make a fool of myself," "Everyone is staring at me"). After completing that, ask your therapist to help you restructure your fear-producing thoughts into thoughts that are more realistic and positive (e.g., "I will do my best and people will respect me for that effort").

        Thought 1: _____

        _____

        Restructured: _____

        _____

        Thought 2: _____

        _____

        Restructured: _____

        _____

        Thought 3: _____

        _____

        Restructured: _____

        _____

Application: How we think about something affects our feelings. By changing our thoughts and perceptions, we change our feelings.

C. **Therapist in Your Pocket:** Ask your therapist to provide you with three statements that will offer reassurance when you are encountering your phobia. Record them and then either commit them to memory or write them on a card to keep in your pocket at all times.

1. _____

2. _____

3. _____

Application: Reassuring and encouraging statements from people we respect and trust can help us cope with difficult or scary situations.

D. **Relaxing Distraction:** Create a favorite relaxing daydream to use to distract yourself when facing or thinking about the situation your fear. Then choose a relaxing activity to use as a distraction at other times (e.g., sunbathing on the beach).

Daydream: _____

_____

_____

Activity (e.g., quietly singing, relaxation breathing): _____

_____

_____

Application: When distracted, we forget our worries, fears, and troubles.

2. Choose an approach to your fear.

A. Identify which of the four approaches (i.e., A, B, C, D) you feel would be most effective in helping you resolve your fear.

_____

B. Explain briefly the choice you made and why you feel it would be effective.

_____

_____

_____

C. Use an **X** to indicate how sure you feel about the approach working for you.

Very Sure	Sure	Somewhat	A Little	Not at All

3. Make a commitment to use the approach you chose whenever you encounter the fear over the next week and then evaluate how effective it was in dealing with the fear after each time you used it.

A. _____

B. _____

C. _____

D. _____

GRADUALLY REDUCING YOUR PHOBIC FEAR

GOALS OF THE EXERCISE

1. Identify precisely what the feared object or situation is.
2. Describe the emotional, physiological, and behavioral impact that the feared object or situation has had.
3. Undergo repeated exposure to feared or avoided phobic objects or situations.
4. Reduce fear of the specific stimulus object or situation that previously provoked phobic anxiety.

ADDITIONAL PROBLEMS FOR WHICH THIS EXERCISE MAY BE MOST USEFUL

- Childhood Trauma
- Posttraumatic Stress Disorder (PTSD)
- Social Anxiety

SUGGESTIONS FOR PROCESSING THIS EXERCISE WITH THE CLIENT

Systematic desensitization to a phobic object or situation has proven to be a very successful approach to extinguishing a fear response. This assignment focuses the client on the phobic stimulus and its effect on his/her life. Instruct the client to develop a gradual hierarchy of exposure steps to the feared stimulus. You probably will have to be directly involved in constructing this hierarchy with the client. As preparation for beginning the in vivo exposure to the feared stimulus, it is recommended that you teach the client some behavioral and cognitive anxiety-reduction skills, such as deep breathing, progressive relaxation, positive imagery, confidence-building self-talk, and so on. Monitor and reinforce his/her implementation of these skills as the exposure program progresses. Urge the patient to increase exposure as anxiety diminishes to the current step.

GRADUALLY REDUCING YOUR PHOBIC FEAR

Fears that are so strong that they control our behavior need to be faced and overcome. This exercise helps you do just that: Identify what your fear is; describe how it affects you; develop a plan to face it systematically; and, finally, actually take steps to face your fear and win.

1. It is important to clearly identify what you fear and how it affects you emotionally (e.g., feel nervous and tense), behaviorally (such as avoid contact and/or don't talk about the feared stimulus), and physically (for instance, heart pounds, forehead and palms sweat, stomachache, nausea). Describe what the feared object or situation is and then tell how it affects you.

Feared Object or Situation

_____

_____

_____

Reaction to Feared Object or Situation

Emotional reaction: _____

_____

_____

Behavioral reaction: _____

_____

_____

Physical reaction: _____

_____

_____

To overcome a fear, it must be faced in a gradual but systematic fashion. We call this *exposure*. When you practice exposure in the proper way, fear steadily diminishes until it does not control your behavior or affect you physically. The key to the process is to develop a plan for gradually increasing exposure to the feared object or situation. Once the plan is developed, you then expose yourself one step at a time to the feared object or situation. You do not take the next step in the gradual exposure plan until you are quite comfortable with the current level of exposure.

For example, if your fear is that of driving alone on the expressway during heavy traffic, you could design a plan as follows.

Step 1.   Drive on the expressway for 5 minutes at a time of light traffic with a supportive person to give reassurance.

Step 2:   Drive on the expressway for 5 minutes at a time of light traffic, alone.

Step 3:   Drive on the expressway for 10 minutes at a time of light traffic, alone.

Step 4:   Drive on the expressway for 15 minutes at a time of light traffic, alone.

Step 5:   Drive on the expressway for 5 minutes at a time of heavy traffic, alone.

Step 6:   Drive on the expressway for 15 minutes at a time of heavy traffic, alone.

Each next step is taken only after the fear is low or gone in the current step.

2.   Now create a gradual exposure program to overcome your feared object or situation. The steps can increase the time you spend with the feared object or situation, increase your closeness to it, increase the size of the object, or a combination of these things. Use as many steps as you need. Your therapist is available to help you construct this plan, if necessary.

Step 1. _____

_____

_____

Step 2. _____

_____

_____

Step 3. _____

_____

_____

Step 4. _____

_____

_____

Step 5. _____

_____

_____

Step 6. _____

_____

_____

Now it's time for a gradual but steady exposure to your feared object or situation. Stay relaxed. Your therapist may teach you some deep breathing, muscle relaxation, and positive self-talk techniques that you can use to keep yourself relaxed. For each attempt at exposure, record the coping technique you used and rate your degree of fear on a scale of 1 to 100, with 100 representing total panic, the sweats, and heart-pounding shakes. The rating of 1 represents total calm, complete confidence, peace of mind, looseness, and relaxed feeling. When your rating is reduced to 10 or lower on a consistent basis for the exposure to a particular step, then it's time to consider moving on to the next step.

Exposure Steps	**Coping Technique and Fear Rating**
Step 1. _____	First attempt: _____
_____	Second attempt: _____
_____	Third attempt: _____
Step 2. _____	First attempt: _____
_____	Second attempt: _____
_____	Third attempt: _____
Step 3. _____	First attempt: _____
_____	Second attempt: _____
_____	Third attempt: _____
Step 4. _____	First attempt: _____
_____	Second attempt: _____
_____	Third attempt: _____
Step 5. _____	First attempt: _____
_____	Second attempt: _____
_____	Third attempt: _____
Step 6. _____	First attempt: _____
_____	Second attempt: _____
_____	Third attempt: _____

HOW THE TRAUMA AFFECTS ME

GOALS OF THE EXERCISE

1. Identify and clarify the experience of PTSD symptoms.
2. Identify the most distressing symptoms and the frequency of their occurrence.
3. Reduce the negative impact that the traumatic event has had on many aspects of life and return to pretrauma level of functioning.

ADDITIONAL PROBLEMS FOR WHICH THIS EXERCISE MAY BE MOST USEFUL

- Childhood Trauma
- Sexual Abuse Victim

SUGGESTIONS FOR PROCESSING THIS EXERCISE WITH THE CLIENT

This is a simple and straightforward exercise designed to help the client focus his/her thinking on the specific PTSD symptoms he/she has experienced. You may want to review the list with the client within the session to clarify the meaning of some of the symptom descriptions. During your review of the completed exercise, allow the client to elaborate on any of his/her symptoms and explore how these symptoms have affected his/her life.

HOW THE TRAUMA AFFECTS ME

After having been exposed to a serious threat or actual physical trauma or abuse, many people develop a set of emotional, cognitive, or behavioral symptoms. The immediate response of fear, helplessness, or horror often gives way to lingering effects that can be intense at times and can affect your life in many ways. This exercise is designed to help you identify and focus on those specific symptoms of PTSD that you have experienced.

1. Review the items in the two columns and put a check mark in front of the symptoms that you have experienced since the traumatic event occurred.

_____ Intrusive thoughts/images	_____ Sleep pattern abnormal
_____ Disturbing dreams	_____ Irritable
_____ Flashbacks of the trauma	_____ Poor concentration
_____ Reminders of trauma cause distress	_____ On edge
_____ Shakes, sweats, heart racing	_____ Easily startled
_____ Avoid talking about the trauma	_____ Sad or guilty feelings
_____ Avoid trauma places/people	_____ Alcohol/drug abuse
_____ Amnesia regarding trauma	_____ Suicidal thoughts
_____ Withdrawal from activities	_____ Conflict with others
_____ Feel detached from other people	_____ Verbally/physically violent
_____ Emotionally numb	_____ Other: _____
_____ Pessimistic regarding future	_____ Other: _____

2. Which three symptoms that you have placed a check mark next to have caused you the most distress? _____

_____

_____

3. How frequently does each of the symptoms that you noted in number 2 occur?

   _____

   _____

4. When was the last occurrence of a PTSD symptom and what was that symptom?

   _____

   _____

SHARE THE PAINFUL MEMORY

GOALS OF THE EXERCISE

1. Describe the traumatic experience in some detail.
2. Identify the ways that the trauma has impacted life.
3. Communicate the feelings associated with the traumatic event.
4. Review treatment options designed to help people recover from PTSD.
5. Recall the traumatic event without becoming overwhelmed with negative thoughts, feelings, or urges.

ADDITIONAL PROBLEMS FOR WHICH THIS EXERCISE MAY BE MOST USEFUL

• Childhood Trauma
• Sexual Abuse Victim

SUGGESTIONS FOR PROCESSING THIS EXERCISE WITH THE CLIENT

It is always a delicate clinical decision as to when and how to encourage the client to explore the details of severe trauma that he/she has experienced. If there is any question about the ability of the client to focus on the details of the traumatic event outside of the supportive therapeutic relationship, allow the client to answer the first question within a therapy session. Allow the client to begin to express his/her feelings associated with the trauma, both those that were immediately precipitated by the event and those feelings that can be stirred after the event. You may have to review the list of treatment strategies found in item 6 to provide further explanation for the client.

SHARE THE PAINFUL MEMORY

It is not unusual for someone who has experienced a physical and/or emotional trauma to want to avoid anything and everything that is associated with that trauma. A common reaction is "I don't want to talk about it." However, refusing to deal with a traumatic event by attempting to bury it will only increase the negative consequences of that trauma and prolong its effects. You need to share, when the time is right, as much detail about the experience as you possibly can. This exercise is designed to help you share what happened and how you feel about it.

1. Describe the traumatic incident, giving as many specifics as possible (e.g., your age, the place of occurrence, details of what happened, who was present at the time of the trauma). If necessary, use additional paper to describe your experience.

   _____

   _____

   _____

2. What other events have you experienced in your life that are similar to the traumatic event you described in item number 1? _____

   _____

   _____

   _____

3. What are the harmful ways that you have attempted to cope with your emotional reaction to the trauma (e.g., substance abuse, avoid thoughts of the incident, avoid people/places associated with the incident, social withdrawal, sleeping)?

   _____

   _____

   _____

4. How have the trauma and your reaction to it affected your life (e.g., intimate partner relationship, relationships with friends, work performance, family relationships, social/recreational activities, spiritual journey, physical health)?

_____

_____

_____

5. For each of the following emotions, use an **X** to indicate the strength of your feeling on the continuum:

Anger

| Very Strong | Strong | Somewhat | Barely | Never |

Sadness

| Very Strong | Strong | Somewhat | Barely | Never |

Fear

| Very Strong | Strong | Somewhat | Barely | Never |

Guilt/Shame

| Very Strong | Strong | Somewhat | Barely | Never |

Embarrassment

| Very Strong | Strong | Somewhat | Barely | Never |

Tension/On Edge

| Very Strong | Strong | Somewhat | Barely | Never |

6. Review various treatment strategies described and mark those that you believe can help you overcome this trauma.

_____ Slowly retelling and gradually reliving the details of the incident in a safe therapy environment.

_____ Learning new ways to think about the trauma.

_____ Learning to manage and control anger and other strong emotions.

_____ Taking medication to deal with depression and anxiety.

_____ Developing a recovery program to end substance abuse as an escape from pain.

_____ Learning relaxation skills to reduce tension, stress, and panic.

_____ Slow, systematic exposure to the memory of the traumatic event while staying calm and relaxed.

_____ Sharing your experience in a group setting with others who have been through a trauma.

_____ Sharing the experience with family members who can be understanding and supportive.

_____ Learning communication and conflict resolution skills to apply to a strained intimate relationship.

_____ Developing a sleep induction routine that will reduce fatigue and restlessness.

_____ Implementing problem-solving skills with vocational conflicts to stabilize employment.

_____ Implementing an exercise regimen to reduce stress and increase energy level.

_____ Relying on spiritual faith to build confidence and foster forgiveness and peace.

7. Explain why you believe each of the treatment selections you made in number 6 will be of benefit to you. _____

_____

_____

_____

WHAT DO YOU HEAR AND SEE?

GOALS OF THE EXERCISE

1. Describe the type and history of the psychotic symptoms.
2. Reduce anxiety associated with the experience of hallucinations.
3. Identify stressors that increase the frequency or intensity of hallucinations.
4. Separate reality from hallucination experience.

ADDITIONAL PROBLEMS FOR WHICH THIS EXERCISE MAY BE MOST USEFUL

- Bipolar—Mania
- Paranoid Ideation
- Unipolar Depression

SUGGESTIONS FOR PROCESSING THIS EXERCISE WITH THE CLIENT

This exercise provides an opportunity for the client to describe the history, nature, and precipitating circumstances surrounding his/her hallucinations. It may be necessary to administer this exercise verbally within a therapy session because the client may not be capable of staying focused enough to complete this as a writing assignment. The therapist should clearly label these hallucination experiences as the result of the client's illness, not a reflection of reality. Suggestions could be made as to coping techniques (distraction, medication adjustment, sharing with supportive individuals, etc.).

WHAT DO YOU HEAR AND SEE?

Hallucinations are those private experiences of hearing voices or sounds, or seeing visions, that others do not experience. You may hear voices that others cannot hear or see people or objects that others cannot see. This can be a very scary experience and it can seem as if the experience is very real, not a result of your mind being confused. This exercise encourages you to describe these private experiences that are not shared by others. Please be as open and honest as you feel comfortable with as you answer these questions.

1. Do you hear voices that others do not hear? Yes _____ No _____ If yes,

   A. When did you first hear such voices? _____
   _____
   _____

   B. What do the voices say to you? (use additional paper, if necessary) _____
   _____
   _____
   _____

   C. Does it seem like the voices come from outside or inside your head? _____
   _____
   _____
   _____

   D. Do the voices ever command you to do anything? If so, what do they tell you to do? Do you do what they tell you? _____
   _____
   _____
   _____

   E. What circumstances seem to bring on the hearing of voices (when you are tired, afraid, tense, alone, with a crowd, etc.)? _____
   _____
   _____
   _____

F. How does taking your medication affect your hearing of voices? _____

_____

_____

_____

G. On a separate piece of paper, draw a picture of what you imagine the person speaking to you looks like.

2. Do you see people or objects that others cannot see? Yes _____ No _____ If yes,

A. When did you first experience these visions? _____

_____

_____

_____

B. Please describe what you see that others cannot see. _____

_____

_____

_____

C. What circumstances seem to bring on the visions? _____

_____

_____

_____

D. How does taking your medication affect your seeing these people or objects?

_____

_____

_____

E. On a separate piece of paper, draw a picture of what you see that others do not see.

A BLAMING LETTER AND A FORGIVING LETTER TO PERPETRATOR

GOALS OF THE EXERCISE

1. Express feelings to and about the perpetrator including the impact that the sexual abuse has had.
2. Clearly place responsibility for the abuse on the perpetrator, absolving self of any blame.
3. Begin the process of forgiveness in order to relieve self of bitter anger.
4. Clarify current feelings toward the perpetrator and expectations held for him/her.
5. Begin the process of moving away from being a victim of sexual abuse toward becoming a survivor of sexual abuse.

ADDITIONAL PROBLEMS FOR WHICH THIS EXERCISE MAY BE MOST USEFUL

- Dissociation
- Low Self-Esteem

SUGGESTIONS FOR PROCESSING THIS EXERCISE WITH THE CLIENT

This exercise focuses on two important steps in the recovery process for the survivor of sexual abuse. First, the client must place clear responsibility on the perpetrator for the sexual abuse and absolve himself/herself of any responsibility. Second, the client must begin a process of forgiveness to reduce feelings of anger or revenge that may cripple the recovery process. The letter of forgiveness cannot be assigned too early in the counseling process, and the therapist must be careful that such a letter does not imply that the perpetrator is excused from responsibility for his/her actions.

A BLAMING LETTER AND A FORGIVING LETTER TO PERPETRATOR

It is very important for your recovery from the trauma of sexual abuse that you sort out your feelings about the abuse and clearly identify the perpetrator as the responsible party. You must resist the common tendency to take some responsibility for the sexual abuse, even in some indirect way or small measure. It is also important during later stages of recovery that you begin to grapple with the concept of forgiveness toward the perpetrator. You will need to discuss the concept of forgiveness and how this is a process that takes time. It is important to develop an understanding of why forgiveness can be a healthy practice for you that brings considerable benefit in terms of replacing bitter anger with a sense of peace. This assignment is designed to help you think through writing a letter of blame, for this is an important step in your recovery, and a letter of forgiveness, a step not to be confused with excusing the perpetrator or absolving him/her of guilt.

1. Blame Letter: On the following lines, compose a letter of blame to the perpetrator and consider including the following elements in your letter.

   - Tell the perpetrator what your accusations are regarding his/her abuse of you.

   - Explain why the perpetrator is solely responsible for this abuse.

   - Describe how the sexual abuse made you feel at the time it occurred and now.

   - Describe how the sexual abuse has affected your life.

   - Describe how you felt toward the perpetrator before, during, and immediately after the sexual abuse.

   - Describe how you feel toward the perpetrator now.

   _____

   _____

   _____

   _____

   _____

   _____

   _____

   _____

   _____

2. Forgiving Letter: On the following lines, compose a letter of forgiveness and consider including the following elements.

    - Tell the perpetrator that he/she is solely responsible for the sexual abuse.
    - Explain why you are attempting to forgive him/her.
    - Explain that forgiveness does *not* mean that his/her abuse was excusable.
    - Explain that forgiveness is a process that may take a long time to complete and you are only beginning it now.
    - Tell the perpetrator what you expect from him/her now and in the future.
    - Tell the perpetrator what type of relationship you may want with him/her, if any, in the future.

_____

PICTURING THE PLACE OF THE ABUSE

GOALS OF THE EXERCISE

1. Identify the location of the abuse and all those that were in reasonable proximity.
2. Acknowledge avoidance practices associated with the place of the abuse.
3. Increase feelings of empowerment, decrease avoidance practices.
4. Work successfully through the issues related to being sexually abused with consequent understanding and control of feelings.

ADDITIONAL PROBLEMS FOR WHICH THIS EXERCISE MAY BE MOST USEFUL

- Dissociation
- Posttraumatic Stress Disorder (PTSD)

SUGGESTIONS FOR PROCESSING THIS EXERCISE WITH THE CLIENT

The client who has been through the trauma of sexual abuse often practices avoidance. This avoidance can be demonstrated in trying not to think about the incident, refusing to discuss the incident, staying away from the location of the abuse, and shunning any contact with the perpetrator. As recovery progresses, the client must terminate these avoidance practices and become more confident of his/her ability to cope with these reminders of the abuse. Encourage the client to face these stimuli that are associated with the trauma of the past. If recollection of the trauma begins to lead to decompensation, it is very important that support be given to the client and he/she not be pressured to deal with these stimuli prematurely.

PICTURING THE PLACE OF THE ABUSE

A common practice of those who have suffered a traumatic experience is to avoid anything associated with the trauma. However, this practice does not promote healing and may exaggerate the negative consequences that occur after a trauma. Healthy recovery requires that you are able to encounter the details of the trauma without being overwhelmed with negative emotions. This exercise is designed to help you come face to face with the traumatic experience, at least in terms of the specific environment in which it occurred.

1. On a separate sheet of paper, draw a floor plan or diagram of the place where the sexual abuse occurred (e.g., house, church, car, park). Indicate on the diagram where you and the perpetrator were and where any other people were who were reasonably close by. If the abuse occurred in several different locations, you may draw more than one diagram on this page or use other pieces of paper to draw your diagrams.

2. Describe any flashbacks, nightmares, or other thoughts you have had about the place of the abuse.

   _____

   _____

   _____

   _____

3. Describe the feelings you have when you remember the place of the abuse.

   _____

   _____

   _____

   _____

4. Describe what steps you have taken to avoid seeing, coming close to, or even thinking about the place of the abuse.

   _____

   _____

   _____

   _____

5. As you recover from this trauma, you will overcome your avoidance of this place, discussions of the incident, feeling ashamed, or being crippled in relationships. Rate your degree of desire for this type of recovery.

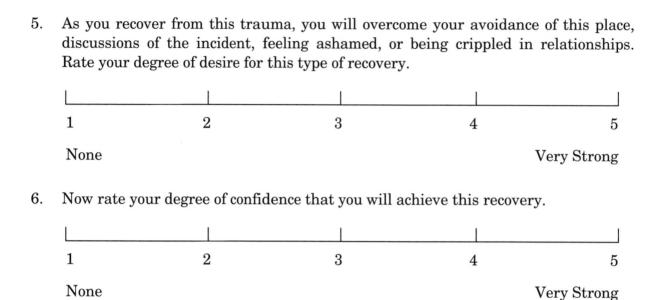

| 1 | 2 | 3 | 4 | 5 |

None   Very Strong

6. Now rate your degree of confidence that you will achieve this recovery.

| 1 | 2 | 3 | 4 | 5 |

None   Very Strong

JOURNAL OF SEXUAL THOUGHTS, FANTASIES, CONFLICTS

GOALS OF THE EXERCISE

1. Increase the awareness of sexual thoughts, feelings, and fantasies.
2. Clarify the direction of sexual attraction feelings.
3. Clarify causes for conflict regarding feelings of sexual attraction.
4. Reduce the overall frequency and intensity of the anxiety associated with sexual identity so that daily functioning is not impaired.

ADDITIONAL PROBLEMS FOR WHICH THIS EXERCISE MAY BE MOST USEFUL

- Female Sexual Dysfunction
- Intimate Relationship Conflicts
- Male Sexual Dysfunction

SUGGESTIONS FOR PROCESSING THIS EXERCISE WITH THE CLIENT

The client must be given the opportunity to indicate the degree of his/her confusion or anxiety associated with feelings of sexual arousal and attraction. If homosexual feelings are dominant, the client will need to clarify any feelings of conflict over these urges. If heterosexual feelings are predominant, there may also be feelings of conflict over experiencing such sexual feelings. Process the client's feelings as they arise and encourage self-acceptance and positive regard.

JOURNAL OF SEXUAL THOUGHTS, FANTASIES, CONFLICTS

This exercise helps you become more aware of your own sexual thoughts, feelings, fantasies, and desires. If we experience conflict over our sexual feelings, we tend to repress those feelings and try to deny their existence. Try to overcome a natural tendency toward inhibiting the expression of these thoughts and feelings. Remember, at this point you are only writing about what you think and feel, you are not acting on these impulses without thought or consideration of values. To clarify your own sexuality, you first need to identify the naturally occurring urges and desires within you.

1. Journal Task: Use the form to enter information on a daily basis regarding your sexual thoughts, any accompanying trigger situations that stimulate those thoughts or fantasies, the degree of arousal you experience associated with your sexual thoughts, and finally, describe any internal moral conflict that may inhibit these thoughts or internal approval that may encourage these thoughts.

Entry 1 Day/Date and Time: _____ _____	Sexual Thoughts	
	Trigger Situation	
	Degree of Arousal	1 None 2 3 4 5 Very Strong
	Internal Conflict or Approval	

Entry 2 Day/Date and Time: _____ _____	Sexual Thoughts	
	Trigger Situation	
	Degree of Arousal	1 2 3 4 5 None Very Strong
	Internal Conflict or Approval	

Entry 3 Day/Date and Time: _____ _____	Sexual Thoughts	
	Trigger Situation	
	Degree of Arousal	1 2 3 4 5 None Very Strong
	Internal Conflict or Approval	

Entry 4 Day/Date and Time: _____ _____	Sexual Thoughts	
	Trigger Situation	
	Degree of Arousal	1 — 2 — 3 — 4 — 5 None Very Strong
	Internal Conflict or Approval	

Entry 5 Day/Date and Time: _____ _____	Sexual Thoughts	
	Trigger Situation	
	Degree of Arousal	1 — 2 — 3 — 4 — 5 None Very Strong
	Internal Conflict or Approval	

Entry 6 Day/Date and Time: _____ _____	Sexual Thoughts	
	Trigger Situation	
	Degree of Arousal	1 2 3 4 5 None Very Strong
	Internal Conflict or Approval	

Entry 7 Day/Date and Time: _____ _____	Sexual Thoughts	
	Trigger Situation	
	Degree of Arousal	1 2 3 4 5 None Very Strong
	Internal Conflict or Approval	

2. Rate the average degree of sexual arousal felt toward same-sex individuals during the week.

1	2	3	4	5

No
Attraction

Strong
Attraction

3. Rate the average degree of sexual arousal felt toward the opposite sex during the week.

1	2	3	4	5

No
Attraction

Strong
Attraction

4. How sure are you that the ratings you gave in number 2 and number 3 above are accurate and reliable?

1	2	3	4	5

Unsure

Certain

If you are not sure, what contributes to your confusion on this issue? _____

_____

_____

5. What type of person triggers your feelings of sexual attraction? _____

_____

6. At what point in your life did you first become aware of your feelings of sexual attraction that are described in number 2 or number 3 above? _____

_____

7. How comfortable are you with your feelings of sexual attraction and arousal?

1	2	3	4	5

Very   Very
Uncomfortable   Comfortable

Explain: _____

_____

TO WHOM AND HOW TO REVEAL MY HOMOSEXUALITY

GOALS OF THE EXERCISE

1. Identify trusted people who could receive and accept information about the homosexual orientation.
2. Anticipate the thoughts and feelings of the recipient of the disclosure.
3. Carefully prepare a statement of disclosure and identify the most appropriate time for sharing it.
4. Disclose sexual orientation to significant others.

ADDITIONAL PROBLEMS FOR WHICH THIS EXERCISE MAY BE MOST USEFUL

- None

SUGGESTIONS FOR PROCESSING THIS EXERCISE WITH THE CLIENT

After clarifying his/her own homosexual identity, the client still has a major task in front of him/her. The client must think through the process of disclosure of his/her sexual orientation with significant people in his/her life. This exercise is designed to help the client through that process of deciding where, when, and to whom the information will be disclosed, as well as possible questions and reactions the recipients may have. Process the completed assignment with the client, allowing him/her to revise his/her statement of disclosure, as well as giving him/her the opportunity to work through the feelings of anxiety and fear of rejection that most often accompany this step. Help the client reach out to develop a support network to reduce feelings of isolation and alienation.

TO WHOM AND HOW TO REVEAL
MY HOMOSEXUALITY

If you are convinced of your sexual orientation, you now must work through the feelings associated with that realization. When you are convinced that you are homosexual, and you have clarified, expressed, and worked through the feelings associated with that fact, then you must formulate a plan for disclosure of this fact to significant people in your life. This exercise is designed to help you think through the process of disclosure or coming out. This is a difficult but important step in declaring who you are and seeking acceptance.

1. Who are all of the people you think should eventually be told of your sexual orientation?_____

_____

_____

_____

_____

2. Who is the first person you are going to tell about your sexual orientation who is not already aware of it? _____

_____

_____

_____

_____

3. When do you believe you should tell your parents of your sexual orientation?

_____

_____

_____

4. Do you believe your parents already have some idea that you may be homosexual? Why or why not? _____

_____

_____

_____

5. Who already knows about your sexual orientation? _____

_____

_____

6. When you tell your parents about your sexual orientation, what reaction do you expect from your mother regarding your disclosure? _____

_____

_____

_____

_____

7. What reaction do you expect from your father regarding your disclosure? _____

_____

_____

_____

_____

8. What reaction do you expect from other important family members like siblings, grandparents, cousins, and so on? (Name the person and his/her expected reaction.)

_____

_____

_____

9. What reaction do you expect from your friends? (Name friend and his/her expected reaction.) _____

_____

_____

_____

10. On the following lines, write out a presentation you might make to your friends and/or family regarding your discovery and belief in your sexual orientation. In your written statement, include telling them about when you first had feelings of homosexual arousal, your emotional struggle connected with this sexual identity discovery, your current degree of certainty regarding your homosexuality, your current feelings about your future life as a homosexual, and any fears you may have about their reaction to your disclosure. Use additional paper, if necessary.

_____

_____

_____
_____
_____
_____
_____
_____
_____
_____
_____
_____
_____
_____
_____
_____
_____
_____
_____
_____
_____
_____
_____

11. What questions might the recipients of this information have after they hear your disclosure? _____

_____
_____
_____
_____

12. Describe an exact person, time, and setting when you would be most comfortable making such a disclosure. _____

_____
_____
_____
_____

SLEEP PATTERN RECORD

GOALS OF THE EXERCISE

1. Increase awareness of effective sleep induction routines.
2. Implement a sleep induction routine.
3. Keep a daily record of stress, sleep pattern, disturbing dreams, and sleep inductions used.
4. Practice good sleep hygiene.
5. Restore restful sleep pattern.

ADDITIONAL PROBLEMS FOR WHICH THIS EXERCISE MAY BE MOST USEFUL

- Anxiety
- Bipolar—Mania
- Substance Use
- Unipolar Depression

SUGGESTIONS FOR PROCESSING THIS EXERCISE WITH THE CLIENT

Establishing an effective sleep routine is essential to breaking through the pattern of sleep disturbance that plagues many clients. Help the client establish a routine that will be consistently implemented. You may want to review the suggestions in the first section of this assignment and you may want to add some techniques that are not listed. The client's journal may produce additional information about anxiety-producing events in his/her life that interfere with restful sleep. Provide the client with additional copies of the journal page containing two entries.

SLEEP PATTERN RECORD

Insomnia is a widespread problem, especially in our fast-paced culture. Some people delude themselves into thinking they need only 4 or 5 hours of sleep when most adults need about 7 hours of sleep on a regular basis. Other people think they do not sleep at all, but people who observe them discover that they do sleep for several hours during the night even though they may awaken periodically. There are techniques that can help people develop a better sleep routine. The most important techniques involve establishing a consistent sleep and wake-up time every day, exercising regularly, and avoiding alcohol. The following list will give you ideas about other sleep induction ideas that have been successful for many people. Review each of these and place a check mark next to those that you are willing to implement on a consistent daily basis to establish a sleep induction routine.

1. Sleep Induction Procedures:

    _____ Engage in daily vigorous exercise during the afternoon for 20 to 30 minutes.

    _____ Avoid spicy foods at night.

    _____ Take a warm bath/shower 30 minutes prior to bed.

    _____ Drink milk 30 minutes prior to bed (or take a melatonin tablet).

    _____ Avoid conflict issues prior to bed.

    _____ Read a book while in bed.

    _____ Go to bed and get out of bed at the same time every day.

    _____ Use deep muscle relaxation techniques to reduce tension.

    _____ Imagine relaxing scenes while in bed rather than thinking about the next day.

    _____ Avoid coffee, tea, colas, chocolate, and other foods or drinks containing caffeine.

    _____ Write down disturbing thoughts to get them off your mind.

_____ Focus on diaphragm breathing, counting each deep breath backward from 100.

_____ Avoid alcohol 4 to 5 hours prior to bed.

_____ Play soothing, quiet music or "white noise."

2. Keep a daily record of stressful events, sleep pattern, disturbing dreams, and sleep induction techniques used.

Day/Date _____ _____	Stressful Events	
	Sleep Pattern	Start time : _____ End time: _____ Number of times awakened: _____ Total time awake: _____ Total time sleeping: _____
	Disturbing Dreams	
	Sleep Induction Techniques Used	

Day/Date _____ _____	Stressful Events	
	Sleep Pattern	Start time :_____ End time : _____ Number of times awakened: _____ Total time awake: _____ Total time sleeping: _____
	Disturbing Dreams	
	Sleep Induction Techniques Used	

3. What sleep induction technique(s) proved to be helpful in improving your sleep?

   _____

   _____

   _____

   _____

4. Describe the relationship between stress and sleep disturbance or bad dreams.

   _____

   _____

   _____

   _____

5. Rate the effectiveness of your sleep induction routines.

1	2	3	4	5
Not Effective				Very Effective

BECOMING ASSERTIVE

GOALS OF THE EXERCISE

1. Demonstrate improved self-esteem through more assertiveness, greater eye contact, and identification of positive traits in self-talk messages.
2. Establish an increased sense of self-worth, confidence, and competence.
3. Decrease dependence on relationships while beginning to meet own needs, build confidence, and practice assertiveness.
4. Develop an awareness of current angry behaviors, clarifying origins of and alternatives to aggressive anger.

ADDITIONAL PROBLEMS FOR WHICH THIS EXERCISE MAY BE MOST USEFUL

- Anger Control Problems
- Dependency
- Low Self-Esteem
- Substance Use

SUGGESTIONS FOR PROCESSING THIS EXERCISE WITH THE CLIENT

A significant part of the processing will be centered around psychoeducation, teaching, feedback, and encouragement/praise. Initially the client will need to be assessed for where he/she is on the assertiveness continuum (aggressive, passive-aggressive, passive, assertive). It would be expected that he/she starts with a general area that he/she can have success in (i.e., saying no as to a specific life situation such as saying no to a boss). As a client gains experience, confidence, and skill, he/she can be encouraged to take on more difficult areas where assertiveness skills can be applied.

BECOMING ASSERTIVE

None of us are born "assertive." It is a set of skills we must acquire. Read the definition of assertive behavior below and then answer the questions that follow.

> *Assertive behavior enables a person to act in his or her own best interests, to stand up for herself or himself without undue anxiety, to express honest feelings comfortably, or to exercise personal rights without denying the rights of others.*
>
> —Alberti and Emmons

1. On the continuum below, place an **X** where you see yourself in terms of being assertive and place an **O** where you would like to see yourself in the future regarding being assertive.

Not very good (worse than most people)	So-so (like most people)	Great (always assertive)

2. What do you see as the factors in your not being more assertive?_____

_____

_____

_____

3. When you think of being assertive in most situations, what feelings do you experience? _____

_____

_____

_____

4. In what specific ways do you see becoming more assertive helping you? _____

_____

_____

_____

5. Further knowledge on being more assertive. Answer True (T) or False (F) to the following questions and then process your choices with your therapist.

      T   F   Most people believe that they have the right to be assertive.

      T   F   Most people are not anxious or fearful about being assertive.

      T   F   Many people do not have the skills to effectively express themselves.

6. Points to remember in being assertive:

      Pause and take several deep breaths before responding.

      Make consistent eye contact with the person you are addressing.

      Use "I" statements (begin each response with "I").

      Keep responses brief and to the point (no long explanations).

      Be respectful.

7. Now choose one of the following situations to role-play with your therapist:

      Saying no to a request for a favor

      Returning an item to a store

      Stating your opinion on a topic

      Starting a conversation with a stranger

      Receiving a compliment or positive feedback

      Receiving negative feedback or criticism

      Giving helpful positive feedback to a friend

      Someone cuts in front of you in line

      Receiving the wrong change

After you have completed the role-play, answer these questions before processing the role-play with your therapist.

How did this experience feel for you? _____

_____

_____

What did you think went well? _____

_____

_____

What is one thing you would like to improve on? _____

_____

_____

8. Now using the list in number 7, choose one to do during the coming week.

    Situation _____

    _____

    How did this experience feel for you? _____

    _____

    _____

    What did you think went well? _____

    _____

    _____

    What is one thing you would like to improve on? _____

    _____

    _____

9. Remember as you work toward becoming assertive:

    Assertiveness is learned.

    Change is hard but possible.

    Take small steps.

    Give yourself credit for trying.

RESTORING SOCIALIZATION COMFORT

GOALS OF THE EXERCISE

1. Identify, challenge, and replace biased, fearful self-talk with reality-based, positive self-talk.
2. Identify possible root causes for the pattern of negative thinking.
3. Interact socially without undue fear or anxiety.

ADDITIONAL PROBLEMS FOR WHICH THIS EXERCISE MAY BE MOST USEFUL

- Low Self-Esteem
- Panic/Agoraphobia
- Sexual Abuse Victim
- Unipolar Depression

SUGGESTIONS FOR PROCESSING THIS EXERCISE WITH THE CLIENT

This exercise is designed around cognitive therapy principles. The client must first identify negative, automatic thoughts that feed his/her social anxiety. Then the client must work to discover some past experiences that contribute to these negative thinking patterns. Finally, the client is challenged to begin to think positively as a means of overcoming fear and social withdrawal. You may want to review some of the examples of distorted, automatic thoughts that feed fear and add some of your own to the list in item 1. You may also have to help the client develop and write positive, realistic statements that build confidence and counteract fear.

RESTORING SOCIALIZATION COMFORT

Fear of being around other people is based in the automatic interpretative thoughts that rise when one considers the social situation. The distorted thoughts lead to negative emotions that lead to maladaptive behavior. In the case of social discomfort, the unrealistic thoughts lead to fear, which leads to social withdrawal and isolation behavior. This exercise is designed to help you identify your distorted thoughts and think about their origins as well as discover ways to replace them with more realistic thoughts.

1.   View the common distorted, automatic thoughts that are listed and that lead to fear and social withdrawal. Check those thoughts that you have experienced.

_____ I never know what to say.

_____ I'll make a fool of myself if I speak up.

_____ These people are much brighter than I am.

_____ This person does not like me.

_____ I'm going to have a panic attack.

_____ People are mean and critical.

_____ I can't speak to people unless I have a few drinks first.

_____ Every time I'm in a group situation, people ignore me.

_____ I can tell by the way she is looking at me that she thinks I'm stupid.

_____ I've never been good with words.

2.   What other negative thoughts go through your mind when you consider a social encounter? _____

_____

_____

_____

_____

3.   Why do you think so negatively about interacting with others? What experiences have taught you to lack confidence? _____

_____

_____

_____

_____

4. Describe any childhood experiences with critical or rejecting parents, siblings, or peers that you believe still contribute to your current anxiety around people.

    _____

    _____

    _____

    _____

5. What is your greatest fear about social interaction?

    _____

    _____

    _____

    _____

6. Rate the strength of your desire to overcome your social fears.

    |_____|_____|_____|_____|
    1   2   3   4   5

    No   Strong
    Desire   Desire

7. Recall a time when you felt good about and enjoyed your social interaction. What was different in that situation? What made you able to overcome your anxiety?

    _____

    _____

    _____

    _____

8. How could you apply the coping skill you used in the situation described in item 7 to new social encounters?

    _____

    _____

    _____

    _____

9. Write three positive statements that are the opposite of the distorted, automatic thoughts that commonly lead to your fear of social interaction. Use these thoughts to build confidence and counteract the negative thoughts that build fear.

    A. _____

    B. _____

    C. _____

CONTROLLING THE FOCUS ON PHYSICAL PROBLEMS

GOALS OF THE EXERCISE

1. Decrease physical complaints, doctor visits, and reliance on medication while increasing assessment of self as able to function normally and productively.
2. Identify emotional stresses that underlie the focus on physical complaints.
3. Increase social and productive activities rather than being preoccupied with self and physical complaints.

ADDITIONAL PROBLEMS FOR WHICH THIS EXERCISE MAY BE MOST USEFUL

- Anxiety
- Chronic Pain
- Medical Issues

SUGGESTIONS FOR PROCESSING THIS EXERCISE WITH THE CLIENT

The client with somatization issues is choosing to make his/her bodily concerns the primary or only focus of his/her attention. This can be very disconcerting to significant others around him/her and can also seriously reduce the client's ability to function effectively. This exercise focuses the client on his/her assets and enjoyable activities. It also limits the amount of time given to somatic complaints by structuring the "worry time" to 30 minutes per day. Reinforce the importance of this structured time to the client and encourage him/her to use the rest of the day to focus on other issues. The client may also need help in examining his/her emotional issues that may lie beneath the somatic complaints because these clients often attempt to avoid focusing on underlying issues. Reinforce time and attention given to productive activities that are unrelated to somatic complaints.

CONTROLLING THE FOCUS ON PHYSICAL PROBLEMS

It is important to establish a proper balance to your perspective on life. Although you have concerns about your physical well-being, there is much more to you and your life than those concerns. Your identity as a person is much greater than someone who is only focused on health and bodily worries. You must control the amount of time and energy given to your anxieties about somatic problems and refocus your life on constructive, productive, and enjoyable activities. This exercise attempts to help you regain your focus and broaden your perspective.

1. List five of your favorite interests—areas of life or activities that you enjoy.

   A. _____

   B. _____

   C. _____

   D. _____

   E. _____

2. List five abilities, talents, or skills that you have and enjoy.

   A. _____

   B. _____

   C. _____

   D. _____

   E. _____

3. Considering your interests and abilities, list five activities you could engage in within the next few weeks that would take your mind off your physical health and get you focused on more productive, constructive, stimulating, and enjoyable pursuits.

   A. _____

   B. _____

   C. _____

   D. _____

   E. _____

4. To make sure your focus on physical problems is decreased while your constructive activity is increased, schedule a specific 30 minutes each day that you will think about, talk about, and write down your physical problems. Even if you have written down your complaint one or more times, keep recording it if it is still on your mind. Do not talk or think about your physical problems at any occasion other than the scheduled time.

Day 1 Date:

Time (30 minutes)   From _____:_____ a.m./p.m. to _____:_____ a.m./p.m.

My physical complaints or problems: _____

_____

_____

_____

Day 2 Date:

Time (30 minutes)   From _____:_____ a.m./p.m. to _____:_____ a.m./p.m.

My physical complaints or problems: _____

_____

_____

_____

Day 3 Date:

Time (30 minutes)   From _____:_____ a.m./p.m. to _____:_____ a.m./p.m.

My physical complaints or problems: _____

_____

_____

_____

Day 4 Date:

Time (30 minutes)   From _____:_____ a.m./p.m. to _____:_____ a.m./p.m.

My physical complaints or problems: _____

_____

_____

_____

Day 5 Date:

Time (30 minutes)   From _____:_____ a.m./p.m. to _____:_____ a.m./p.m.

My physical complaints or problems: _____

_____

_____

_____

Day 6 Date:

Time (30 minutes)   From _____:_____ a.m./p.m. to _____:_____ a.m./p.m.

My physical complaints or problems: _____

_____

_____

_____

Day 7 Date:

Time (30 minutes)   From _____:_____ a.m./p.m. to _____:_____ a.m./p.m.

My physical complaints or problems: _____

_____

_____

_____

5. What concerns or conflicts are you experiencing that are not related to your physical health (e.g., fears, worries, hurts, frustrations)? _____

_____

_____

_____

6. Do you think that at times you focus on your physical complaints rather than face your emotional struggles listed in item 5? If so, why do you think you do this?

_____

_____

_____

7. Ask your family and close friends what they think you should do to cope with your physical concerns. Record their responses (use additional paper if needed).

_____

_____

_____

_____

_____

_____

_____

_____

MY HISTORY OF SPIRITUALITY

GOALS OF THE EXERCISE

1. Describe the story of the spiritual quest/journey.
2. Examine how life experiences have influenced beliefs about a higher power.
3. Take steps to deepen spiritual life.
4. Clarify spiritual concepts and instill a freedom to approach a higher power as a resource for support.

ADDITIONAL PROBLEMS FOR WHICH THIS EXERCISE MAY BE MOST USEFUL

- Medical Issues
- Substance Use
- Suicidal Ideation
- Unipolar Depression

SUGGESTIONS FOR PROCESSING THIS EXERCISE WITH THE CLIENT

Research has shown the positive impact that an active and meaningful spiritual life can have on physical and mental health. Explore the client's history of experiences with spiritual concepts and religious practices. Assist him/her in overcoming barriers to a deeper spiritual life if he/she shows an interest in pursuing this. Be respectful of the client's religious and spiritual preferences.

MY HISTORY OF SPIRITUALITY

Begin to explore your spiritual life by writing a biography that focuses on your experiences with learning about and relating to God. Start with your recollection of your childhood understanding of God and trace that understanding to the present. Include any meaningful times of closeness to God, distance from God, anger toward God, questions about God, and worship of God. Then answer some questions that explore experiences that may have influenced your thoughts, beliefs, and feelings about spiritual matters.

1. **My Spiritual Journey—A Focused Biography (use back of sheet if needed)**

    _____
    _____
    _____
    _____
    _____
    _____
    _____
    _____
    _____
    _____
    _____
    _____
    _____
    _____
    _____
    _____
    _____
    _____
    _____
    _____
    _____

2. **Where Am I Now Spiritually and How Did I Get Here?**

A. What do I currently believe about a higher power or God? _____

_____

_____

B. How are my thoughts about God as Father influenced by my experiences with my own father or mother? _____

_____

_____

C. How have my life experiences influenced my beliefs and feelings toward God?

_____

_____

_____

D. What do I think prevents me from developing a more meaningful spiritual life?

_____

_____

_____

_____

E. What is the difference between spirituality and religion? Are they related? ____

_____

_____

_____

F. What positive and negative experiences have I had with religious people? _____

_____

_____

G. Do I believe God is harsh and judgmental or loving and forgiving? How does my belief affect my spiritual relationship? _____

_____

_____

_____

H. What three things could I do to make my life of faith and spirituality more meaningful? _____

_____

_____

_____

YOUR SPIRITUAL INHERITANCE INVENTORY

GOALS OF THE EXERCISE

1. Resolve issues that have prevented faith or belief from developing and growing.
2. Identify the benefits, blessings, and baggage of personal and family spiritual histories.
3. Increase awareness of the benefits and blessings of present beliefs and spiritual heritage.
4. Let go of past spiritual baggage that has prevented spiritual growth.

ADDITIONAL PROBLEMS FOR WHICH THIS EXERCISE MAY BE MOST USEFUL

- Anxiety
- Grief/Loss Unresolved
- Low Self-Esteem
- Substance Use
- Unipolar Depression

SUGGESTIONS FOR PROCESSING THIS EXERCISE WITH THE CLIENT

Before having the client do the assignment, it is strongly recommended that the client's thoughts and feelings connected to looking into this area be processed. This will clear the way for the client getting the most out of the assignment. Also, normalizing with the client that this is a difficult area for most of us is important for having him/her be as open as possible. Further, it needs to be pointed out that not having answers is significant in that it helps identify what is perhaps an area of need. Lastly, as is the case in working with adults, the assignment needs to be revisited after it is initially processed as additional information and insights often come to clients once the area has been opened up for examination and reflection.

YOUR SPIRITUAL INHERITANCE INVENTORY

Answer the questions in each of the areas below to the best of your knowledge or with what first hits you. You can also choose to ask these family members if they are available and you are comfortable doing so.

Maternal Grandparents

Religious/Church Affiliation _____

Level of Involvement:

_____ Regular attender

_____ Semiregular attender

_____ Occasional attender

_____ Nonattender

View of God:

_____ Punishing God

_____ Accepting God

_____ Noninvolved God

_____ Nonexistent God

Comments: _____

_____

Their beliefs regarding faith, good and evil, life and death, prayer, and so on: _____

_____

_____

_____

Note differences present between grandfather and grandmother for any of these questions: _____

_____

_____

_____

Paternal Grandparents

Religious/Church Affiliation _____

Level of Involvement: _____ Regular attender

                                                _____ Semiregular attender

                                                _____ Occasional attender

                                                _____ Nonattender

View of God: _____ Punishing God

                                                _____ Accepting God

                                                _____ Noninvolved God

                                                _____ Nonexistent God

Comments: _____

_____

Their beliefs regarding faith, good and evil, life and death, prayer, and so on: _____

_____

_____

_____

Note differences present between grandfather and grandmother for any of these questions: _____

_____

_____

_____

Parents

Religious/Church Affiliation _____

Level of Involvement: _____ Regular attender

                                                _____ Semiregular attender

                                                _____ Occasional attender

                                                _____ Nonattender

View of God: _____ Punishing God

                                                _____ Accepting God

                                                _____ Noninvolved God

                                                _____ Nonexistent God

Comments: _____

_____

Their beliefs regarding faith, good and evil, life and death, prayer, and so on: _____

_____

_____

_____

Note differences present between father and mother for any of these questions: ____

_____

_____

_____

Yourself

Religious/Church Affiliation _____

Level of Involvement: _____ Regular attender

                                 _____ Semiregular attender

                                 _____ Occasional attender

                                 _____ Nonattender

View of God: _____ Punishing God

                                 _____ Accepting God

                                 _____ Noninvolved God

                                 _____ Nonexistent God

Comments: _____

_____

Your beliefs regarding faith, good and evil, life and death, and so on: _____

_____

_____

_____

Who are the people who have been the most influential to you in the development of your faith? _____

_____

_____

_____

What are your beliefs regarding prayer? _____

_____

_____

_____

How often do you pray?

_____ Continually

_____ Daily

_____ Frequently

_____ Sometimes

_____ Seldom

_____ Never

_____ During difficult times

Now looking and thinking over your spiritual inheritance, what do you see as:

The benefits/blessings:

1.

2.

3.

4.

5.

The baggage (barriers/obstacles):

1.

2.

3.

4.

5.

AFTERCARE PLAN COMPONENTS

GOALS OF THE EXERCISE

1. Acknowledge that the maintenance of sobriety requires many different life changes and support components.
2. Identify the specific aftercare components that will support recovery.
3. Maintain long-term sobriety.
4. Establish a sustained recovery free from the use of all mood-altering substances.

ADDITIONAL PROBLEMS FOR WHICH THIS EXERCISE MAY BE MOST USEFUL

- None

SUGGESTIONS FOR PROCESSING THIS EXERCISE WITH THE CLIENT

Recovery from substance abuse requires a multifaceted approach. The client must be reminded often of the need for many different support systems to overcome his/her natural tendency to relapse. A structured aftercare plan should be completed by the client at the early to middle stage of treatment. Assist the client with filling in any of the necessary information requested on the form. Add additional information that you believe will be necessary to support the client's recovery.

AFTERCARE PLAN COMPONENTS

Maintenance of long-term sobriety requires an aftercare plan with various components that support the recovery endeavor. This assignment allows you to stipulate what components you will rely on to help you maintain sobriety for the long term. Sobriety will never be maintained if the only component of recovery is "I'm going to stop using a specific substance." Pure willpower has never been, nor will it ever be, enough to maintain sobriety once substance abuse has been such a dominating force in a person's life. You need many different components to keep the plan strong and moving forward.

Fill in all the blanks with the pertinent information regarding the resources that you will be making use of during your recovery.

A. AA/NA Meetings

Where? _____

Times? _____

How many times per week? _____

B. Sponsor

Who? _____ Phone number _____

C. Counseling

With whom? _____ Phone number _____

How often? _____

D. Family Counseling

With whom? _____ Day and time _____

E. Spiritual Support Group

Where? _____ How often? _____

F. Employment

Where? _____ Hours per week _____

G. Employment Search

How conducted? _____

How often will you search? _____

H. Recreation

What will it be? _____

When will you do it? _____

I. New Sober Friends

Who are they? _____

What will you do together? _____

How will you make new friends? _____

J. Exercise Program

What will you do? _____

When will you do it? _____

How many times per week? _____

K. Probation/Parole Contact

With whom? _____ How often? _____

L. Child Visitation

Where? _____ Date and time _____

M. Sleep Schedule

Bedtime? _____ Arise time? _____

N. Meal Schedule

Breakfast time? _____

Lunchtime? _____

Dinnertime? _____

O. Other Important Component: _____

_____

P. Another Important Component: _____

_____

List the three most important components of your aftercare recovery plan and tell how you will ensure that you will follow through on these things. _____

_____

_____

_____

_____

_____

IDENTIFYING RELAPSE TRIGGERS AND CUES*

GOALS OF THE EXERCISE

1. Increase awareness of personal situational triggers and cues to relapse.
2. Recognize high-risk situations involving increased risk of relapse.
3. Develop alternative coping strategies to manage relapse triggers, cues, and warning signs.

ADDITIONAL PROBLEMS FOR WHICH THIS EXERCISE MAY BE MOST USEFUL

- None

SUGGESTIONS FOR PROCESSING THIS EXERCISE WITH THE CLIENT

This activity is designed to help the newly recovering client identify both environmental and internal relapse triggers and plan strategies to identify them quickly and cope with them when they occur. Follow-up may include completing the "Relapse Prevention Planning" activity, keeping a journal about working with the information gained in this exercise, and reporting to the therapist or group on outcomes of any strategies that are identified.

---

* This assignment has been adapted from *Addiction Treatment Homework Planner* by J. R. Finley and B. S. Lenz, 2009, Hoboken, NJ: Wiley. Copyright © by John Wiley & Sons, Inc. Reprinted with permission.

IDENTIFYING RELAPSE TRIGGERS AND CUES

Relapse is common, but it is preventable. Preventing relapse requires awareness of things that can trigger us to behave addictively and willingness to do something about it when one of them happens. The purpose of this exercise is to ask yourself questions to increase your awareness of possible relapse triggers and make a plan to cope with them and prevent relapse.

Risky Situations

1. Relapse is often triggered by sights, sounds, and situations that have been associated with addictive behaviors in the past. Many recovering people find that, unless they are on guard, their thoughts automatically turn back to old behavior patterns when they are around the people with whom they drank, used, or gambled. Who are the people, or the kind of people, with whom you usually practiced addictive behaviors in the past?

    _____

    _____

2. Because addictive behaviors are sometimes social activities, you may know people who will expect you to continue your old habits with them. They may not understand or care about your recovery, and may use persuasion, teasing, or argument to try to get you to relapse. In your life, who are the people most likely to exert social pressure on you to relapse? (This list may include all or some of the people you listed for Question 1.)

    _____

    _____

3. Many recovering people find that others—family members, friends, or coworkers— had been enabling their addictions (i.e., these people had helped them avoid the consequences or made it easier in other ways for them to keep using). Please list any people who have enabled your addiction.

    _____

    _____

4. For each of the people listed previously—drinking/using/gambling companions, people pressuring you to relapse, and enablers—describe how you will avoid relapse triggered by their actions.

_____

_____

_____

_____

5. What are the social situations that you think will place you at the greatest risk to relapse?

_____

_____

6. Many people also use addictions to cope with stress, and sometimes relationship issues can be extremely stressful. When you think about your future, what relationship difficulties might put you at risk for returning to addictive patterns?

_____

_____

_____

_____

7. We also find that for many of us our addictions had become part of our daily routine, something we did automatically at certain times, such as just after work. Reviewing your former daily routines, at what times of the day are you most likely to relapse?

_____

_____

8. Many people feel the desire to test their ability to maintain recovery in challenging situations, such as being with drinking friends, going to old hangouts, and so forth. This often leads to relapse and is an unnecessary risk. Describe any ways in which you've tested your ability to stay in recovery.

_____

_____

_____

_____

9. As another way to guard against stress-induced relapse, please think about both current situations and future life events that you need to be prepared to handle without escaping into addictions. What are they?

_____

_____

_____

_____

10. What's your plan to handle these situations? What changes are you willing and able to make to handle the pressures and temptations to relapse in the situations you listed previously?

_____

_____

_____

_____

_____

Internal Triggers

11. When you experience urges or cravings to act out addictively, how does your body feel?

_____

_____

12. When you experience urges to act out addictively, what emotions do you usually feel?

_____

_____

13. As mentioned earlier, addictions are often tools for coping with stress (i.e., ways to change feelings that we dislike to ones with which we are more comfortable). What unpleasant feelings will place you at greatest risk for relapse?

_____

_____

_____

14. Following are some common feelings for which people have used chemicals to cope. It's important not only to be determined not to drink or use to cope, but also to know what you will do—not having an alternative to replace substance abuse increases your risk of relapse. Next to each feeling, describe what you will do instead of using to cope with that feeling.

Feeling	What You Will Do to Cope
Anger	_____
Anxiety	_____
Boredom	_____
Sadness	_____
Fatigue	_____
Fear	_____
Frustration	_____
Loneliness	_____
Indifference	_____
Self-pity	_____
Shame	_____
Depression	_____
Other feelings	_____

RELAPSE PREVENTION PLANNING*

GOALS OF THE EXERCISE

1. Develop a plan of action to deal with relapse triggers and warning signs.
2. Assess commitment to recovery.
3. Take greater responsibility for recovery and increase the chances of success through planning.

ADDITIONAL PROBLEMS FOR WHICH THIS EXERCISE MAY BE MOST USEFUL

- None

SUGGESTIONS FOR PROCESSING THIS EXERCISE WITH THE CLIENT

This activity provides clients (either those who are beginning in recovery or experiencing stresses that increase the risk of relapse) with a structured framework to create a personalized plan to anticipate relapse triggers and cues; plan coping or avoidance strategies; spot early warning signs of the relapse process; and identify resources, strategies, and relationships to use to maintain recovery. For best results, have the client complete "Identifying Relapse Triggers and Cues" (see Exercise 39.B in this book) before assigning this activity. Follow-up may include having the client present his/her plan to the therapist, treatment group, and program sponsor; keep a log or journal on plan compliance; and report on the outcomes of his/her uses of the strategies planned.

---

* This assignment has been adapted from *Addiction Treatment Homework Planner* by J. R. Finley and B. S. Lenz, 2009, Hoboken, NJ: Wiley. Copyright © by John Wiley & Sons, Inc. Reprinted with permission.

RELAPSE PREVENTION PLANNING

If you have identified your own personal relapse triggers and relapse warning signs, you have a good understanding of your relapse process and how to spot it early, before it leads you to an actual return to your addiction. Now it's time to take this information and plan specific strategies to put it to use. The more work you do on this plan and the more specific you are, the more prepared you will be to deal with day-to-day living and unexpected stressful events without reliance on alcohol, drugs, or other addictive behavior patterns.

1. First, evaluate your thoughts and feelings about sobriety. Are you ready to take any action needed, to go to any lengths to live your life without using mind-altering chemicals or addictive behaviors to block painful feelings or seek pleasure? Describe your attitude about this.

    _____

    _____

2. What will the consequences be if you return to your addiction?

    _____

    _____

3. Refer to the exercises on relapse triggers and warning signs, or draw on whatever information you have about the process of relapse. List what you consider to be your 10 most important personal triggers and warning signs for relapse and what you will do to cope with them.

Triggers/Warning Signs

**Specific Plan to Avoid
Drinking/Using/Addictive Behavior**

Example: Feeling hopeless

Review progress; ask others what growth they see

Example: Urge to use

Attend meetings; contact sponsor; meditate

_____   _____

_____   _____

_____   _____

_____   _____
_____   _____
_____   _____
_____   _____
_____   _____

4. Recovery is not a solo process, which is why people who try to quit without help
    from others usually relapse. Whom will you contact for support and assistance?
    List six people.

    Name   **Phone Number**

    _____   _____
    _____   _____
    _____   _____
    _____   _____
    _____   _____
    _____   _____

5. Emergency planning: Your relapse prevention plan should include what you will do
    if you encounter a stressful situation or a sudden crisis that triggers a strong urge
    to use or drink or return to addictive behavior. Write a plan that is simple and can
    be started immediately.

    _____
    _____
    _____

6. Changing your routine is important in managing addictive behavior. How will you
    begin and end each day to help you maintain sobriety?

    _____
    _____
    _____

7. Your relapse prevention plan should include attending support groups—Alcoholics
    Anonymous, Narcotics Anonymous, Gamblers Anonymous, and so forth. List
    meetings you will commit yourself to attend regularly.

    Name of Group   **Day and Time**   **Location**

    _____   _____   _____
    _____   _____   _____
    _____   _____   _____

8. Do you foresee any obstacles or barriers to implementing this plan? If so, what are they?

   _____

   _____

   _____

9. What will you do about these roadblocks to your recovery or any others you experience?

   _____

   _____

   _____

10. If your plan isn't enough, and you relapse, what will you do to get back on track in your recovery?

    _____

    _____

    _____

11. Are there parts of this plan that you are already carrying out? What are they, and how well have they worked?

    _____

    _____

    _____

12. Now that you have made your plan, it's important to monitor your success in using it and correct it or add to it as needed. When and with whom will you make regular progress checks?

Person	**When You Will Talk About Your Progress**
_____	_____
_____	_____
_____	_____
_____	_____

RELAPSE TRIGGERS

GOALS OF THE EXERCISE

1. Increase awareness of potential relapse triggers.
2. Identify coping techniques for each relapse trigger.
3. Accept powerlessness over mood-altering substances and the need for a structured recovery program that includes the help of others.
4. Acquire the necessary skills to maintain long-term sobriety from all mood-altering substances.

ADDITIONAL PROBLEMS FOR WHICH THIS EXERCISE MAY BE MOST USEFUL

- None

SUGGESTIONS FOR PROCESSING THIS EXERCISE WITH THE CLIENT

Although the client may be able to identify the people, places, and things that are the strongest potential triggers for relapse, he/she may need significant guidance in listing coping techniques for each of these triggers. Let the client struggle on his/her own to identify these coping skills before providing support and additional guidance. More than one coping technique may be recommended for a particular trigger situation.

RELAPSE TRIGGERS

Alcoholics Anonymous (AA) refers to people, places, and things that can initiate a relapse into substance abuse as "relapse triggers." It is very important that you try to identify those people or situations that may increase your vulnerability to the temptation to return to substance use. Identifying the triggers for substance use is a first step that must be followed by a plan for coping with each of these triggers if you are to minimize the power of their influence over you in the future.

1. List at least eight people, places, or things that your experience has taught you will tempt you to return to the use of mood-altering substances. Consider such things as friends or associates, family members, drug or alcohol-using locations, places to purchase drugs or alcohol, strong emotions that have been associated with drug or alcohol use, recreational activities associated with use, financial situations that provide opportunities for use, and so on.

    A. _____
    _____

    B. _____
    _____

    C. _____
    _____

    D. _____
    _____

    E. _____
    _____

    F. _____
    _____

    G. _____
    _____

    H. _____
    _____

2. Consider each of the triggers that you have listed and write down a positive way that you can cope with this situation, person, or emotion in order to not return to substance use. You may need to consult with your counselor about coping techniques, but attempt to come up with some of these on your own. Consider such things as AA meetings, sponsor contact, higher-power meditation, positive support groups, positive relationships, one-to-one counseling, avoidance of specific friends or places, keeping money out of your hands, increasing recreation, and so on.

   A. _____
   _____

   B. _____
   _____

   C. _____
   _____

   D. _____
   _____

   E. _____
   _____

   F. _____
   _____

   G. _____
   _____

   H. _____
   _____

3. What are the three most important triggers that you need to be alert for in order to avoid their powerful influence?

   A. _____
   B. _____
   C. _____

4. What are the three most important coping skills that you believe will help you maintain your sobriety?

   A. _____
   B. _____
   C. _____

SUBSTANCE ABUSE'S NEGATIVE IMPACT VERSUS SOBRIETY'S POSITIVE IMPACT

GOALS OF THE EXERCISE

1. Break down denial and minimization by acknowledging the negative consequences of substance abuse.
2. Increase hope and motivation for sobriety by recognizing the potential positive consequences of recovery.
3. Commit to a recovery program that will promote sobriety.
4. Establish and maintain total abstinence while increasing knowledge of the disease and the process of recovery.

ADDITIONAL PROBLEMS FOR WHICH THIS EXERCISE MAY BE MOST USEFUL

- None

SUGGESTIONS FOR PROCESSING THIS EXERCISE WITH THE CLIENT

Breaking through denial for a chemically dependent client is a difficult task. This assignment provides an opportunity for the client to assess the devastating effects of substance use on his/her life and the lives of others. Confrontation may be used if minimization or denial prevents honest acknowledgment of the negative consequences surrounding the client's substance abuse pattern. Reinforcement and support should be given as honesty is demonstrated. Assistance may be necessary to provide the chemically dependent client with a vision of the positive impact of sobriety on his/her future since it is not unusual for hopelessness and helplessness to predominate.

SUBSTANCE ABUSE'S NEGATIVE IMPACT VERSUS SOBRIETY'S POSITIVE IMPACT

To maintain a life of sobriety, you need to acknowledge without denial and minimization the negative impact that substance use has had on your life and the lives of others, and in contrast to that, to accept that sobriety will have a positive impact on your life and the lives of others. This assignment gives you an opportunity to honestly evaluate the negative consequences of your history of substance use and project how sobriety will produce positive consequences for you and others.

1. List at least eight ways that your substance use has negatively impacted your life. Consider such things as health, relationships, self-esteem, employment, legal entanglements, finances, friendships, family relations, children, and so on.

    A. _____

    _____

    B. _____

    _____

    C. _____

    _____

    D. _____

    _____

    E. _____

    _____

    F. _____

    _____

    G. _____

    _____

    H. _____

    _____

2. List at least eight ways that your substance use has had a negative impact on the lives of others. Consider friends, family, employers, children, coworkers, neighbors, counselors, clergy, AA members, sponsors, and so on. (Be sure to indicate not just who was affected by your substance use, but *how* they were affected.)

A. _____

_____

B. _____

_____

C. _____

_____

D. _____

_____

E. _____

_____

F. _____

_____

G. _____

_____

H. _____

_____

3. List at least eight positive impacts that being sober will have on your life. Consider the same areas that you reviewed in number 1.

A. _____

_____

B. _____

_____

C. _____

_____

D. _____

_____

E. _____

_____

F. _____

_____

G. _____
_____

H. _____
_____

4. List at least eight ways that being sober will have a positive impact on the lives of others. Consider those same people that you thought of for number 2.

A. _____
_____

B. _____
_____

C. _____
_____

D. _____
_____

E. _____
_____

F. _____
_____

G. _____
_____

H. _____
_____

5. List the three most important negative consequences of your substance use on your life. Select these from number 1.

A. _____
B. _____
C. _____

Why have you chosen these as the most important? _____
_____
_____

6. List the three most important negative consequences that your substance use has had on others. Select these from number 2.

A. _____
B. _____
C. _____

Why have you chosen these as the most important? _____

_____

_____

7. List the three most important positive consequences of sobriety in your personal life. Select these from number 3.

   A. _____

   B. _____

   C. _____

   Why have you chosen these as the most important? _____

   _____

   _____

8. List the three most important positive consequences of sobriety on the lives of others. Select these from number 4.

   A. _____

   B. _____

   C. _____

   Why have you chosen these as the most important? _____

   _____

   _____

9. What changes can you make in your life to reduce the probability that substance use will continue along with its negative consequences and increase the probability that sobriety will be maintained along with its positive consequences?

   _____

   _____

   _____

   _____

JOURNAL OF DISTORTED, NEGATIVE THOUGHTS

GOALS OF THE EXERCISE

1. Identify life factors that preceded the suicidal ideation.
2. Identify distorted cognitions and discouraging thoughts that lead to suicidal urges.
3. Identify and replace negative thinking patterns that mediate feelings of hopelessness and helplessness.

ADDITIONAL PROBLEMS FOR WHICH THIS EXERCISE MAY BE MOST USEFUL

- Borderline Personality
- Unipolar Depression

SUGGESTIONS FOR PROCESSING THIS EXERCISE WITH THE CLIENT

After the client has completed a journal that identifies trigger situations and distorted cognitions that lead to suicidal urges, it is most important that the lack of accuracy in his/her thinking should be challenged. Each of his/her dysfunctional thoughts must be replaced with one that is positive and self-enhancing. You may need to assist the client in replacing the negative or discouraging thoughts with more positive or reality-based messages. Provide additional copies of the daily journal from this assignment for future incidents.

JOURNAL OF DISTORTED, NEGATIVE THOUGHTS

When you are caught in the web of depression and hopelessness, you need to identify those situations and thoughts that are pushing you to the edge of life. This exercise helps you discover those distorted, discouraging thoughts and the situations that seem to trigger them. It is also important that you attempt to gain some perspective on your life by identifying the positive aspects of your situation and those people who support and care for you.

1. Keep a daily record of the trigger situations and your self-defeating, negative thoughts that lead to consideration of suicide.

Incident One Day/Date: _____ _____	Trigger Situation	
	Discouraging Thought	

Incident **Two** Day/Date: _____ _____	Trigger Situation	
	Discouraging Thought	

Incident _____ Day/Date: _____ _____	Trigger Situation	
	Discouraging Thought	

Incident _____ Day/Date: _____ _____	Trigger Situation	
	Discouraging Thought	

Incident _____ Day/Date: _____ _____	Trigger Situation	
	Discouraging Thought	

2. What are the most commonly occurring discouraging thoughts? _____
   _____
   _____
   _____

3. After reviewing the list of discouraging thoughts, replace these with more positive or reality-based self-talk. _____
   _____
   _____
   _____

4. What situations are causing you the most conflict and hopelessness? _____
   _____
   _____
   _____

5. What are the positive aspects of your present life that provide a sense of hope?
   _____
   _____
   _____
   _____

6. Who are the people you can turn to for help and support? _____
   _____
   _____
   _____

NO SELF-HARM CONTRACT

GOALS OF THE EXERCISE

1. Develop an action plan to follow if suicidal thoughts or urges to harm self are experienced.
2. Verbalize a promise to contact the therapist or some other emergency helpline if a serious urge toward self-harm arises.
3. Establish support network of individuals and agencies that can be turned to when experiencing suicidal thoughts or urges to harm self.
4. Reestablish a sense of hope for self and the future.

ADDITIONAL PROBLEMS FOR WHICH THIS EXERCISE MAY BE MOST USEFUL

- Bipolar—Mania
- Sexual Abuse Victim
- Unipolar Depression

SUGGESTIONS FOR PROCESSING THIS EXERCISE WITH THE CLIENT

In this intervention, the client must sign a formal contract, whereby he/she agrees to contact specific individuals or agencies in the event that he/she experiences suicidal thoughts or the urge to harm himself/herself. The contract reminds the client that there is a support network available if he/she becomes suicidal. Furthermore, the contract helps to mobilize significant persons when the client is in distress. First, assess the client's suicidal risk and determine whether there is a need for inpatient hospitalization. The contract is not meant to take the place of inpatient hospitalization if that intervention is necessary. The client, parents, and therapist should sign the contract only after the client has given his/her verbal commitment not to engage in any acts of self-harm and has agreed to inform others when he/she experiences suicidal thoughts or urges. The client's refusal to sign the contract is a strong indicator that inpatient hospitalization is necessary, but willingness to sign should not be interpreted as a singular indication that hospitalization is not necessary to protect the client from self-harm. Obtain important phone numbers of agencies or individuals, such as a crisis hotline or the emergency room at a local hospital, in the event that the client becomes suicidal in the future.

NO SELF-HARM CONTRACT

This intervention is designed to keep you safe. You will be asked to sign a no self-harm contract in which you agree not to harm yourself in any way and/or to inform agencies or people important to you if you experience suicidal thoughts or urges to injure yourself. By signing the contract, you are recognizing that your life is important and that you are a person of worth. The contract also reminds you that there are other people or agencies that you can turn to in times of sadness or hurt.

1. The following suicide contract involves two important commitments on your part. First, you will pledge not to harm yourself in any way. Second, the contract calls for you to inform other important persons or agencies if you experience suicidal thoughts or urges in the future. The contract contains the names and phone numbers of important individuals or agencies that you can turn to if you experience suicidal thoughts. Place the contract in a private but easily accessible place where you can quickly locate the important telephone numbers if you need them. For example, place the contract in the top drawer of your desk or in a folder close to the telephone. Do not hesitate to contact the individuals or agencies identified on the contract if you experience suicidal thoughts or the urge to harm yourself.

2. After signing the contract, follow through by attending your counseling sessions. Your therapist or counselor may talk to you about the need for medication. Talk carefully with your therapist about this option and feel free to ask any questions.

    Therapy or counseling can be hard work, and sometimes requires you to get in touch with painful thoughts, feelings, or memories. Your therapist will explore the factors contributing to your suicidal thoughts or urges. By identifying these factors, you can find more effective ways to solve or handle your problems. Likewise, your therapist can help identify constructive ways to meet your needs. Although therapy or counseling can be hard work, it is hoped that in the end you will come out of it a stronger person.

NO SELF-HARM CONTRACT

I, _____, agree that I will not harm or hurt myself in any way.
(Name of client)

I, _____, further agree that I will successfully contact at least one of the
(Name of client)
agencies or individuals listed in the event that I experience suicidal thoughts or the urge to injure myself.

_____   _____
Signature of Client   Signature of Spouse/Significant Other

_____   _____
Signature of Parent or Friend   Signature of Therapist

Names of Individuals or Agencies   **Telephone Numbers**

Spouse: _____   Cell/Home: _____   Work: _____

Parent: _____   Cell/Home: _____   Work: _____

Friend: _____   Cell/Home: _____   Work: _____

Therapist: _____   Phone: _____
                  (Name)

Crisis Hotline: _____   Phone: _____
                        (Name of agency)

Emergency Room: _____   Phone: _____
                          (Name of hospital)

Psychiatric Hospital: _____   Phone: _____

Significant Others: _____   Phone: _____
                          (Name)

_____   Phone: _____
              (Name)

STRATEGIES TO RESIST SUICIDAL THOUGHTS AND FEELINGS

GOALS OF THE EXERCISE

1. Develop strategies to successfully resist the urge to harm oneself when suicidal urges appear.
2. Identify and verbalize reasons for living when suicidal thoughts and feelings emerge.
3. Engage in calming, comforting activities to alleviate suicidal urges.
4. Stabilize the suicidal crisis.
5. Reestablish a sense of hope for self and the future.

ADDITIONAL PROBLEMS FOR WHICH THIS EXERCISE MAY BE MOST USEFUL

- Bipolar—Depression
- Bipolar—Mania
- Borderline Personality
- Unipolar Depression

SUGGESTIONS FOR PROCESSING THIS EXERCISE WITH THE CLIENT

This assignment employs three different strategies that can help the client resist the urge to harm himself/herself. The client is first asked to identify his/her specific reasons for living. This list will hopefully provide the client with a sense of meaning and purpose. Next, the client is instructed to identify a list of calming or soothing activities than can help him/her overcome the suicidal urge. Finally, the client is also asked to identify a list of supportive individuals whom he/she can turn to in times of distress. This assignment can be completed in the therapy session. Instruct the client to place the assignment sheet with his/her responses in a readily accessible place at home so that it can be reviewed if and when suicidal thoughts emerge. This assignment can be used in conjunction with the other assignments in this chapter to help formulate a suicide safety plan. The client should be strongly encouraged to contact his/her therapist, a 24-hour hotline, or other supportive family members and friends if the strategies do not prove to be helpful in overcoming the suicidal urges.

STRATEGIES TO RESIST SUICIDAL THOUGHTS AND FEELINGS

Having a sense of purpose and meaning in life can provide renewed hope. Hope, in turn, can be a powerful ally when it comes to combating depression and resisting the urge to harm oneself. This assignment highlights three different strategies that you can use to resist the urge to harm yourself if suicidal thoughts emerge.

1. First, you are asked to reflect on your reasons for living. You can do this alone or with the help of another supportive person. After spending some time in reflection, please list your reasons for living below. (Please add more reasons on the back of this page if you need more space.)

   A. _____
   B. _____
   C. _____
   D. _____
   E. _____

2. Next, you are asked to identify a list of activities that you can do to comfort yourself when you are feeling distraught or greatly upset. What could I do to calm or comfort myself when I am feeling suicidal? (Please add more activities on the back of this page if you need more space.)

   A. _____
   B. _____
   C. _____
   D. _____

3. Many times, it helps to talk to a supportive or understanding person when you are distraught or upset. Who can you turn to when you are feeling upset or stressed? Please list at least five individuals below along with their phone numbers.

Name: _____ Phone #: _____

Name: _____ Phone #: _____

Name: _____ Phone #: _____

Name: _____ Phone #: _____

Name: _____ Phone #: _____

Please keep this sheet in a readily accessible place at home so that you can review your reasons for living, comforting activities, and supportive individuals when and if suicidal thoughts and feelings emerge.

THE AFTERMATH OF SUICIDE

GOALS OF THE EXERCISE

1. Identify the devastating effects that suicide can have on family members and significant others.
2. Identify unmet needs that lie beneath the suicidal urges and self-destructive behavior.
3. Reestablish a sense of hope for self and the future.
4. Identify a supportive network of people who can be turned to when experiencing suicidal thoughts or urges to harm self.

ADDITIONAL PROBLEMS FOR WHICH THIS EXERCISE MAY BE MOST USEFUL

• Unipolar Depression

SUGGESTIONS FOR PROCESSING THIS EXERCISE WITH THE CLIENT

In this assignment, the client is asked to identify the effects that the decision to take his/her life would have on his/her family members and other key individuals. The responses to the questions can help provide insight into the factors contributing to the emergence of the suicidal thoughts or urges. More specifically, the responses may reveal the client's unmet needs, internal conflicts, or fantasies that lie beneath the suicidal urges. It is strongly recommended that this assignment be completed within the therapy session. The therapist should be ready to refer the client for inpatient hospitalization if this step is believed necessary. If the client's suicide risk is not assessed to be high enough to warrant hospitalization, the therapist is encouraged to establish a suicide prevention contract, arrange for 24-hour supervision by a significant other, and/or provide him/her with phone numbers for agencies or individuals (e.g., crisis hotline) in the event that he/she may become suicidal in the future.

THE AFTERMATH OF SUICIDE

It is not uncommon for people who have had thoughts of suicide to wonder what would happen if they were to take their own life. Sometimes, people daydream or fantasize about how other people would respond if they were to choose to end their life. This exercise looks at the impact that the decision to take your own life would have on others. Please answer the following questions.

1. What problems would be created for others if you took your life?

   _____
   _____
   _____
   _____

2. What impact would your decision to take your life have on your:

   Spouse/Partner? _____
   _____
   _____

   Children? _____
   _____
   _____

   Mother? _____
   _____
   _____

   Father? _____
   _____
   _____

   Siblings? _____
   _____
   _____

Grandparents? _____

_____

Other key family members (please provide names)? _____

_____

_____

_____

_____

Friends? _____

_____

Enemies?_____

_____

_____

3. What are your spiritual beliefs about what would happen to you should you choose to take your life?

_____

_____

_____

4. What would people say about you at your funeral if you took your life?

_____

_____

_____

5. What would you *want* people to say about you at your funeral?

_____

_____

_____

6. What would you like to tell others about why you have wanted to die?

_____

_____

_____

7. Whom can you turn to for emotional support to deal with your problems and painful emotions?

_____

_____

_____

8. What can others *say* to you that would help you feel emotionally stronger and less depressed?

_____

_____

_____

_____

9. What could others *do* to help you feel emotionally stronger and less depressed?

_____

_____

_____

_____

10. What can you do to help yourself become more hopeful about the future?

_____

_____

_____

_____

11. Rate the strength of the urge to kill yourself.

1	2	3	4	5

No
Urge

Uncontrollable
Urge

DEVELOPING NONCOMPETITIVE VALUES

GOALS OF THE EXERCISE

1. Accept that life is out of balance with too great an emphasis on drive, achievement, and competition.
2. Reprioritize values resulting in being less oriented toward achievement and more toward relaxation and relationship building.
3. List and commit to engagement in noncompetitive activities.
4. Reach a balance between work/competitive and social/noncompetitive time in daily life.

ADDITIONAL PROBLEMS FOR WHICH THIS EXERCISE MAY BE MOST USEFUL

*   Phase of Life Problems
*   Spiritual Confusion

SUGGESTIONS FOR PROCESSING THIS EXERCISE WITH THE CLIENT

This exercise will help the client clarify values and focus on engagement in activities that lead to new priorities. The client will have to be held accountable for following through with implementing these planned activities because the inclination will be to avoid them. Review the activity list the client produces and suggest additional activities that may be helpful in developing a more relaxed, spiritual, relational, and inner focus.

DEVELOPING NONCOMPETITIVE VALUES

A person who is constantly driven and preoccupied with getting ahead, winning at all costs, and dominating all social or business situations has lost balance. This person is typically impatient with others and cannot sit quietly and relax. The need for balance calls for less self-focus, a greater orientation toward others, less competition and impatience with others, and more nurturing of and valuing friendships. Use this exercise to reflect on ways that you can restore balance to your life and reduce the drive to achieve more and more.

1. **Relationships:** List the relationships in your life that are important to you. Next to each name, write an activity you could engage in with that person that would nurture and strengthen the closeness of the relationship.

Name	Activity
A. _____	_____
	_____
	_____
B. _____	_____
	_____
	_____
C. _____	_____
	_____
	_____
D. _____	_____
	_____
	_____

2. **Recreation:** List the recreational activities that would be relaxing, enjoyable, and serve to calm your spirit. Write a date that you could initiate such an activity.

Activity	Date
A. _____	_____
_____	
B. _____	_____
_____	
C. _____	_____
_____	

3. **Spiritual Growth:** List activities that you could engage in that would foster the spiritual aspect of your character. List a date to begin this activity.

    Activity   **Date**

    A. _____   _____

    _____

    B. _____   _____

    _____

    C. _____   _____

    _____

4. **Reflection and Aesthetics:** List activities that you could engage in that would develop your ability to reflect, relax, and enjoy the art of life. Write a date to begin.

    Activity   **Date**

    A. _____   _____

    _____

    B. _____   _____

    _____

    C. _____   _____

    _____

5. **Giving to Others:** List activities that you could participate in that would be a service to others. Write a date to begin.

    Activity   **Date**

    A. _____   _____

    _____

    B. _____   _____

    _____

    C. _____   _____

    _____

IDENTIFY AND SCHEDULE PLEASANT ACTIVITIES

GOALS OF THE EXERCISE

1. Identify, schedule, and participate in enjoyable activities.
2. Utilize behavioral strategies to overcome depression.
3. Enjoy the pleasant feelings that social, leisure, and recreational activities can bring.
4. Report a lift in mood resulting from increased social and recreational activity.
5. Alleviate depressed mood and return to previous level of effective functioning.

ADDITIONAL PROBLEMS FOR WHICH THIS EXERCISE MAY BE MOST USEFUL

- Family Conflict
- Intimate Relationship Conflicts
- Type A Behavior

SUGGESTIONS FOR PROCESSING THIS EXERCISE WITH THE CLIENT

The client's depression may interfere with his/her ability to recall pleasant activities and he/she may avoid many of these activities, feeling he/she does not have the energy for them. Encourage him/her to brainstorm freely. If it is necessary, this assignment can be done within the counseling session rather than relying on a depressed and unmotivated client to fulfill the requirements of the assignment outside the session. Perhaps the brainstorming and scheduling need to be done within the session and the homework can be that of implementing the activity and recording its impact. It is recommended that the client monitor his/her mood before, during, and after the event to focus him/her on the positive effect that the event has on mood. Review and reinforce the client's success in improving his/her mood using the satisfying activities.

IDENTIFY AND SCHEDULE PLEASANT ACTIVITIES

People who are depressed almost always withdraw from participation in activities that they once found satisfying, rewarding, pleasurable, or just plain fun. It is very important to break this cycle of withdrawal and to begin reinvesting in the activities of life, the relationships around you, and the things you do well. A starting point for this task of reinvestment or reinvolvement is to create an inventory of all those things that you found to be pleasant events in the past.

1. On the lines that follow, write down a description in only a few words of those activities that you found pleasurable and pleasant in the past. These enjoyable activities should include (1) positive social interactions (e.g., spending time with a good friend), (2) useful or productive activities (e.g., caring for your child, doing a job well), and (3) intrinsically pleasant activities (e.g., a meal at your favorite restaurant, listening to favorite music, taking a warm bath). During this brainstorming session, allow yourself to freely recall any pleasant and enjoyable activities without censoring them based on whether you think you have the energy for them or whether they are feasible. You may want to ask significant others to give input to your list, but please remember that this is your list of personal pleasant activities and must reflect events that *you* find enjoyable.

Positive Social Interactions	Useful Activities	Intrinsically Pleasant Activities
___	___	___
___	___	___
___	___	___
___	___	___
___	___	___
___	___	___
___	___	___
___	___	___
___	___	___

2. Now select from your list of pleasant events seven that you believe are most likely for you to engage in. In the seven lines, list those activities and then write a few words that describe what was positive about the activity or why you found it pleasant or enjoyable.

    Most Likely Activities   **Why Pleasant?**

    1. _____   _____

    2. _____   _____

    3. _____   _____

    4. _____   _____

    5. _____   _____

    6. _____   _____

    7. _____   _____

3. On the following lines, schedule one pleasant activity per day to which you are committed. Include the time of the day and with whom you might share the activity.

    Activity   **When and With Whom**

    Day 1 _____   _____

    Day 2 _____   _____

    Day 3 _____   _____

    Day 4 _____   _____

    Day 5 _____   _____

    Day 6 _____   _____

    Day 7 _____   _____

4. On the following lines, record the activity engaged in and the degree of satisfaction on a scale of 1 (low) to 10 (high) that was felt during and after the engagement with the pleasant event. Also record the effect that the pleasant event had on your mood using a scale of 1 (no positive effect) to 10 (strong uplifting effect on mood).

    Activity   **Satisfaction**   **Effect on Mood**

    Day 1 _____   _____   _____

    Day 2 _____   _____   _____

    Day 3 _____   _____   _____

    Day 4 _____   _____   _____

    Day 5 _____   _____   _____

    Day 6 _____   _____   _____

    Day 7 _____   _____   _____

NEGATIVE THOUGHTS TRIGGER NEGATIVE FEELINGS

GOALS OF THE EXERCISE

1. Verbalize an understanding of the relationship between distorted thinking and negative emotions.
2. Learn key concepts regarding types of distorted thinking.
3. Apply key concepts regarding distorted thinking to own experience.
4. Identify and replace cognitive self-talk that is engaged in to support depression.

ADDITIONAL PROBLEMS FOR WHICH THIS EXERCISE MAY BE MOST USEFUL

*   Anxiety
*   Eating Disorders and Obesity
*   Grief/Loss Unresolved
*   Intimate Relationship Conflicts
*   Low Self-Esteem
*   Panic/Agoraphobia
*   Paranoid Ideation
*   Social Anxiety
*   Suicidal Ideation

SUGGESTIONS FOR PROCESSING THIS EXERCISE WITH THE CLIENT

The concepts of cognitive therapy can be difficult to explain to a client in the abstract. This assignment defines and gives life examples for each of the common types of distorted thinking. The content of this assignment leans heavily on the work of cognitive/behavior therapists such as Beck, Burns, and Lazarus. You may use this assignment as a stepping-stone for educating the client on the importance of controlling and changing thoughts. Help him/her find examples of distorted thinking from his/her own life experience as it has been revealed to you in previous or current sessions. Then assist in generating positive replacement thoughts for the client's negative thoughts. After this tutoring, send the client home with the assignment again to try to identify and replace negative thoughts.

NEGATIVE THOUGHTS TRIGGER NEGATIVE FEELINGS

We used to believe that it was depression or anxiety that made people think negatively, but psychologists and psychiatrists have discovered that most people who struggle with anxious or depressed feelings first had negative, pessimistic, distorted thoughts that produced those feelings. People often have completely different reactions to the same situation. For example, John and Jack both heard their supervisor say to their production group, "We have to work harder and be more productive. Too much time is being wasted on trivial matters and we need to get focused." John thinks, "The supervisor is trying to increase production and make us more efficient. I'd better do my part." But Jack thinks, "The supervisor is blaming me for our low productivity numbers. I'm worried that I'm going to get fired. He never did like me." Jack returns to work feeling depressed and anxious and his preoccupation with these negative feelings reduces his productivity. John, after hearing the same statement from the supervisor, returns to work more focused and confident that the situation can improve. The thoughts and interpretations that you make regarding a circumstance have a very strong influence on the feelings that are generated. Psychologists have identified several negative thinking patterns that are common to people who struggle with feelings of anxiety and depression. These distorted thinking patterns trigger the negative feelings and can lead to chronic states of depression and anxiety.

1. Study the following list of the types of negative thinking patterns that have been identified and defined. These distorted thinking patterns are common to people who suffer from depression, anxiety, and low self-esteem.

DISTORTED THINKING

Type	Definition	Example
Black or white	Viewing situations, people, or self as entirely bad or entirely good—nothing in between.	When Mary brought her vegetable salad to the neighborhood potluck, a hostess commented, "That's our third salad." Mary immediately thought, "She's criticizing me. She doesn't like me."

Type	Definition	Example
Exaggerating	Making self-critical or other-critical statements that include terms like *never, nothing, everything,* or *always.*	Jack was accidentally overlooked when coworkers joined to make plans for lunch together. Jack thought, "They never ask me to do anything. Nobody wants me around here."
Filtering	Ignoring the positive things that occur to and around self but focusing on and accentuating the negative.	Kate had her hair cut short and styled differently. After receiving several compliments from friends and family, one person was mildly critical. Kate thought, "I knew I shouldn't have gotten it cut short. I look like a freak. People are laughing at me."
Discounting	Rejecting positive experiences as not being important or meaningful.	Tyler was complimented by his boss for his good work on a project. He thought, "Anybody could have done that. She doesn't know anything about this project and I didn't do anything special with it."
Catastrophizing	Blowing expected consequences out of proportion in a negative direction.	The teacher told Mary that her son was struggling a bit with math. Mary thought, "This is awful. Johnny is going to fail. I knew I should have worked with him more."
Judging	Being critical of self or others with a heavy emphasis on the use of *should have, ought to, must, have to,* and *should not have.*	Jill made a sales presentation to a client. The client was very attentive and made comments about being impressed with the product. Jill thought, "He knows I stumbled over my words. I should have been more prepared. I have to be more relaxed or no client will ever buy from me."

Type	Definition	Example
Mind reading	Making negative assumptions regarding other people's thoughts and motives.	Aaron inquired about a transfer to a new department. When he was told the position was already filled, he thought, "This manager never did like me. He knew I wanted that position but he just ignored me."
Forecasting	Predicting events will turn out badly.	Kelly just finished an important job interview. She immediately predicted that she would not get hired. "I'll never get this job. That interview was awful and I'm sure I blew it," she thought.
Feelings are facts	Because you feel a certain way, reality is seen as fitting that feeling.	Jim did not have plans for activity with any friends for the weekend. He felt lonely and inferior. He thought, "No one likes me. I have a terrible personality."
Labeling	Calling self or others a bad name when displeased with a behavior.	Joan had a disagreement with her friend about where to meet for lunch. Joan thought, "Betty is such a controller. She never listens to anyone and insists on always getting her own way."
Self-blaming	Holding self responsible for an outcome that was not completely under one's control.	Paula's friend had a minor traffic accident while she and Paula were riding to the mall. Paula thought, "This accident was my fault. I should not have been talking to Jackie while we were driving. Even though that other car hit us, I'm sure Jackie could have avoided it if I would have kept my mouth shut."

2. Apply these 11 common types of distorted thinking to your own way of thinking. List at least three examples of your own thoughts that have led you to feeling depressed and anxious. First, describe the event that prompted you to feel depressed and then describe the thoughts that promoted the bad feelings.

What Happened?   **Negative Thoughts You Had**

A. _____   _____

   _____   _____

   _____   _____

B. _____   _____

   _____   _____

   _____   _____

C. _____   _____

   _____   _____

   _____   _____

D. _____   _____

   _____   _____

   _____   _____

3. It is important to try to replace negative, distorted thoughts with positive, more realistic thoughts that can help you feel happier. Refer to each of your examples listed in number 2 and write a positive thought that you could have used to make you feel better.

What Happened?   **Replacement Positive Thoughts**

A. _____   _____

   _____   _____

   _____   _____

B. _____   _____

   _____   _____

   _____   _____

C. _____   _____

   _____   _____

   _____   _____

D. _____   _____

   _____   _____

   _____   _____

POSITIVE SELF-TALK

GOALS OF THE EXERCISE

1. Increase the frequency of positive thinking and talking about self, the world, and the future.
2. Report a positive shift in mood based on the implementation of positive self-talk.
3. Identify and replace cognitive self-talk that is engaged in to support depression.

ADDITIONAL PROBLEMS FOR WHICH THIS EXERCISE MAY BE MOST USEFUL

- Anxiety
- Grief/Loss Unresolved
- Low Self-Esteem
- Suicidal Ideation

SUGGESTIONS FOR PROCESSING THIS EXERCISE WITH THE CLIENT

Explain to the client that our thoughts greatly influence our mood. He/she will tend to think that his/her mood dictates his/her thoughts rather than the reverse that we know is true. Help the client find positive statements to apply to his/her life if the client is unsuccessful at writing them himself/herself. Reinforce the client's daily review of the positive statements to counteract the distortions that feed the depression.

POSITIVE SELF-TALK

How soon we forget. This statement is especially true for people struggling with depression. They forget how to think positively and they forget about their worth as individuals, their contribution to society in general, and friends and family in particular. The cloud of depression blocks out the positive and distorts their vision into seeing themselves, the world, and their future as negative. This assignment is designed to help you break out of that self-defeating, unrealistic, negative thinking cycle. It will take effort and focused attention to break the bad habit of distorted thinking.

1. List five positive mood-enhancing statements regarding yourself (e.g., "I am a competent person who has had successes"), the world (e.g., "Other people are basically kind and want to be helpful"), and the future (e.g., "As I increase my activity, the future looks brighter"). You must force yourself to focus in on your successes, positive traits, the goodness of people, and an optimistic view of the future. Your tendency will be to think of failures and discount or ignore successes as well as seeing the future as hopeless. In other words, you must think contrary to your natural depressive inclination and return to the realistic, positive way of thinking that characterized you before bad habits got a stranglehold on your thoughts.

Positive View of Me

_____

_____

_____

_____

_____

Positive View of the World

_____

_____

_____

_____

_____

Positive View of the Future

_____

_____

_____

_____

_____

2. Each day select one mood-enhancing thought from your lists and write it on a piece of paper to be posted somewhere in your house so that it will be easily visible (e.g., on the refrigerator, on a mirror).

3. Stand in front of a mirror each day for 3 minutes and look yourself in the eye while repeating the positive self-talk that you have written in item 1.

4. Explain the impact that the positive self-talk has had on your mood.

_____

_____

_____

_____

_____

5. Rate the degree of improvement in your mood when you think positively versus when you think negatively.

1	2	3	4	5

No Impact		Moderate Impact		Great Impact

A VOCATIONAL ACTION PLAN

GOALS OF THE EXERCISE

1. Overcome immobilizing feelings of helplessness, anxiety, and resentment.
2. Identify and replace negative, distorted cognitive messages that foster stress.
3. List proactive steps to be taken to reduce the vocational stress.
4. Pursue employment consistently with a reasonably hopeful and positive attitude.

ADDITIONAL PROBLEMS FOR WHICH THIS EXERCISE MAY BE MOST USEFUL

- Financial Stress

SUGGESTIONS FOR PROCESSING THIS EXERCISE WITH THE CLIENT

Clients who have experienced failure, rejection, confrontation, or conflict related to employment can easily become immobilized with fear and helplessness. Whether the client is in job jeopardy, has been terminated, or is in conflict with personnel at work, he/she needs to accept responsibility for taking constructive action to improve the situation. You may need to assist the client in identifying and replacing his/her self-defeating cognitions in number 2 ("Identify Self-Defeating Messages"). Hold the client accountable and reinforce action taken to implement the proactive steps of number 3 ("Replace Self-Defeating Messages").

A VOCATIONAL ACTION PLAN

It is common for a person to feel overwhelmed by vocational stress and to then develop a feeling of hopelessness and helplessness. You may feel you are not in control of your situation and that others are pulling all of the strings. But you must recapture a sense of controlling those things that you can and should control. You must develop a plan of action to respond proactively to your circumstance rather than to be immobilized by the events around you. Other people may have made decisions and implemented actions that affect you directly, but you do not have to be passive in response. You have choices before you in terms of how to respond assertively and constructively to reduce conflict and/or open new avenues for exploration.

1. **Resource People:** List three people you can rely on to help you through this stressful time by providing support and constructive suggestions for action.

    A. _____

    B. _____

    C. _____

2. **Identify Self-Defeating Messages:** First, list the negative, pessimistic, self-defeating, and distorted thoughts that cause you to feel hopeless, anxious, and helpless about your vocational situation (e.g., "Nothing I can do will help the situation," "Everything I have tried has failed," "I am only going to be rejected again").

    A. _____

    _____

    B. _____

    _____

    C. _____

    _____

    D. _____

    _____

    E. _____

    _____

3. **Replace Self-Defeating Messages:** Now challenge these negative thoughts that fill your mind and cause you to be angry, depressed, worried, or immobilized. Replace each thought with a more realistic, energizing thought that can move you into constructive action to improve your circumstance (e.g., "I have choices regarding what I can do to try to improve the situation," "I need to try again at implementing change," "There are people who do believe in me so I can take risks to reach out").

   A. _____

   _____

   B. _____

   _____

   C. _____

   _____

   D. _____

   _____

   E. _____

   _____

4. **Proactive Steps:** Write five actions you will take to improve your situation and reduce vocational stress.

   A. _____

   _____

   B. _____

   _____

   C. _____

   _____

   D. _____

   _____

   E. _____

   _____

APPENDIX A:
ALTERNATE ASSIGNMENTS FOR
PRESENTING PROBLEMS

ANGER CONTROL PROBLEMS

Antisocial Behavior	How I Have Hurt Others
Antisocial Behavior	Letter of Apology
Antisocial Behavior	Three Acts of Kindness
Attention Deficit Disorder (ADD)—Adult	Problem-Solving: An Alternative to Impulsive Action
Borderline Personality	Plan Before Acting
Family Conflict	Applying Problem-Solving to Interpersonal Conflict
Legal Conflicts	Accept Responsibility for Illegal Behavior
Legal Conflicts	Crooked Thinking Leads to Crooked Behavior
Parenting	The Two Sides of Parenting
Parenting	Using Reinforcement Principles in Parenting
Social Anxiety	Becoming Assertive

ANTISOCIAL BEHAVIOR

Anger Control Problems	Alternatives to Destructive Anger
Anger Control Problems	Anger Journal
Anger Control Problems	Assertive Communication of Anger
Attention Deficit Disorder (ADD)—Adult	Self-Monitoring/Self-Reward Program
Dissociation	Describe the Trauma
Family Conflict	Applying Problem-Solving to Interpersonal Conflict
Legal Conflicts	Accept Responsibility for Illegal Behavior
Legal Conflicts	Crooked Thinking Leads to Crooked Behavior

ANXIETY

Borderline Personality	Journal and Replace Self-Defeating Thoughts
Childhood Trauma	Deep Breathing Exercise
Low Self-Esteem	Replacing Fears With Positive Messages

Obsessive-Compulsive Disorder (OCD)	Interrupting Your Obsessions/Compulsions
Obsessive-Compulsive Disorder (OCD)	Making Use of the Thought-Stopping Technique
Panic/Agoraphobia	Coping Card
Panic/Agoraphobia	Monitoring My Panic Attack Experiences
Phobia	Four Ways to Reduce Fear
Sleep Disturbance	Sleep Pattern Record
Somatization	Controlling the Focus on Physical Problems
Spiritual Confusion	Your Spiritual Inheritance Inventory
Unipolar Depression	Negative Thoughts Trigger Negative Feelings
Unipolar Depression	Positive Self-Talk

ATTENTION DEFICIT DISORDER (ADD)—ADULT

Anger Control Problems	Alternatives to Destructive Anger
Antisocial Behavior	Three Acts of Kindness
Bipolar—Mania	Recognizing the Negative Consequences of Impulsive Behavior
Bipolar—Mania	Why I Dislike Taking My Medication
Borderline Personality	Plan Before Acting
Cognitive Deficits	Memory Aid—Personal Information Organizer
Cognitive Deficits	Memory Enhancement Techniques
Impulse Control Disorder	Impulsive Behavior Journal

BIPOLAR—DEPRESSION

Attention Deficit Disorder (ADD)—Adult	Self-Monitoring/Self-Reward Program
Bipolar—Mania	Keeping a Daily Rhythm
Bipolar—Mania	What Are My Good Qualities?
Bipolar—Mania	Why I Dislike Taking My Medication
Suicidal Ideation	Strategies to Resist Suicidal Thoughts and Feelings

BIPOLAR—MANIA

Anger Control Problems	Assertive Communication of Anger
Attention Deficit Disorder (ADD)—Adult	Problem-Solving: An Alternative to Impulsive Action
Attention Deficit Disorder (ADD)—Adult	Self-Monitoring/Self-Reward Program
Bipolar—Depression	Early Warning Signs of Depression
Borderline Personality	Plan Before Acting
Impulse Control Disorder	Impulsive Behavior Journal
Low Self-Esteem	Acknowledging My Strengths

Medical Issues   The Impact of My Illness
Psychoticism   What Do You Hear and See?
Sleep Disturbance   Sleep Pattern Record
Suicidal Ideation   No Self-Harm Contract
Suicidal Ideation   Strategies to Resist Suicidal Thoughts and Feelings

BORDERLINE PERSONALITY

Anger Control Problems   Alternatives to Destructive Anger
Anger Control Problems   Anger Journal
Bipolar—Mania   Keeping a Daily Rhythm
Bipolar—Mania   Recognizing the Negative Consequences of Impulsive
                                         Behavior
Dependency   Satisfying Unmet Emotional Needs
Dissociation   Describe the Trauma
Impulse Control Disorder   Impulsive Behavior Journal
Suicidal Ideation   Journal of Distorted, Negative Thoughts
Suicidal Ideation   Strategies to Resist Suicidal Thoughts and Feelings

CHILDHOOD TRAUMA

Bipolar—Depression   Identifying and Handling Triggers
Dissociation   Describe the Trauma
Parenting   The Two Sides of Parenting (Being Parented and Being
                                         a Parent)
Phobia   Gradually Reducing Your Phobic Fear
Posttraumatic Stress   How the Trauma Affects Me
    Disorder (PTSD)
Posttraumatic Stress   Share the Painful Memory
    Disorder (PTSD)

CHRONIC PAIN

Phase of Life Problems   What's Good About Me and My Life?
Somatization   Controlling the Focus on Physical Problems

COGNITIVE DEFICITS

Dissociation   Staying Focused on the Present Reality

DEPENDENCY

Anxiety   Analyze the Probability of a Feared Event
Intimate Relationship   How Can We Meet Each Other's Needs and Desires?
    Conflicts

Low Self-Esteem	Replacing Fears With Positive Messages
Phase of Life Problems	What's Good About Me and My Life?
Social Anxiety	Becoming Assertive

DISSOCIATION

Cognitive Deficits	Memory Aid—Personal Information Organizer
Sexual Abuse Victim	A Blaming Letter and a Forgiving Letter to Perpetrator
Sexual Abuse Victim	Picturing the Place of the Abuse

EATING DISORDERS AND OBESITY

Female Sexual Dysfunction	Study Your Body: Clothed and Unclothed
Obsessive-Compulsive Disorder (OCD)	Making Use of the Thought-Stopping Technique
Obsessive-Compulsive Disorder (OCD)	Reducing the Strength of Compulsive Behaviors
Unipolar Depression	Negative Thoughts Trigger Negative Feelings

EDUCATIONAL DEFICITS

| Cognitive Deficits | Memory Enhancement Techniques |

FAMILY CONFLICT

Anger Control Problems	Alternatives to Destructive Anger
Anger Control Problems	Anger Journal
Anger Control Problems	Assertive Communication of Anger
Antisocial Behavior	Letter of Apology
Financial Stress	Plan a Budget
Parenting	Learning to Parent as a Team
Parenting	Using Reinforcement Principles in Parenting
Unipolar Depression	Identify and Schedule Pleasant Activities

FEMALE SEXUAL DYSFUNCTION

Intimate Relationship Conflicts	How Can We Meet Each Other's Needs and Desires?
Intimate Relationship Conflicts	Positive and Negative Contributions to the Relationship: Mine and Yours
Male Sexual Dysfunction	Journaling the Response to Nondemand Sexual Pleasuring (Sensate Focus)
Sexual Identity Confusion	Journal of Sexual Thoughts, Fantasies, Conflicts

FINANCIAL STRESS

Educational Deficits	My Academic and Vocational Strengths
Educational Deficits	The Advantages of Education
Impulse Control Disorder	Impulsive Behavior Journal
Vocational Stress	A Vocational Action Plan

GRIEF/LOSS UNRESOLVED

Bipolar—Depression	Early Warning Signs of Depression
Dependency	Making Your Own Decisions
Dependency	Satisfying Unmet Emotional Needs
Spiritual Confusion	Your Spiritual Inheritance Inventory
Unipolar Depression	Negative Thoughts Trigger Negative Feelings
Unipolar Depression	Positive Self-Talk

IMPULSE CONTROL DISORDER

Anger Control Problems	Assertive Communication of Anger
Antisocial Behavior	Three Acts of Kindness
Anxiety	Past Successful Anxiety Coping
Attention Deficit Disorder (ADD)—Adult	Problem-Solving: An Alternative to Impulsive Action
Attention Deficit Disorder (ADD)—Adult	Self-Monitoring/Self-Reward Program
Bipolar—Mania	Recognizing the Negative Consequences of Impulsive Behavior
Legal Conflicts	Accept Responsibility for Illegal Behavior

INTIMATE RELATIONSHIP CONFLICTS

Antisocial Behavior	Letter of Apology
Dependency	Satisfying Unmet Emotional Needs
Family Conflict	Applying Problem-Solving to Interpersonal Conflict
Female Sexual Dysfunction	Factors Influencing Negative Sexual Attitudes
Grief/Loss Unresolved	Creating a Memorial Collage
Grief/Loss Unresolved	Dear _____: A Letter to a Lost Loved One
Paranoid Ideation	Check Suspicions Against Reality
Parenting	Using Reinforcement Principles in Parenting
Sexual Identity Confusion	Journal of Sexual Thoughts, Fantasies, Conflicts
Unipolar Depression	Identify and Schedule Pleasant Activities
Unipolar Depression	Negative Thoughts Trigger Negative Feelings

LEGAL CONFLICTS

Antisocial Behavior   How I Have Hurt Others
Antisocial Behavior   Letter of Apology
Antisocial Behavior   Three Acts of Kindness
Impulse Control Disorder   Impulsive Behavior Journal

LOW SELF-ESTEEM

Anxiety   Analyze the Probability of a Feared Event
Anxiety   Worry Time
Bipolar—Depression   Early Warning Signs of Depression
Bipolar—Mania   What Are My Good Qualities?
Borderline Personality   Journal and Replace Self-Defeating Thoughts
Childhood Trauma   Feelings and Forgiveness Letter
Dependency   Making Your Own Decisions
Dependency   Satisfying Unmet Emotional Needs
Dependency   Taking Steps Toward Independence
Female Sexual Dysfunction   Study Your Body: Clothed and Unclothed
Sexual Abuse Victim   A Blaming Letter and a Forgiving Letter to Perpetrator
Social Anxiety   Becoming Assertive
Social Anxiety   Restoring Socialization Comfort
Spiritual Confusion   Your Spiritual Inheritance Inventory
Unipolar Depression   Negative Thoughts Trigger Negative Feelings
Unipolar Depression   Positive Self-Talk

MALE SEXUAL DYSFUNCTION

Female Sexual Dysfunction   Factors Influencing Negative Sexual Attitudes
Intimate Relationship   How Can We Meet Each Other's Needs and Desires?
   Conflicts

Intimate Relationship   Positive and Negative Contributions to the Relationship:
   Conflicts   Mine and Yours
Sexual Identity Confusion   Journal of Sexual Thoughts, Fantasies, Conflicts

MEDICAL ISSUES

Bipolar—Depression   Early Warning Signs of Depression
Chronic Pain   Pain and Stress Journal
Somatization   Controlling the Focus on Physical Problems
Spiritual Confusion   My History of Spirituality

OBSESSIVE-COMPULSIVE DISORDER (OCD)

Anxiety   Analyze the Probability of a Feared Event
Anxiety   Past Successful Anxiety Coping

| Anxiety | Worry Time |
| Panic/Agoraphobia | Coping Card |

PANIC/AGORAPHOBIA

Anxiety	Past Successful Anxiety Coping
Anxiety	Worry Time
Low Self-Esteem	Replacing Fears With Positive Messages
Phobia	Four Ways to Reduce Fear
Social Anxiety	Restoring Socialization Comfort
Unipolar Depression	Negative Thoughts Trigger Negative Feelings

PARANOID IDEATION

Bipolar—Mania	Why I Dislike Taking My Medication
Psychoticism	What Do You Hear and See?
Unipolar Depression	Negative Thoughts Trigger Negative Feelings

PARENTING

| Family Conflict | A Structured Parenting Plan |

PHASE OF LIFE PROBLEMS

Anxiety	Past Successful Anxiety Coping
Chronic Pain	Pain and Stress Journal
Cognitive Deficits	Memory Aid—Personal Information Organizer
Educational Deficits	My Academic and Vocational Strengths
Family Conflict	Applying Problem-Solving to Interpersonal Conflict
Financial Stress	Plan a Budget
Grief/Loss Unresolved	Dear _____: A Letter to a Lost Loved One
Type A Behavior	Developing Noncompetitive Values

PHOBIA

Anxiety	Analyze the Probability of a Feared Event
Anxiety	Past Successful Anxiety Coping
Anxiety	Worry Time
Childhood Trauma	Deep Breathing Exercise
Panic/Agoraphobia	Coping Card
Panic/Agoraphobia	Monitoring My Panic Attack Experiences

POSTTRAUMATIC STRESS DISORDER (PTSD)

| Anger Control Problems | Alternatives to Destructive Anger |
| Anger Control Problems | Anger Journal |

Bipolar—Depression	Identifying and Handling Triggers
Childhood Trauma	Changing From Victim to Survivor
Childhood Trauma	Deep Breathing Exercise
Childhood Trauma	Feelings and Forgiveness Letter
Dissociation	Describe the Trauma
Dissociation	Staying Focused on the Present Reality
Parenting	The Two Sides of Parenting (Being Parented and Being a Parent)
Phobia	Gradually Reducing Your Phobic Fear
Sexual Abuse Victim	Picturing the Place of the Abuse

PSYCHOTICISM

Bipolar—Mania	Why I Dislike Taking My Medication
Cognitive Deficits	Memory Aid—Personal Information Organizer
Dissociation	Staying Focused on the Present Reality
Medical Issues	How I Feel About My Medical Treatment
Medical Issues	The Impact of My Illness
Paranoid Ideation	Check Suspicions Against Reality

SEXUAL ABUSE VICTIM

Bipolar—Depression	Identifying and Handling Triggers
Bipolar—Mania	What Are My Good Qualities?
Childhood Trauma	Changing From Victim to Survivor
Childhood Trauma	Deep Breathing Exercise
Childhood Trauma	Feelings and Forgiveness Letter
Dissociation	Describe the Trauma
Dissociation	Staying Focused on the Present Reality
Low Self-Esteem	Replacing Fears With Positive Messages
Posttraumatic Stress Disorder (PTSD)	How the Trauma Affects Me
Posttraumatic Stress Disorder (PTSD)	Share the Painful Memory
Social Anxiety	Restoring Socialization Comfort
Suicidal Ideation	No Self-Harm Contract

SEXUAL IDENTITY CONFUSION

| Female Sexual Dysfunction | Factors Influencing Negative Sexual Attitudes |
| Female Sexual Dysfunction | Study Your Body: Clothed and Unclothed |

SLEEP DISTURBANCE

| Bipolar—Depression | Early Warning Signs of Depression |
| Paranoid Ideation | Check Suspicions Against Reality |

SOCIAL ANXIETY

Anxiety	Analyze the Probability of a Feared Event
Anxiety	Past Successful Anxiety Coping
Bipolar—Mania	What Are My Good Qualities?
Borderline Personality	Journal and Replace Self-Defeating Thoughts
Childhood Trauma	Deep Breathing Exercise
Dependency	Satisfying Unmet Emotional Needs
Low Self-Esteem	Acknowledging My Strengths
Low Self-Esteem	Replacing Fears With Positive Messages
Panic/Agoraphobia	Coping Card
Panic/Agoraphobia	Monitoring My Panic Attack Experiences
Paranoid Ideation	Check Suspicions Against Reality
Phobia	Four Ways to Reduce Fear
Phobia	Gradually Reducing Your Phobic Fear
Unipolar Depression	Negative Thoughts Trigger Negative Feelings

SOMATIZATION

Chronic Pain	Pain and Stress Journal

SPIRITUAL CONFUSION

Type A Behavior	Developing Noncompetitive Values

SUBSTANCE USE

Antisocial Behavior	How I Have Hurt Others
Antisocial Behavior	Letter of Apology
Bipolar—Mania	Recognizing the Negative Consequences of Impulsive Behavior
Bipolar—Mania	What Are My Good Qualities?
Educational Deficits	The Advantages of Education
Impulse Control Disorder	Impulsive Behavior Journal
Obsessive-Compulsive Disorder (OCD)	Reducing the Strength of Compulsive Behaviors
Parenting	The Two Sides of Parenting (Being Parented and Being a Parent)
Sleep Disturbance	Sleep Pattern Record
Social Anxiety	Becoming Assertive
Spiritual Confusion	My History of Spirituality
Spiritual Confusion	Your Spiritual Inheritance Inventory

SUICIDAL IDEATION

Anxiety	Analyze the Probability of a Feared Event
Anxiety	Past Successful Anxiety Coping
Borderline Personality	Journal and Replace Self-Defeating Thoughts
Dependency	Satisfying Unmet Emotional Needs
Low Self-Esteem	Acknowledging My Strengths
Low Self-Esteem	Replacing Fears With Positive Messages
Phase of Life Problems	What Needs to Be Changed in My Life?
Phase of Life Problems	What's Good About Me and My Life?
Spiritual Confusion	My History of Spirituality
Unipolar Depression	Negative Thoughts Trigger Negative Feelings
Unipolar Depression	Positive Self-Talk

TYPE A BEHAVIOR

Antisocial Behavior	Three Acts of Kindness
Borderline Personality	Plan Before Acting
Impulse Control Disorder	Impulsive Behavior Journal
Unipolar Depression	Identify and Schedule Pleasant Activities

UNIPOLAR DEPRESSION

Anxiety	Analyze the Probability of a Feared Event
Anxiety	Worry Time
Attention Deficit Disorder (ADD)—Adult	Self-Monitoring/Self-Reward Program
Bipolar—Depression	Early Warning Signs of Depression
Bipolar—Mania	Keeping a Daily Rhythm
Bipolar—Mania	What Are My Good Qualities?
Bipolar—Mania	Why I Dislike Taking My Medication
Borderline Personality	Journal and Replace Self-Defeating Thoughts
Cognitive Deficits	Memory Aid—Personal Information Organizer
Dependency	Making Your Own Decisions
Dependency	Satisfying Unmet Emotional Needs
Grief/Loss Unresolved	Creating a Memorial Collage
Grief/Loss Unresolved	Dear _____: A Letter to a Lost Loved One
Low Self-Esteem	Acknowledging My Strengths
Low Self-Esteem	Replacing Fears With Positive Messages
Obsessive-Compulsive Disorder (OCD)	Interrupting Your Obsessions/Compulsions
Phase of Life Problems	What Needs to Be Changed in My Life?
Phase of Life Problems	What's Good About Me and My Life?
Psychoticism	What Do You Hear and See?
Sleep Disturbance	Sleep Pattern Record
Social Anxiety	Restoring Socialization Comfort

Spiritual Confusion	My History of Spirituality
Spiritual Confusion	Your Spiritual Inheritance Inventory
Suicidal Ideation	Journal of Distorted, Negative Thoughts
Suicidal Ideation	No Self-Harm Contract
Suicidal Ideation	Strategies to Resist Suicidal Thoughts and Feelings
Suicidal Ideation	The Aftermath of Suicide

VOCATIONAL STRESS

Educational Deficits	My Academic and Vocational Strengths
Educational Deficits	The Advantages of Education
Family Conflict	Applying Problem-Solving to Interpersonal Conflict
Grief/Loss Unresolved	Dear _____: A Letter to a Lost Loved One

APPENDIX B:
ALPHABETICAL INDEX OF EXERCISES

ABOUT THE CD-ROM

INTRODUCTION

This appendix provides you with information on the contents of the CD that accompanies this book. For the latest information, please refer to the ReadMe file located at the root of the CD.

SYSTEM REQUIREMENTS

- A computer with a processor running at 400 Mhz or faster
- At least 64 MB of total RAM installed on your computer; for best performance, we recommend at least 128 MB
- A CD-ROM drive
- Adobe Flash Player 9 or later (free download from Adobe.com)
- Microsoft Word or Word Reader
- A web browser

Note: Many popular word processing programs are capable of reading Microsoft Word files. However, users should be aware that a slight amount of formatting might be lost when using a program other than Microsoft Word.

USING THE CD WITH WINDOWS

To access the content from the CD, follow these steps:

1. Insert the CD into your computer's CD-ROM drive. Select Home.html The interface won't launch if you have autorun disabled. In that case, click Home.html or for Windows Start > All Programs > Accessories > Run). In the dialog box that appears, type D:\Home.html. (Replace D with the proper letter if your CD drive uses a different letter. If you don't know the letter, see how your CD drive is listed under My Computer.) Click OK.

2. Read through the license agreement, and then click the Accept button if you want to use the CD. The CD interface appears. Simply select the material you want to view.

USING THE CD WITH A MAC

1. Open the disc image.
2. Double click Home.html.

WHAT'S ON THE CD

The following sections provide a summary of the software and other materials you'll find on the CD.

Content

92 ready-to-use, between-session assignments designed to fit virtually every therapeutic mode.

Troubleshooting

If you have difficulty installing or using any of the materials on the companion CD, try the following solutions:

- Turn off any anti-virus software that you may have running. Installers sometimes mimic virus activity and can make your computer incorrectly believe that it is being infected by a virus. (Be sure to turn the anti-virus software back on later.)
- Close all running programs. The more programs you're running, the less memory is available to other programs. Installers also typically update files and programs; if you keep other programs running, installation may not work properly.
- Reboot if necessary. If all else fails, rebooting your machine can often clear any conflicts in the system.

Customer Care

If you have trouble with the CD-ROM, please contact Wiley Product Technical Support through Wiley's web page at http://support.wiley.com or call the Wiley Product Technical Support phone number at (800) 762-2974. Outside the United States, call 1(317) 572-3994. You can also contact Wiley Product Technical Support at http://support.wiley.com. John Wiley & Sons will provide technical support only for installation and other general quality control items. For technical support of the applications themselves, consult the program's vendor or author.

To place additional orders or to request information about other Wiley products, please call (877) 762-2974.